D0230089

FIELD GUIDE
TO THE
BIRDS
OF BRITAIN & EUROPE

ORDER OF BIRDS

The birds in this book are arranged in systematic order. This scientifically accepted system arranges birds in their approximate order of evolution. To the beginner, this order may seem chaotic compared with arranging the birds in, say, order of size, or by habitat, or alphabetically. The systematic order does, however, have one great advantage – it generally groups similar birds together and facilitates comparison. Where this does not happen, the book departs from the strict order to allow similar species to be grouped together.

Use the coloured square at the corner of the pages to help you find the different groups as you flick through the book.

	Divers and Grebes		Owls
	Shearwaters, Cormorants, Gannets and Pelicans		Woodpeckers and Allies
	Herons		Larks, Swallows and Pipits
	Wildfowl		Wrens and Allies
	Birds of Prey		Chats and Thrushes
	Gamebirds, Crakes and Rails		Warblers and Flycatchers
	Waders		Tits, Nuthatches and Treecreepers
	Gulls, Terns and Auks		Shrikes and Crows
	Pigeons and Cuckoos		Sparrows, Finches and Buntings

LAROUSSE

FIELD GUIDE
TO THE
BIRDS
OF BRITAIN & EUROPE

JOHN GOODERS

ILLUSTRATED BY NORMAN ARLOTT
& ALAN HARRIS

LAROUSSE

Larousse plc,

Elsley House,

24-30 Great Titchfield Street,

London W1P 7AD

First Published in 1995 by Larousse plc.

10 9 8 7 6

BRITISH LIBRARY CATALOGUING IN PUBLICATION DATA

GOODERS, JOHN 1937-

ISBN 1-85697-0014-8

Senior Editor: Michèle Byam

Editor: Sylvia Sullivan

Art Editor: Christopher Howson

Front and back cover illustrations: Alan Harris and Norman Arlott

Maps: Christopher Howson, Martyn Foote

Art Director: Paul Wilkinson

Publishing Director: Jim Miles

Phototypeset by Graphical Innovations, London

Colour separations by Newselle Litho, Milan

Printed in Hong Kong

Contents

Foreword

Little did I know years ago as I sat by a marsh on the Suffolk coast puzzling over the identity of waders, armed only with black and white drawings in what passed as a field guide at that time, that one day I would be asked to write a 'Field Guide' by no less a company than Larousse. Having now completed this guide I find it surprising what one can pick up in thirty-five years of solid birding. During those years 'birdwatching' has become 'birding', more a sport than a scientific endeavour. This alone has had a dramatic effect on our knowledge and understanding of the movements and status of a large number of birds. The accent is now decidedly on identification rather than on biology and behaviour. Field guides have been instrumental in this change and there are several good field guides to the birds of Britain and Europe. Some, I would venture, are too verbose, others over illustrated. Some are out of date simply because identification criteria have developed so fast. And some are too simplistic when it comes to seriously difficult groups of species. In the Larousse guide we have tried to merge text, illustrations and design to create the most practical and up-to-date field guide possible. Along the way we have tried not to sacrifice detail to design by giving additional space to those birds that most need it in various ways.

No book of this nature is ever the work of a single individual. My attempts at drawing birds are, even though I say it myself, dire. Thus I was fortunate to be able to recruit two of the best bird artists working today to paint the birds that I required in the plumages and poses needed. Norman Arlott and Alan Harris not only know their stuff, but have the enviable skill of making their birds look as if they could fly from the page. To say that I was grateful would be an unforgivable understatement.

At Larousse, Jim Miles was as supportive and inspirational as any publisher could be. Michele Byam, bless her, kept track of everything and never forgot that various elements had to be produced by particular times. Without Michele this book would not exist. Christopher Howson performed miracles on his magic machine to make text, maps, art and everything else fit perfectly on the page. While tucked away in the heart of England, Sylvia Sullivan edited my often incoherent typescript into succinct prose that was just what was needed. In deepest Sussex, Marion Waran turned scribble into computer images faster than I could write. Only by stockpiling could I keep output in pace with production. To them all goes the thanks of a very grateful author. I must also thank my wife, the overworked Robbie Gooders, for her understanding (mostly), sympathy (occasional) and criticism (continuous) in helping me to ensure that everything was ready on schedule. Thank you Rob.

John Gooders,

Sussex, England

Introduction

Try, if you can, to imagine birding without a field guide. It was, in fact, only forty years ago that Roger Tory Peterson and his chums produced the first sensible, full-colour guide to the birds of Europe. Before that birders had to struggle along with black and white guides, or resort to a few incomplete pocket-books covering only the commonest of birds. Outside America and Europe there was hardly a field guide to be had. How things have changed! Today the problem is: which guide to choose.

The basic elements of a field guide are almost standard – illustrations, text and maps. But the arrangement of these elements varies enormously. In the *Larousse Field Guide to the Birds of Britain and Europe* we decided that all the elements would be grouped together for each species. Thus each bird receives a full half-page with all the ingredients neatly and standardly arranged for easy reference. Some birds are, however, more difficult to identify than others, so species like the eagles have been treated to full page coverage. For similar reasons, several bird groups rely on direct comparison to identify, so we have added additional pages to show all the confusing species together. Again, the eagles fall into this category, but so do the confusingly plain warblers. In these cases we have used the facility of 'panoramas' to enable all of the species to be placed on a special double page. Wherever necessary space has been found to compare confusing species within the main body of the book as with juvenile terns, winter grebes and so on.

To the basic field guide elements we have added a coloured abundance chart for each bird. This monthly calendar tells you not only when a bird is present, but assesses the likelihood of it being seen. This is partly a statement of its population, but also an estimate of its visibility. Such estimates are purely subjective, but as every birder knows there is a much greater chance of seeing a Fan-tailed than a Cetti's Warbler, or a Griffon Vulture than a Rock Bunting, and so on. We have also added notes around the illustrations to pick out the points to look for in much the same way as birders do in their field notebooks. The combination of illustrations, text, maps, abundance charts and notes should provide sufficient data to name every bird seen. The comparative sections for more confusing species adds another dimension to help clinch the identification.

Every effort has been made to keep the *Larousse Field Guide* as manageable as possible. By keeping the text of this book brief I hope that those who use it will not be daunted, but find the various elements combine to produce a truly useful tool, a field guide that is both comprehensive and portable.

Among my collection of field guides to various parts of the world, the better ones can be picked out by their well-used feel. These are among my most valued possessions. I have every hope that the *Larousse Field Guide* will find the same place in the pockets, car glove compartments and suitcases of all readers. Use it, improve it, even abuse it, but please never throw it away! Field guides are tools that should be honed and improved.

There is inevitably a tendency to ignore introductions and get straight to the heart of the matter. May I respectfully request here and now that you read the rest of the material that lies between here and the Red-throated Diver. By doing so you will, I believe, improve not only the usefulness of the guide, but also improve your birding.

Bird Names

The subject of bird names causes ornithologists to get hot under the collar and brings confusion to the users of bird books. *Panurus biarmicus*, for example, has, within a few brief years changed from Bearded Tit to Bearded Reedling, to Bearded Parrotbill and back to Bearded Tit. Throughout this period birders have always referred to it as Bearded Tit, despite the fact that it is neither a tit, nor is it bearded. It is, in fact, a parrotbill, a sub-grouping of the widespread Old World family Timaliidae, the babblers.

In one of my previous books I attempted to be ahead of the field by using the new English names proposed by *British Birds* magazine. While agreeing that a review is not the right place to debate such names, one reviewer, rather than concentrating on what the book was about and whether it achieved its purpose, then proceeded to 'hammer' the book for using them. Today, *British Birds* uses a published list that, while differing from common usage, is non-confusing and becoming ever more widely accepted. By and large, the English names used in this book follow that list with a few idiosyncratic differences, mainly in line with what birders call the birds, of my own. I have, for long, advocated the adoption of a list of standard English names covering all the birds of the world. There are, for example, two Black Vultures in the world, one in Europe and Asia, the other in America. Thus there is a case for changing the names of one to avoid confusion in everyday 'bird-speak'. But this does not mean that we have to change both in a form of transatlantic *quid pro quo*. The proposed use of 'Cinereous Vulture' for our European bird seems to me doomed to failure.

All birds have both an English and a scientific name. The latter consists of two parts – a generic name and a specific name. The generic name is the first word and it is customary to begin it with a capital letter. All closely related birds have the same generic name. Many of the woodpeckers, for example, belong to the genus *Dendrocopus*. The second word is the specific name and this begins with a small letter. The specific name picks out one member of a genus from another. The scientific name of the Great Spotted Woodpecker is *Dendrocopus major* while that of its close relative the Lesser Spotted Woodpecker is *Dendrocopus minor*.

Many scientific names refer to the characteristics of the species – *cristata*, for example, means crested. Other names, such as *Larus audouinii* (Audouin's Gull), commemorate the person who discovered the bird. Others still are creations of ornithologists and may be obscure, humorous or even disgusting.

Knowing scientific names is useful because they form an excellent guide to a bird's relationships and therefore to similarities in structure and appearance. They are also a universally acceptable international language. Swedish or Dutch birdwatchers, for example, may have a perfect command of English except for bird names. So, in order to communicate, one has to resort to the international language of scientific names.

As with English names, the scientific names used here largely follow those adopted by *British Birds* magazine which, in turn, largely follow those proposed by Voous in *List of Recent Holarctic Bird Species*, published by the British Ornithologists' Union and reprinted from *Ibis*, 1977. The order of birds is also based on these sources, save only that minor adjustments have been made to bring together similar species, that may be confused in the field. The scientific order may take a short time to learn, but once understood it facilitates the use of every other sensible bird book published anywhere in the world.

Geographical Scope

Europe is a historical, rather than a geographical entity, that is far from easy to define. Surrounded by sea in three directions, it has a lengthy land boundary with Asia to the east. For many purposes, that area of the former USSR lying to the west of the Ural Mountain chain can be regarded as part of Europe. But, even with the breakdown of the former Soviet Union, much of Russia and the other autonomous republics remain out of bounds to casual birders. In contrast, most of eastern Europe, the former Soviet satellites, are open and of easy access. Similarly, Turkey and Cyprus have always welcomed visitors and their place within the 'European' framework has never been questioned.

For these reasons, this guide draws its eastern boundary to coincide with that of Turkey, from the north-eastern corner of the Mediterranean to the Black Sea. It crosses to include the Crimea and mouth of the Volga and then heads northwards to the Norwegian border on the Varanger Fjord. This is the area that is freely available to European birders. To venture further east would be to add a number of exciting species that are never seen in Europe; mouth-watering, but frustrating.

Virtually every bird that will be encountered within the boundaries of this huge area is fully covered, but not every waif and stray that has ever been seen in Europe. So, most American vagrants are not included; those who would identify them are recommended to acquire one of the several excellent guides available to the birds of North America. Nevertheless, some transatlantic birds are covered because they bear a strong resemblance to related European species. Thus, though there are no American warblers, several waders that are easily confused with European species are included. Similarly, many Asiatic and southern waifs have been omitted, though others, such as the *Phylloscopus* warblers, are included.

Rarities are, of course, the very birds that the birder wants to see. However, that does not mean that all rarities are difficult to identify. What matters is that, having found a bird that is not in this book, you have located a rarity, and all rarities need thorough noting and confirmation. That, I believe, is a specialist job requiring a specialist book.

1 SLOVENIA
2 CROATIA
3 BOSNIA-HERZEGOVINA
4 SERBIA
5 ALBANIA
6 SWITZERLAND
7 LUXEMBOURG
8 BELGIUM
9 NETHERLANDS
10 CZECH REPUBLIC
11 SLOVAKIA
12 MOLDOVA

Using This Guide

Each of the birds in this book is allocated either a half or a whole page, depending on how much space is required to detail its identification. Within the space allocated each has the same elements and a similar design. When you see an unfamiliar bird, the first thing is to check the list of general types of bird (Waders, Birds of Prey and so on) on page 2. Then turn to the appropriate pages and leaf through the illustrations to see if your bird is there. If you spot it, or one that looks very similar, check the labels around the illustrations to see if your bird showed the same features. Then consult the text, map and monthly abundance chart to confirm your identification. If still unsure, check the 'Similar Species' heading at the foot of the entry. This will lead you to confusing species that share several or many of the bird's characteristics. It may also lead you to one of the special comparative sections for difficult-to-identify birds.

This colour shows which group of birds each species belongs to. Use it to help find the different groups as you flick through the book. The colour code is explained on page 2.

Illustrations show major plumages (such as male, female, juvenile, summer and winter), and typical field postures (swimming, perching and so on).

Annotation picks out the best identification features.

Text outlines the most important points about the bird's appearance and behaviour, and distinguishes it from similar species.

Abundance chart from January to December.

unknown

rare

requires serious searching

needs a bit of searching

seen most days

regularly seen every day

impossible to miss

Map shows breeding distribution (yellow) and wintering areas (blue). Where these colours overlap to make green, this indicates that the bird is present throughout the year. Grey maps show the distribution of birds that occur only on migration.

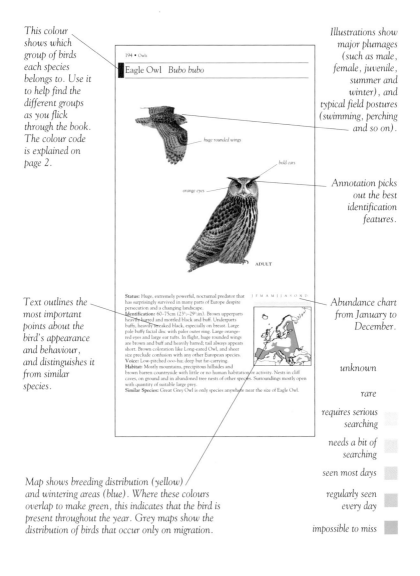

194 • Owls

Eagle Owl *Bubo bubo*

huge rounded wings

bold ears

orange eyes

ADULT

Status: Huge, extremely powerful, nocturnal predator that has surprisingly survived in many parts of Europe despite persecution and a changing landscape.
Identification: 60–75cm (23½–29½in). Brown upperparts heavily barred and mottled black and buff. Underparts buffy, heavily streaked black, especially on breast. Large pale buffy facial disc with paler outer ring. Large orange-red eyes and large ear tufts. In flight, huge rounded wings are brown and buff and heavily barred; tail always appears short. Brown coloration like Long-eared Owl, and sheer size preclude confusion with any other European species.
Voice: Low-pitched ooo-hu; deep but far-carrying.
Habitat: Mostly mountains, precipitous hillsides and brown barren countryside with little or no human habitation or activity. Nests in cliff caves, on ground and in abandoned tree nests of other species. Surroundings mostly open with quantity of suitable large prey.
Similar Species: Great Grey Owl is only species anywhere near the size of Eagle Owl.

J F M A M J J A S O N D

ILLUSTRATIONS

On each page the illustrations will be your first points of reference. Each species is shown in its major plumages and in typical attitudes, as it is usually seen in the field. Wherever possible similar species appear above, below or alongside each other, and in the same postures to make comparison easier. Some birds are treated more diagrammatically than others so that attention can be drawn to finer points of distinction.

LABELS

Around the illustrations are labels, which are based on the sort of notes that most birders make in the field when they see an unfamiliar bird or a bird they do not recognize. The labels draw attention to the most important points to watch for. These are not necessarily the most obvious features; indeed, some are quite subtle. To improve your bird identification, spend time browsing through, studying the illustrations and the labels to familiarize yourself with the major points that separate one species from another.

TEXT

The text seeks to put the bird into the field as a living being by painting a word picture of its appearance and the way it moves within its habitat. It also describes where the bird usually occurs and indicates how to distinguish it from similar species.

MAPS

Using different colours to indicate breeding and wintering areas, the maps show the normal distribution of the bird. Where the areas overlap, the two colours combine to produce a third. Some birds regularly pass through our area, but neither breed nor winter. To keep the maps simple and understandable, information about passage has been omitted from them but is mentioned in the text instead. A small number of birds do not breed or winter in Europe but pass through in spring or autumn, or both. Most of these passage migrants are Arctic breeders, mainly waders. Grey-coloured maps show where they regularly occur. The maps show what the birds regularly do, but, occasionally, birds depart from their normal behaviour: a summer visitor may stay on through the winter, for example. This makes it as much a rarity as the bird that has occured in Europe only or twice a century and should be treated as such.

ABUNDANCE CHARTS

A scale of colour density on the seasonal abundance chart indicates the likelihood of seeing the bird in each month of the year. The density of colour is not so much a measure of the actual number of birds as a combination of number and visibility. Colour densities have been defined in terms of a full day's birding in the right place and habitat by a competent birder.

COMPARISONS

Some birds are so similar that careful comparison may be required to make an accurate identification. Often this is a process of elimination, of dismissing species one after another to narrow the field. Comparative sections are provided for most of these 'species groups'. In summer plumage the grebes, for example, are relatively easy. In winter they form three confusing pairs and have been treated separately for comparison. Similarly, eagles, buzzards, stints, terns, warblers and so on merit separate sections. Each is cross referenced from the individual species' section. As ever with bird identification, knowing what to look for is the key.

Bird Identification

Identifying birds is part art, part science, but always a matter of experience. The beginner is often amazed that a distant speck, or a briefly glimpsed blob can be named with such apparent ease. And it is quite natural to ask 'How did you identify that?' Or even somewhat sceptically 'How can I be sure that you are right?' As every professional bird tour leader knows, the answer is not 'Because I say it is', but to explain carefully and considerately on what basis the bird has been identified. Part of the skill of identification is the ability to put names to birds at greater and greater distances with briefer and briefer views. But this can only come with experience and the beginner (or should we say the less experienced?) must be prepared for the frustration of not naming every bird seen. Of course, if birds were like fashion models they would parade up and down showing off their key features for all to see. This would be great for listers, but essentially boring to those who appreciate the challenge of identification, of developing their skill and of finding an immense satisfaction in solving a problem.

Lest it be thought that every bird presents an identification challenge it should be stressed that the vast majority of birds are relatively simple to identify. Everyone knows what a Mute Swan, a Blackbird and a Starling looks like. Similarly, most find little difficulty in placing a bird into a category such as duck-like, hawk-like, crow-like, and so on. It is then relatively simple to progress to naming the species that fall within such categories. The inexperienced will soon pick up the differences between Carrion Crow and Raven, between Rook and Jackdaw. It may take a little longer to work out why a bird of prey is a harrier rather than a buzzard, a falcon rather than a hawk. The essential ingredient is knowledge and studying a field guide is as good a way as any of gaining such knowledge.

WHAT TO LOOK FOR

Identification, then, is largely a matter of knowledge, of knowing what to look for. See a gull and check the wingtips; see a bunting – check the head pattern; see a diver – check the bill shape. Competent birders do this automatically while the less experienced are taking in all sorts of features that may be enjoyable but are completely irrelevant to a correct identification. Skill and

Self-testing
The picture below contains a number of different winter waterbirds at sea. See if you can find six species…then name them all without reading the answers on page 13.

Broad white supercilium, dark cap, streaked back, reed habitat add up to Moustached Warbler at a glance, once you know what to look for.

knowledge improve. Catch the birding bug and faster progress will be made... practice, as they say, makes perfect (well almost).

Sometimes a bird can be missed not through a lack of skill, but by a simple lack of knowledge. A flock of black birds on the sea look like duck and are identified as Common Scoter. To the inexperienced, correctly finding the flock and correctly identifying them is satisfaction enough. But the competent birder will wait and watch to see one of the birds rise from the water to flap its wings. It shows a white patch on the wings and identification is confirmed as Velvet Scoter.

This is a relatively simple and straightforward example. But suppose the bird had been found among scrub and reeds along a wetland margin? Suppose it had been brown and featureless? Then what? Differences between many of these 'marshy' birds are often very slight. Nevertheless, a quick examination should eliminate Reed Bunting and Bearded Tit, and establish that we have a thin-billed warbler. But which? The route here, as always, is to narrow down the search by eliminating as many species as possible. Its back is unstreaked, it has a bold supercilium, it has a short tail – check leg colour. Yes! It's a Paddyfield Warbler and you are either very, very lucky, or you are on the Black Sea coast in summer, or both.

Knowledge, knowing what to look for, is the key to identification and much more important than good eyesight, the finest binoculars, the very best telescope and tripod, and even the right jacket with a multitude of bird badges all over it.

Answers: A flock of Common Scoter with at least two Velvet Scoter (white wings on one); Black-headed Gull flying left; Slavonian Grebe right foreground; two Long-tailed Duck right background; followed by female Goldeneye.

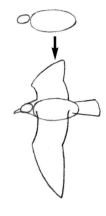

Watch, examine, note – these are the three most important elements when starting to identify a bird. Combined, they form one of the most important skills that must be learned, a skill that will prove invaluable as long as you go birding. The field description is not only the backbone of the rare bird system (no written description = no record), but also the only sensible way of investigating or checking an identification. While memory makes fools of us all, a description taken in the field, preferably with the bird in view, cannot lie. Note every part of a bird's plumage working systematically from bill to tail, upperparts then underparts. Add bill and legs, plus behaviour, habitat, date, time and place and you have the field description.

By far the best way to take notes is to draw an outline of the bird and mark its features. I cannot draw birds but have found that two ovals (sometimes with the addition of lines)

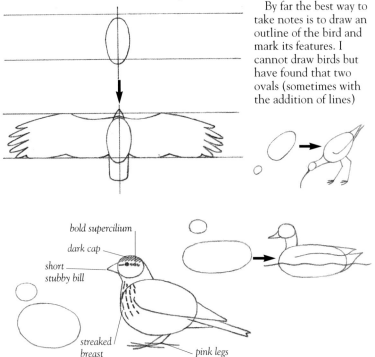

bold supercilium

dark cap

short stubby bill

streaked breast

pink legs

work quite satisfactorily if I add legs, bill and tail. Should the bird fly, try to note the pattern on both the upperwing and underwing. However, if that is impossible, don't worry – an incomplete description is far better than an inaccurate one.

Having made your field notes and drawings, check through the guide to find the bird you have seen. If you have difficulty finding it, do not immediately assume that you have found a major rarity. Go back over the pages checking notes and drawings against possible species. If it cannot be found, delve into the text checking and cross checking. If identification still eludes you ask other birders for their views and when they give you the name ask why. Then check the book again.

Making Field Notes

The field description is the basis of all identification. Of course, it will not be necessary to take full notes on every individual bird seen, but practising on common birds, or on birds that are easy to identify but not familiar, will prove of great help when the occasion arises, as it will, when an unknown bird is encountered for the first time. The most important thing to remember is that it is better to note down too much information than too little, for even insignificant features may make all the difference. Above all be accurate. Never find features that do not exist.

The more birding you do the sooner you will come across examples of other birdwatchers hoodwinking themselves and each other into seeing what is not really there. Occasionally a mass hoodwink, comprising a hundred or more people, may be encountered. Always make up your own mind rather than accepting the proffered view.

finch-like

duck-like

wader-like

hawk-like

swallow-like

thrush-like

WHAT TYPE OF BIRD?

We do not have to be interested in birds to recognize a duck, a swan, a swallow, a thrush, or a sparrow. Dividing birds into groups is not only easy, it is also very useful. The birds in this book are grouped according to natural relationships, and it is worth familiarizing yourself with these groups, if only to see how many you already know. By deciding quite clearly that a particular bird is, say, a swallow, you have reduced the possibilities enormously and concentrated attention on the relevant bird group.

Some years ago I was asked to design a questionnaire to form the basis of a computer bird identification system. When testing the finished program there was much enjoyment (and not a little education) to be had in seeing just how the number of possibilities tumbled by answering a single question. Though I never got to a single answer producing a complete identification, entering 'bird of prey-like' and 'forked tail' did produce Red Kite.

THE BIRD'S SHAPE

These 'types of bird' are often recognizable by their shape rather than by a particular feature; for not all finches have thick bills, nor do all waders have long bills. So we describe birds as plump or slim, elegant, or chunky. Overall shape and 'type of bird' have much in common, but they are not the same thing. Describing a wader as slim and elegant leads to a different identification than would calling it plump and chunky, yet both are found within the wader group. Thus in two steps we have moved from bird, to wader, and to a slim and elegant wader like a Greenshank, rather than a plump and chunky one like a Ringed Plover.

Wing Shape

The shape of a bird's wings not only determines the way it flies, but is also an invaluable aid to its identity. Some birds, of course, live a mainly aerial lifestyle, but even terrestrial foraging birds may have a particular wing shape that picks them out from similar species. Swallows, shearwaters, birds of prey and swifts all have characteristic wing shapes, are most often seen in flight and are easy to identify down to generic (group) level. Thereafter swallows are relatively easy; shearwaters need care; birds of prey may prove easier than when resting; and swifts have to be identified in flight simply because they are virtually never seen at rest. Birds of prey are generally easier to identify in flight when they show their wing shape. Indeed some species are better separated by this criterion than any other. Spotted and Lesser Spotted Eagles are both featureless, all-dark eagles, but the former has broad wings and a short tail, the latter relatively narrow wings and a longer tail. The wing:tail ratio of Spotted is 100:50, the Lesser Spotted 100:75. Similarly, the European Sparrowhawk has broad, rounded wings like a Northern Goshawk, but the latter has a pronounced secondary bulge lacking in the former. The Common Kestrel has long pointed wings, but these are broader-based than those of the Hobby. Whereas the former hovers and pounces, the latter is an aerial hunter.

Wing shape is even a useful identification aid with species that are seldom identified in flight. Melodious Warblers have short, rounded wings that, while they can be picked out in flight, are just as obvious when folded and the bird is at rest. In this species the primaries are bunched and the exposed portion that extends beyond the tips of the covering tertial feathers forms only a quarter of the folded wing. In the similar and closely related Icterine Warbler the proportion of folded wing is nearer a third.

Wing shape, then, can be used to place a particular bird in an appropriate group, but it may also be useful in separating similar and related birds one from another. Check Marsh and Blyth's Reed Warblers, or Little and Baillon's Crakes. Even if birds share a common wing shape, like the gulls and shearwaters, the way that the wing is held may be completely different. Gulls have long wings that are angled and swept back from the carpal joint, and held bowed. Shearwaters hold their wings straight, stiff and flat. Thus, while the Fulmar is very similar to a gull on plumage characters, its stiff flight identifies it as a close relative of the shearwaters.

Are they broad like a buzzard?

Are they straight like a Fulmar?

Are they rounded like a partridge?

Or pointed like a kestrel?

Or sharply angled like a swallow?

Or long and thin like a swift?

Wing Pattern

wingbar: Ringed Plover

speculum: Garganey

wing tip: Kittiwake

wing patch: Common Redshank

contrasting coverts: Wigeon

black axillaries: Grey Plover

carpal patch: Rough-legged Buzzard

The wings of both birds and aircraft are highly complex structures. In the case of birds the spread wing can be seen to comprise many different groups of feathers, all of which are essential to flight. But these feathers also serve to communicate, both in flight and on the ground. It is this secondary purpose that creates the distinctive wing patterns that are such useful aids to identification.

The wingtips of gulls, the speculum (secondaries) of duck, wingbars in waders, contrast between flight feathers and coverts in birds of prey, marked axillaries (arm pits) in plovers are all significant aids in separating one species from another, often at considerable range. The 'ink-pot' wingtip of a Kittiwake is a feature not shared with any other gull. Several immature gulls do have black wingtips, but these extend along the primaries rather than being confined to the tip. Many gulls have black wingtips marked by white 'mirrors', but the size and number of mirrors varies from one species to the next. The wingtip of the Common Gull, for example, is black with an almost complete white bar through it created by large 'mirrors' and is quite different from the spotted wingtip of the Herring Gull.

The presence or absence of a wingbar may be vital in separating several wader species. Common and Spotted Redshank, for example. Or Dunlin and Broad-billed Sandpiper. Or Ringed and Little Ringed Plovers. Among the duck, several species have a boldly coloured speculum that shows well in flight and may be visible even at rest. In general drakes are not difficult to identify, but females and eclipse drakes are highly confusing and a glimpse of speculum colour may be the only distinguishing feature. Check female Common Teal and Garganey, for example, where the blue innerwing of the latter contrasts with the green speculum of the Teal. Calandra and Bimaculated Larks are both thickset, broad-winged and chunky birds that inhabit the same sort of open country habitats. At any distance they are virtually identical. But in flight the black and white trailing edge to the wing of the Calandra is obvious.

Tail Size and Shape

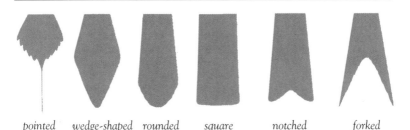

| pointed | wedge-shaped | rounded | square | notched | forked |

Tails come in a wide variety of shapes from the highly pointed to the deeply forked, from the Pintail to the Barn Swallow. All other birds may fall between these extremes, but even subtle differences may serve to separate one species from another. The rounded tails of the *Hippolais* warblers, for example, are quite different from the neatly notched ones of the *Phylloscopus*.

Just as birds' tails vary in shape, so too do they vary in length. Common Starling, Blue Rock Thrush and Waxwing all have short, square-cut tails that are so obvious that these three quite distinctive birds may be confused in flight. Grey, Yellow and Pied Wagtails all have long tails, but the longer tail of the Grey is a useful identification aid. Similarly, though they are much the same shape and size, all wagtails have longer tails than pipits. In general, the large vultures have shorter tails than the large eagles, a useful feature when they are no more than soaring silhouettes against the sky. At the finest level, one of the distinguishing features of Lesser from Common Kestrel, is the former's wedge-shaped tail with its distinctive 'faulted' tail band.

Tail Pattern

Many birds have bold tail and rump marks. Wheatears, for example, show a prominent white rump as they flit away, and white outer-feathers are shown by pipits, wagtails, many waders, tits, and so on. Tail bands are important in birds of prey, and their position and number can help with several confusing species. Among the buzzards, for example, the Common Buzzard has a heavily barred tail; the Long-legged Buzzard an unmarked one; the Rough-legged Buzzard a broad, black terminal band; and the Honey Buzzard a pattern of three clear-cut bands, which helps to identify it.

white outertail feathers   *inverted 'T' shape*

Many waders have characteristic tail and rump patterns, features that remain hidden when at rest or busily feeding. A white-rumped bird among a flock of Dunlin may be a Curlew Sandpiper, but it might be the much more difficult and decidedly rarer White-rumped Sandpiper. A white 'V' extending up the back might be a Greenshank, but it might equally be a Marsh Sandpiper. Two white ovals on the rump is a feature shared by several species of waders, though in none is it so obvious as a Ruff.

black tip   *white outer tips*

Bill Shape and Size

Each of the nine thousand or so living bird species in the world differs in one way or another. All have feathers and most can and do fly, but that is about all they have in common. Over the centuries each species has adapted to its particular environment and nowhere is this adaptation so apparent as in bill shape. A bird's bill is a specialized feeding tool, a tool whereby it can exploit a source of food better or more efficiently that its competitors. It follows that bill shape and size is a very useful means of identification.

Hooked bills are for tearing, be it flesh or fruit. Wedge-shaped bills are for cracking. Long bills are for probing. Chisel-like bills are for hacking. Spoon-shaped bills are for sieving. And serrated bills are for grasping. If we take a highly specialized group like the waders we find a huge variety of sizes and shapes, from the awl of the Avocet to the chisel of the Turnstone. Most waders fall somewhere between these two extremes and, indeed, most have straight, medium-length bills. When comparing these birds it is useful to have some standard of measurement. Often we can say that a wader's bill is longer or shorter than, or several times its head length. With shorter bills, among the stints for example, it is more accurate to compare bill length with loral distance, that is the distance between the base of the bill and the eye.

Even with some smaller birds bill shape may be the crucial identification feature. The thin bills of warblers and pipits are quite different from the thick, chunky bills of finches. There are four species of crossbills found in Europe. One, the Two-barred, has white wingbars, but the others share virtually identical shape, size and plumage. Only by careful observation of the shape of the bill is it possible to separate Common, Scottish and Parrot Crossbills. And there are those who doubt that this is possible in the field.

Tiny like a swallow?

Thin and pointed like a Robin?

Conical like a Greenfinch?

Hooked like a kestrel?

Long and thin like a redshank?

Decurved like a curlew?

Behaviour and Jizz

Tufted Duck dive from the surface

Arctic Terns dive from the air

How birds move around, how they feed, where they perch, whether or not they form flocks are all useful clues to their identity. For while some birds swim, others do not. While some dive, others don't. While some birds hop, others walk. Thus a Tufted

Black Terns pick food from the water

Stonechats perch atop gorse

Duck perched in a tree is just as impossible as a diving Red Grouse. And a flock of Robins is as unlikely as swimming Stonechat. Understanding what birds do and do not do is another stage in the elimination process.

A flock of small waders running up and down a beach following the movements of the waves is Sanderling. A wader systematically turning stones is a Turnstone. A bird hacking at a tree trunk is either a woodpecker or a nuthatch. These are, of course, simple classic examples that even non-birders know. But to understand that a tern diving into the sea is not a Black Tern; that a bird perched on top of a gorse bush is probably a Whinchat or a Stonechat; that an owl quartering a marsh in daylight is a Short-eared, are all somewhat more sophisticated examples of birds identified by knowledge of their behaviour.

'Jizz' is a birding term that encapsulates the very character, shape and behaviour of an individual species. A wader searching the margins of a fast-running stream is a Common Sandpiper. If it bobs continuously and the season is summer, it is certainly this species. In autumn the bird could be a Wood Sandpiper, in winter a Green Sandpiper. A bird of prey that plunges into water is either an Osprey or a White-tailed Eagle. A bird that hangs out its wings to dry is one of the cormorants. A 'marsh' tern typically feeds by picking insects from the surface of water. It swoops, it hangs, it changes direction violently, it is erratic, graceful, light, elegant, angular and it's either a Black, White-winged Black, or a Whiskered Tern. Describing jizz is far from easy, but whenever possible we have tried within the species' text.

Turnstones turn stones

Sanderling run before waves

House Sparrows hop

Meadow Pipits walk

Flight

Straight line like a Turtle Dove?

Undulate like a Mistle Thrush?

Hang in the air like a gull?

Glide like a shearwater?

Hover like a kestrel?

Dive like a Gannet?

Soar like a buzzard?

Quarter like a harrier?

Birds 'soar', 'glide', 'stoop', 'hover', 'dive', and 'quarter', but no single bird does all of these. We think of eagles soaring, shearwaters gliding, falcons stooping, kestrels hovering, gannets diving and harriers quartering. In many cases, only certain kinds of birds fly in a particular way – only birds of prey stoop and only harriers and owls quarter. To say that we saw a Robin soaring is as unlikely as to describe a stooping Stonechat.

Some birds fly in a straight line, like the starlings. Others, like the woodpeckers and larks, have a very undulating, bouncy flight. The Mistle Thrush, for example, has a deeply undulating flight, whereas the similar Song Thrush is a direct flier. Among difficult groups of birds to identify are birds of prey. But while many species use rising air to gain height by soaring, the way in which they hold themselves can be a vital clue to their identity.

For some species flight is essential to feeding, whereas for others it is a useful way of avoiding danger and of moving from one location to another. Birds as variable as Gannet, Peregrine, Spotted Flycatcher and swift rely on flight to catch their food; Gannets dive into the sea; Peregrines stoop through the air; Spotted Flycatchers sally out to grab their food; and swifts whizz around all day long scooping up their flying food.

Knowing how birds fly is another element in identification, another factor that eliminates a range of species as possibilities – like the soaring Robin.

Range and Distribution

Maps are an important element in every good field guide, and it is usually possible to see at a glance whether a bird can be reasonably expected in a particular area. If not, then the bird becomes a rarity and should be treated with caution. Sardinian Warblers, for example, are common year-round residents in many parts of the Mediterranean. In northern Europe, they are major rarities. Some species are so tied to a particular region or area, that they are completely unknown elsewhere like the Black-shouldered Kite outside Iberia.

Knowing what birds are likely to be seen in a particular area, especially when travelling, is not only a great help in identifying any bird observed, but also essential if species are not to be missed because they overlap in range with very similar species. For example, you will miss the Syrian Woodpecker in eastern Europe unless you are aware that it exists alongside the Great Spotted Woodpecker. Before setting out on a journey abroad, all good birders create a list of the 'possibilities'.

Of course, all maps of bird distribution are based on where birders have previously observed them. That does not mean to say that the bird does not occur elsewhere, merely that no birder has yet seen them there. Our understanding of bird distribution has improved enormously over the past twenty years as a result of the various 'atlas' projects that have covered so many countries. Even so a bird may regularly breed miles, perhaps hundreds of miles, out of its known range just waiting for a birder to find it. Although I doubt if we shall find Azure-winged Magpies breeding in Greece, we might well find Tengmalm's Owls in Italy.

Call or Songs

The value of learning the different bird songs and calls cannot be overstated. The ability to recognize a bird from its song or call, sometimes even a brief twitter coming from the middle of a dense thicket saves a great deal of time and effort. If an unknown bird calls, write down a phonetic rendering or perhaps put it into words.

Another solution is to carry a tape recorder with you in the field and record calls and songs you don't know. Then, with the aid of a good set of bird recordings try to find the owner. The use of calls to identify birds is not confined to picking out the more widespread birds in dense woodland when they are difficult to see. The calls of most waders are reasonably distinct and are relatively easy to learn. The *tu-tu-tu* of a Greenshank or the nasal *treep* of a Dunlin not only help to identify the bird, but may prove an invaluable aid in locating it in the first place. Similarly, at migration watch points, the hard *swee* of a Yellow-browed Warbler is responsible for locating more of these Asiatic strays than sightings of them. Even non-vocal sounds, such as the drumming of woodpeckers, vary from one species to another. The high frequency of the Lesser Spotted is quite different from that of the Great Spotted Woodpecker.

I have been fortunate enough to travel several times with a lady who has mastered most of the songs and calls of European birds. As a result she continually locates 'invisible' birds which we are then able to track down. Her secret, she tells me, is to listen to tape recordings while doing the family ironing! While I do not advocate that all birders immediately take up ironing, there are many other opportunities to use a 'Walkman' to pass the time.

Field Marks

Field marks are conspicuous plumage patches, usually confined to particular groups of feathers, that are an invaluable aid to identification. The diagram shows the position and name of each feather group and, in particular, picks out the complex feather structure of the wing both when folded (on the main diagram) and when spread. The way in which even large groups of feathers on an open wing disappear when the wing is closed should be fully understood. It is crucial to the identification of many bird groups and may involve a field mark on the flying bird being invisible when the bird is at rest. A separate diagram shows details of the field markings on the head. A full, working knowledge of a bird's anatomy is essential to produce an accurate field description, which, in turn, leads to an accurate identification.

Of course, such diagrams appear in almost every good book on bird identification and are largely ignored as being too technical, even off-putting in their use of 'foreign' terms. I cannot, however, over stress the usefulness of understanding which feathers are which: the primaries, secondaries, tertials, coverts, scapulars and so on. To miss an opportunity to identify a bird simply because you do not know which group of feathers on the folded wing of a bird are the scapulars, seems short-sighted or even foolish.

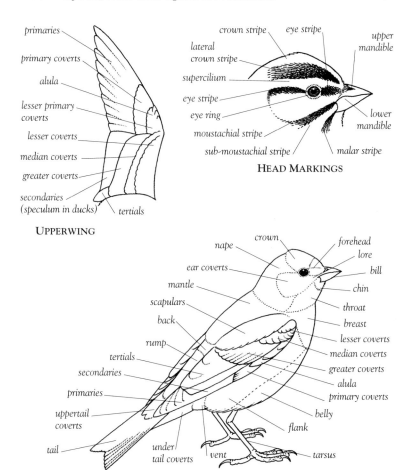

UPPERWING

HEAD MARKINGS

Size

Size is difficult to judge and everyone, experienced or not, is prone to error. So by far the best measure of size is to compare an unidentified bird with a known species, such as a thrush or a sparrow. Better still is to compare it with a bird with which it associates. Here, however, error is possible because viewing through binoculars distorts perspective, making birds that are farther away appear larger than closer ones. This optical illusion can easily be seen by looking directly along a pair of parallel lines, such as a railway track, with binoculars. Instead of the lines appearing to converge as they do when seen with the naked eye, they seemingly diverge. (If you do test this, please do not use an operating railway line!)

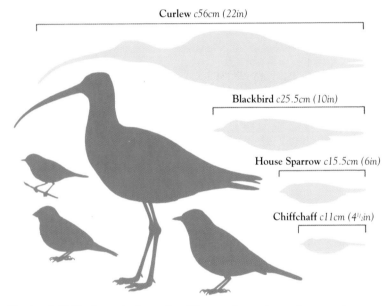

Curlew *c56cm (22in)*

Blackbird *c25.5cm (10in)*

House Sparrow *c15.5cm (6in)*

Chiffchaff *c11cm (4¹⁄₂in)*

The size of a bird is taken as the distance from bill tip to tail tip, and is usually measured using dead specimens. In life, the apparent size may differ due to the bird's posture.

If an unidentified bird is observed for any length of time and it associates with other, more common, birds, then it should be possible to estimate its size with a fair degree of accuracy. But always take into account the effect that broken tail feathers in particular can have on a bird's overall length, as well as changes in size owing to changes in posture. Tail-less Blackbirds and Starlings are, for example, occasionally seen and may cause problems for the inexperienced. Tail-less skuas on the other hand are virtually the norm in autumn. Similarly, winter birds such as finches and thrushes, often puff up their feathers to increase their insulation against the cold. What are often slim and elegant birds can then appear fat and chubby. A factor that may lead to an incorrect identification of a relatively well known and common bird.

Size is useful in identification, but because of the factors outlined above, it should never be used as the main criterion. It is, for example, far less use than determining the 'type' of bird and, in my opinion, size is of far less value than 'structure'.

Structure

Picking out a species by its structure is largely a matter of experience. It is the most difficult feature to describe and appreciate – even though it is arguably the most important. Even within closely related groups of birds, structure may differ considerably. The most common waders, for instance, are divided into two groups based on their structure. Although there are differences within each group, their overall structure is similar. The *Tringa* sandpipers are slim, long-legged, elegant birds; the *Calidris* sandpipers are rather dumpy and stocky. Once appreciated, there should be no possibility of confusion between, say, a Wood Sandpiper (*Tringa*) and a Dunlin (*Calidris*), although their plumage may, at times, be quite similar.

A Calidris *sandpiper – dumpy structure*
Little Stint

A Tringa *sandpiper – elegant structure*
Wood Sandpiper

Even within a genus, however, structural differences exist and may be quite pronounced. For example, a 'species pair' of waders that often causes confusion are the Little and Temminck's Stint. Both belong to the genus *Calidris*, but whereas the Little Stint is a bustling Dunlin-type, Temminck's is a more delicate, even elegant bird. Among gulls, too, structure is often the easiest means of separating what is a confusing group of species. The Black-headed Gull and the Herring Gull, for example, are quite different in structure. But so are the Herring Gull and Audouin's Gull, even though it may appear that the latter is no more than a red-billed version of the former. In fact, Audouin's Gull is almost as different from a Herring Gull as is a Black-headed Gull. They can be confused on grounds of size and of plumage, but structurally they are poles apart. Structure is largely a matter of proportion. Thus closely related birds may have longer or shorter tails, longer or shorter legs, and broader or narrower wings. Thus while all gulls have long wings these are much broader and less pointed than all terns. In general, gulls have long legs and terns short ones; but the Kittiwake, which is a gull, has short legs and the Caspian Tern long ones.

It is, however, with the birds of prey that structure becomes of paramount importance as a criterion of identification. Knowing the structural differences between a vulture, eagle, buzzard, hawk, harrier and falcon is not so much a matter of 'what type of bird' but more a recognition of its structure. Eagles are bulky with prominent heads and tails; vultures are all wings with small heads and tails. Hawks are round-winged and long-tailed; falcons have pointed wings and 'regular' tails, though kestrels are exceptional in also having long tails. Harriers are slim, long-winged and long-tailed, but some are more heavily built than others and, when soaring, may cause confusion with other groups of birds of prey.

Structure as an identification criterion has one major advantage over the more usual field marks–plumage detail approach. For whereas a bird's plumage may change with age, sex and season, its structure remains the same. So getting structure right can save time in checking plumage details.

Wing Formula

Just as each human being can be recognised by his or her fingerprints, so can a bird species be identified by its wing formula. Wing formula is no more than the relationship between the primary feathers of the wing, especially the outer ones. Thus a Marsh Warbler always has its third primary as its wing point, whereas the similar Blyth's Reed Warbler has the third and fourth primaries equal in length. This may sound somewhat technical, but the effect is to give Blyth's Reed a much shorter and more rounded wing than Marsh Warbler. And this can be seen in the field.

Short-toed Lark   **Lesser Short-toed Lark**

Marsh Warbler   **Blyth's Reed Warbler**

Similarly, while Short-toed and Lesser Short-toed Larks have similar wing formulae, but the Short-toed has very long tertials, which cover its primaries on the folded wing, whereas Lesser Short-toed shows a considerable length of exposed primaries. This is known as the bird's primary projection and is equally useful in species as varied as the small crakes.

Unfortunately, wing formulae can only accurately be read on a bird in the hand, but it can be seen with a close approach to a static bird and, as in the examples above, may be quite obvious in some species.

Plumage Variations

Long-tailed Duck

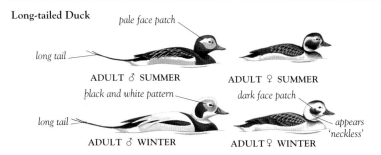

pale face patch

long tail

ADULT ♂ SUMMER

ADULT ♀ SUMMER

black and white pattern

dark face patch

long tail

appears 'neckless'

ADULT ♂ WINTER

ADULT ♀ WINTER

Understanding the way that plumage varies according to season, age and sex is essential if every bird seen is to be accurately identified. Birds differ in these ways for good reasons: for camouflage and display; to indicate adulthood; and to inform potential partners of their masculinity or femininity. In many species the male is more boldly marked or coloured than the female and immature birds are similarly more subdued. Such immature birds, particularly juvenile and first winter ones, are the most likely to get lost and turn up as vagrants out of range. A thorough knowledge of immature plumages is not only sensible, but often critical to autumn and winter birding. A scaly brown shrike may be a Red-backed, but it could be a Woodchat or a Masked. Besides which if each 'plumage' is treated as if it were a 'species' then there's even more enjoyment to be had going birding. Why not keep a checklist of plumages alongside the checklist of species?

Habitat Guide

Birds are creatures of habit, or perhaps we should say, habitat. Many have very specialized requirements found only in highly specific land forms. They may have specific food requirements, specialized hunting or foraging techniques, particular nest site needs and so on. Such species may, as a result, be found only in a very particular habitat. A knowledge of an individual species' habitat requirements is not only a great help in locating it, but also an invaluable aid to identification. Birds are, however, the most mobile group of animals in the world and, during their journeys, may be forced to occupy habitats that are far from perfect. Thus, to rely solely on habitat as a key is to miss the very essence of birding and, what's more, to make big identification howlers.

Gannets may be seen from shore, but are widespread at sea.

OPEN SEA

Seabirds must return to land each year to breed, but some of them seldom stray far from the shoreline. Nevertheless, there are some species that are seldom, if ever, seen except at sea. Such birds are pelagic in the true meaning of the term. The shearwaters and petrels are 'classic seabirds' in this sense, feeding and resting at sea. Most gulls are, in contrast, coastal, though some like Kittiwake and Sabine's Gull are truly seabirds. The Gannet is similarly a proper seabird as are two species of phalaropes in winter. These pelagic birds feed near the water's surface on fish, crustaceans or plankton and can thus range over the open oceans. Though many of the auks, terns, skuas and cormorants are seabirds, they mostly prefer inshore waters rather than open seas. Similarly, seaduck and divers spend their winters at sea, but they too are seldom found far from land. These birds find their food in shallow water and many are bottom feeders, seeking out mussels and other molluscs that are out of reach in deep water.

CLIFFS AND ROCKS

European shorelines, apart from those of the Mediterranean, are swept twice daily by the tides and, as a result, are among the richest of all habitats in the provision of food. In some places huge areas of sand and mud are uncovered on each tide. In others the shoreline is sheer or rocky and bird feeding opportunities are reduced as a result. Cliffs do, however, offer some birds safe breeding sites adjacent to the rich feeding grounds of the sea itself. Cliff-breeding birds, having no delimiting feeding territories, may cram closely together to nest, forming spectacular colonies. Guillemots stand side by side on narrow ledges, Kittiwakes construct their nests on the tiniest ledges, Fulmars nest near the cliff-tops and Puffins hide away in burrows. Rocky shorelines do, however, offer feeding to waders such as Purple Sandpiper and Turnstone, which are seldom found elsewhere, as well as Redshank and Curlew.

More at home on estuaries, Greenshank and Redshank also frequent beaches.

BEACHES

Beaches of sand and shingle are built up by the action of sea and local currents and offer both feeding and nesting opportunities for a variety of birds. Sadly, beach-nesting species have suffered significantly since human mobility turned such areas into summer playgrounds. As a result, there has been a notable decline among the terns that were the previous occupants. Little Terns, in particular, have suffered and are now endangered in Europe. More and more the terns are confined to difficult-to-reach beaches and to nature reserves. Other beach nesting species such as Oystercatcher and Ringed Plover are more catholic in their choice of nest sites and have suffered less. Though many waders regularly feed on beaches, most are also found along other shores. The Sanderling is the beach 'expert', feeding between each wave as it rolls back from the shoreline.

TIDAL FLATS

In many parts of north-western Europe, large tides combine with low-lying coasts to form huge intertidal areas of mud and sand. At each tide huge quantities of planktonic material is deposited over the seashore, providing food for vast numbers of shellfish and crustaceans. These, in turn, provide food for some of the greatest bird gatherings on the continent. The numbers of waders on the German and Dutch Waddensea, or the English Wash and Morecambe Bay are monumental. Knot, Dunlin, Oystercatcher, Ringed Plover, Bar-tailed Godwit, Grey Plover, Redshank, Curlew, Avocet and Little Stint occur in their thousands in winter or on passage. Some like Knot and Grey Plover are seldom found in any number away from these staggeringly rich and vitally important habitats. For some the existence of the land between the tides is crucial to their very survival.

ESTUARIES AND DELTAS

Where large rivers die as they meet the sea, they deposit silt and other material that they have eroded and carried from their hilly or mountain origins. Where they meet the North Sea or Atlantic, they form estuaries that are covered and uncovered twice each day by the tides. Where they join a non-tidal sea like the Mediterranean, they form deltas that gradually build up and extend into what was previously sea. Though similar in origin, deltas and estuaries offer totally different habitats for birds. Estuaries closely resemble tidal flats and differ only in their higher parts where fresh river water has a significant effect. Deltas are mainly freshwater pools and marshes intersected by islands and old river banks colonized by trees. These offer feeding and nesting sites to herons and egrets, ibises and pelicans, but they are also ideally suited to rice growing and are threatened as a result.

HARBOURS AND BARRAGES

Both of these habitats are man-made and more estuaries and tidal flats seem destined to follow suit. They are not, of themselves, poor bird habitats. On the contrary, many are richer in species than the 'land' they replaced. The point is, however, that some species cannot live without the mud- and sand-banks and use them in enormous numbers. So while harbours and barrages may offer a home to a wider variety of species, they do not always hold the number of individual birds. Present-day harbours are usually situated at the mouths of large rivers near large centres of human population. Their construction destroys estuaries. Other estuaries may be enclosed to produce gigantic freshwaters. So while both are destructive, harbours offer little in return except opportunities for gulls, while barrages produce wonderful freshwater lakes and marginal marshes.

Shelduck are found in harbours and estuaries.

LAKES AND RESERVOIRS

Lakes, together with their man-made equivalents, vary enormously in their appeal to birds. Deep waters attract fewer birds than shallow ones and as most deep lakes are situated in mountain, or hilly areas, and most shallow ones in lowlands, it is the latter that prove most rewarding to birders. Sadly, many shallow, lowland lakes have been eroded and reclaimed for agriculture and those that remain are frequently used for recreation. Natural, undisturbed lowland lakes are thus few and far between. The demand for water has, however, accelerated and, as a result, large numbers of reservoirs have been constructed both in mountain and lowland areas. Whereas the former are generally barren and of little interest, the latter are among the richest of bird habitats. Large numbers of wildfowl use them in winter, waders may pour through on passage and breeding birds find them ideal. Herons and egrets often establish colonies on islands and bushy marsh-like margins. Marsh terns may abound and harriers, duck and other waterbirds find new homes in previously barren areas. If they are spared the blight of watersports, these lowland waters may become the most important bird areas for miles; their conservation and protection is important to many species.

RIVERS AND STREAMS

Many European rivers vary season by season. Some, fed by melting snow, form torrents in spring, but are completely dry by summer. Others, that flow throughout the year, flood their banks every spring. While such seasonality is unsuitable for bank or ground-nesting birds, it offers a haven for tree nesting and other waterside species. In their higher reaches streams and young rivers are home to Dipper, Grey Wagtail and Common Sandpiper. More mature rivers have Kingfisher, Grey Heron and Little Grebe. Slow, broad rivers have much in common with lakes and their marginal vegetation may support White-tailed Eagle, Gull-billed Tern and Penduline Tit.

Grey Herons breed among riverside trees.

MOUNTAINS AND TUNDRA

The great permafrost zone of the Arctic tundra is a maze of marshes and lakes sitting on an impermeable layer of frozen land. Vegetation is scant and dwarf, but the wealth of food is prodigious. Mountains below the Arctic Circle offer similar conditions at lower latitudes. Such areas are the breeding grounds of hosts of summer visitors, including many waders, terns, buntings and skuas. They are also home to a few major predators which, like the Snowy Owl, Rough-legged Buzzard and Gyr Falcon, manage to eke out an existence throughout the year. A single species, the Ptarmigan, manages to exist through the harsh winter without reliance on predation. Mountains differ mainly in the sharp differences in altitude and climate exhibited within a relatively short distance, thus enabling birds to descend (rather than migrate) to warmer climes. Red-billed and Alpine Choughs can, therefore, avoid the worst of the winter by dropping down a few thousand feet. Similarly, Wallcreepers can move from cliff faces to valley floors, where quarries and churches offer milder foraging grounds. Mountains are also largely uninhabited and provide sites suitable for birds of prey to nest safe from persecution.

MOORLAND

Moorland is usually associated with mountains and its low ground cover of coarse grasses and heathers is due largely to the poor quality of its soils, coupled with poor drainage. Insects are, however, often abundant and many birds take advantage of the summer abundance as breeding grounds. In the main these are summer visitors such as Dunlin, Curlew, Redshank, Whimbrel and other waders. Meadow Pipits are frequently the most abundant species, but there are Snow and Lapland Buntings, Red and Black Grouse and the predatory Hen Harrier and Short-eared Owl. In winter, the moors are often abandoned, though a wider variety of species 'stays on' than on the otherwise similar tundra of the Arctic. In some areas birds from farther north may actually be winter visitors to moorlands, though they will avoid the worst conditions by moving away during freeze-ups or snow cover.

Black Grouse gather to display on moorland 'leks'.

CONIFEROUS FORESTS

Conifer forests of spruce and pine naturally cover huge areas of northern Europe either side of the Arctic Circle; the boreal forests. Similar forests exist on mountain slopes farther south where similar climatic conditions prevail. Despite man's efforts, vast areas of these forests remain intact. Though areas are clear-felled annually, regeneration and replanting has turned forestry from a simple rape to managed farming during the past hundred years. Elsewhere, conifer forests and belts have been planted as wind breaks, shelter and as an exploitable resource, mainly on poor heath-like soils. Even in southern Europe, islands like Cyprus and Corsica have extensive pine forests clothing the hills. Put together, these coniferous forests are rich in bird species, if not in the actual members of individual birds. Many of the species that inhabit conifers are never found elsewhere. The northern owls, Great Grey, Ural, Hawk, Tengmalm's and Pygmy are all confined to conifers and some to only the boreal zone.

DECIDUOUS FORESTS

Broad-leaved forests once covered vast areas of temperate Europe merging to the north with the conifers, to the south with the prickly evergreens of the Mediterranean. Today only remnants remain. Their clearance drastically reduced birds that could not adapt to the new landscape, yet it is not possible to name a single species that has become extinct as a result. Woodpeckers, nuthatches, warblers, flycatchers, treecreepers and tits are still present, even among small copses and woods. Many were doubtless found among clearings or along forest margins, but others still find a true forest habitat even in small deciduous forests.

Barn Swallows frequent anywhere that provides food to rear a family.

HEATHS AND SCRUB

Heaths exist on poor, sandy soils and are often invaded by broom and gorse, birch and hazel. Modern agriculture has developed means of turning such former 'wastelands' to productive farming and, as a result, many heaths have disappeared. Such landscapes are now scarce in northern Europe, though much of the dry Mediterranean region is still well covered with prickly *maquis*, exploited only by sheep and goats. Typical species of heathlands are the resident Yellowhammer, Stonechat and Dartford Warbler. Mediterranean scrub boasts a host of warblers, including Sardinian, Subalpine, Spectacled, Orphean and Marmora's, some resident, some summer visitors.

GRASSLANDS

Whether any European grasslands can be deemed 'natural' is debatable. The Russian steppes were grazed for generations before being turned to the plough. The Spanish steppes continue to exist, though they too are progressively cultivated. Modern agriculture has turned a patchwork of fields to cereal prairies that, for steppe birds, is little different from grassland. Were it not for harrowing, sowing and harvesting, steppe birds might be doing quite well in deforested Europe. Bustards, sandgrouse, plovers, larks and pipits are all typical steppe birds that require grassland to survive. All are under threat in modern Europe.

FIELDS AND HEDGES

A mixture of hedges and fields provides perfect habitat for vast numbers of birds, many drawn from heaths and woodland margins. Hedgerows provide a wealth of nest sites and winter food for a wide variety of species from Cirl Bunting to Goldfinch. Even the Red-billed Chough relies for survival on cattle being left out in the fields during winter. Barn Owls, in decline virtually everywhere, need ill-kept field margins and fallow as hunting grounds.

Goldfinches delight among hedgerow corners with thistles.

VILLAGES AND TOWNS

Small urban areas are usually strategically sited to exploit the surrounding countryside by acting as a market for the area. For many birds they work in a similar manner and Rooks, White Storks, Lesser Kestrels, swifts and House Martins all nest in urban areas surrounded by suitable feeding grounds. For many species, however, towns and villages meet all their needs. Gardens, often with bird feeders, are planted with a wide variety of trees and shrubs that offer excellent nesting and feeding opportunities and Robin, Blackbird, Song and Mistle Thrushes, Magpie, Hedge Accentor, Goldfinch, Serin and Greenfinch all take advantage.

CITIES

At first sight the high-rise modern city seems to offer little to birds. A city-based birder may concentrate his attention on parks and gardens, but these are no more than woods or parklands within the urban environment. True city birds must be sought within the concrete jungle itself and among the other functions that are essential to contemporary city life. House Sparrow, Starling, Feral Pigeon, Tawny Owl and Kestrel may all scrape a living actually in the city. But every city needs its rubbish dumps, its sewage works and its reservoirs and it is here that the city-based birder finds his birds. Gulls, duck, starlings, wagtails, waders, finches and buntings are all regular, some in very high numbers indeed. Such sites also offer respite to many small migrants and can be viewed as oases within a desert of concrete. There is much to be seen by the city birder who stays at home and much to be learnt of the ways that birds adapt to change.

The
BIRDS
of Britain & Europe

WHICH BIRDS?

Some 700 different species have been seen in Britain and Europe at one time or another, and new species are added to the list every year. Fortunately, many are vagrants that occur once in a while from a part of North Africa, Asia and America. They are in no sense 'European birds'. Most tend to be young, lost birds in rather nondescript juvenile or first-winter plumage. They are often difficult to identify and need a somewhat different approach from the normal field guide.

This book covers the birds that occur every year and are most likely to be seen. These birds either breed regularly, winter regularly or regularly pass through on passage to and from their breeding areas. Of course, things are never static; today's regular breeder may disappear and become a rarity. Conversely, today's vagrant may become tomorrow's breeding species.

Red-throated Diver *Gavia stellata*

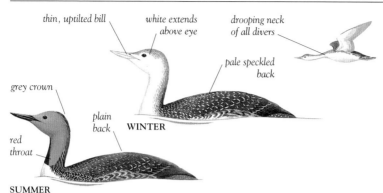

thin, uptilted bill

white extends above eye

drooping neck of all divers

pale speckled back

grey crown

plain back

WINTER

red throat

SUMMER

J F M A M J J A S O N D

Status: Smallest, most widespread and numerous of divers.
Identification: 53–59cm (21–23in). Grey back and thin
uptilted bill are best means of identification. In summer,
head pale grey with difficult-to-see rusty triangle on throat,
and series of black and white stripes on rear of neck. In
winter, grey back is speckled white to create a scaly look.
White of foreneck and lower face extends above dark eye.
Flies fast on long, pointed wings; 'hump-backed'.
Voice: In summer, wails and cackles. In flight, *kuk-kuk-kuk*.
Habitat: In summer, freshwater lakes, within flighting
distance of sea. Winters at sea in inshore waters.
Similar Species: Other divers; none have thin uptilted bill.

Black-throated Diver *Gavia arctica*

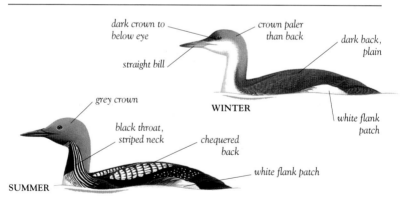

dark crown to below eye

crown paler than back

dark back, plain

straight bill

grey crown

WINTER

black throat, striped neck

chequered back

white flank patch

white flank patch

SUMMER

Status: Medium-sized diver most likely to be confused
with larger Great Northern in all plumages. Circumpolar.
Identification: 56–69cm (22–27in). In summer, largely
black and white with two chequer-board ovals on back. In
winter, upperparts uniform slate-grey in adult; slightly
mottled in juvenile. White patch at waterline on rear
flank often obvious. Dark of crown extends below eye
giving a masked effect.
Voice: Grunts, croaks and wails in summer. Silent at sea.
Habitat: Breeds on large fresh waters; winters inshore at sea.
Similar Species: See other divers. Red-throated always
paler grey. Great Northern more massive head and bill.

J F M A M J J A S O N D

Great Northern Diver   *Gavia immer*

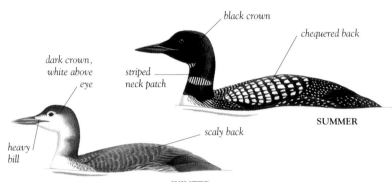

black crown

chequered back

dark crown, white above eye

striped neck patch

SUMMER

heavy bill

scaly back

WINTER

J F M A M J J A S O N D

Status: Largest of common European divers. Winter visitor from Iceland.
Identification: 69–81cm (27–32in). Large angular head and heavy black bill distinguish at all seasons. In summer, black head and neck, broken only by narrow oval of stripes on sides of neck. Chequered back pattern. In winter, darker above than Red-throated: scaly back paler than Black-throated. Dark-crown does not enclose eye. Wingbeats noticeably slower than smaller divers.
Voice: Loud wails, cackling laughs and mournful notes.
Habitat: Freshwater lakes in summer. Winters at sea.
Similar Species: In winter, all other divers as above.

White-billed Diver   *Gavia adamsii*

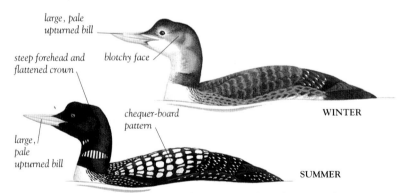

large, pale upturned bill

steep forehead and flattened crown

blotchy face

WINTER

chequer-board pattern

large, pale upturned bill

SUMMER

J F M A M J J A S O N D

Status: High Arctic equivalent of Great Northern Diver; strays southwards into North Sea and Atlantic.
Identification: 75–90cm (29–35in). Similar to Great Northern, but with longer, paler and distinctly shaped bill; straight upper mandible and sharply angled gonys give uptilted impression. Summer plumage much as Great Northern. Winter, very similar to Great Northern; with paler neck and smudgy paler face. Steep forehead and flattened crown always apparent.
Voice: Usually silent away from breeding grounds.
Habitat: Breeds tundra lakes. Winters at sea, inshore.
Similar Species: Great Northern Diver as above.

Pied-billed Grebe *Podilymbus podiceps*

deep chunky bill

large head

'sawn-off rear end'

bill ring

prominent eye ring

WINTER

SUMMER

J F M A M J J A S O N D

Status: Vagrant from America that has become virtually annual in Britain since 1963 and is often a 'long stay' visitor.
Identification: 31–38cm (12–15in). Very similar to, but larger than Little Grebe, with 'sawn-off' rear end and plume-less plumage. Large, wedge-shaped bill and heavy head create bulky appearance, obvious even at distance. In summer shows black bill ring and difficult-to-see throat patch.
Voice: Brief *whit-whit*.
Habitat: Freshwater lakes, reservoirs and marshes.
Similar Species: Little Grebe as above.

Little Grebe *Tachybaptus ruficollis*

red sides to head

stubby bill

pale bill patch

SUMMER

'sawn-off' tail

buffy neck

WINTER

Status: Most widespread and numerous of the regular grebes.
Identification: 25–29cm (10–11in). Buoyant small grebe that sits, cork-like, on the water with 'sawn-off' rear end. In summer, rust-red cheeks, throat and neck, with bold, yellowish spot at base of bill. In winter, dark cap and upperparts; white throat; buffy neck and flanks. Dives easily and often to re-emerge at considerable distance.
Voice: Very vocal, far-carrying winnowing calls.
Habitat: Breeds on ponds, lakes and slow-flowing rivers. Winters larger waters and estuaries.
Similar Species: Winter Slavonian and Black-necked Grebes lack square-cut tail. Transatlantic Pied-billed Grebe.

J F M A M J J A S O N D

Great Crested Grebe *Podiceps cristatus*

JUVENILE

striped head

ear tufts and crest

ADULT SUMMER

white above eye

white foreneck

ADULT WINTER

J F M A M J J A S O N D

Status: Largest grebe; widespread resident; summer and winter visitor to fresh waters and the sea. Increasing.
Identification: 45–51cm (18–20in). In summer, resplendent with golden-russet head plumes and crest erected to great effect in display. In winter, black cap extends to just above eye, forming prominent white eyebrow; foreneck white. Juvenile heavily streaked on head and neck. Dives expertly; flies laboriously after lengthy pattering over water's surface.
Voice: Barking and croaking calls.
Habitat: Breeds at lakes and reservoirs among emergent vegetation. Winters large waters and sea coasts.
Similar Species: See Red-necked Grebe.

Red-necked Grebe *Podiceps grisegena*

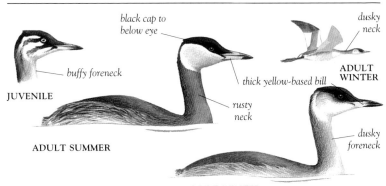

black cap to below eye

buffy foreneck

JUVENILE

ADULT SUMMER

thick yellow-based bill

rusty neck

dusky neck

ADULT WINTER

dusky foreneck

ADULT WINTER

J F M A M J J A S O N D

Status: Summer visitor, passage migrant and winter visitor that breeds in eastern and central Europe.
Identification: 40–46cm (16–18in). Slightly smaller than Great Crested Grebe. Marked in summer by black cap, white cheek patch and rust-red neck. In winter, neck becomes dusky-grey and cheeks less white, smudged grey. At all seasons bill is yellow with extensive black tip, and black cap extends below eye.
Voice: Loud wailing breeding season. Silent rest of year.
Habitat: Small, inland fresh waters. Winters coastal waters and large inland natural and artificial waters.
Similar Species: Great Crested Grebe in winter.

Slavonian Grebe   *Podiceps auritus*

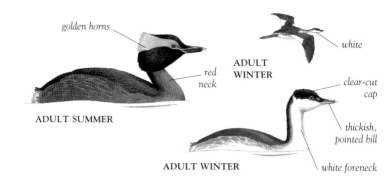

golden horns

white

ADULT
WINTER

*clear-cut
cap*

*red
neck*

*thickish,
pointed bill*

ADULT SUMMER

ADULT WINTER

white foreneck

J F M A M J J A S O N D

Status: Small grebe; easily confused with Black-necked.
Identification: 31–36cm (12–14in). Summer; black head
with bold golden 'horns' forming hindcrest. Front of neck
and underparts rich rust-red. Winter; clear-cut black cap,
white foreneck and flanks; back almost black. Sits low in
water seldom, if ever, raising tail. Bill stout.
Voice: Rippling call when breeding, silent in winter.
Habitat: Shallow lakes in boreal zone during breeding
season. In winter, most move to larger fresh waters,
estuaries or sheltered seas.
Similar Species: Summer Black-necked Grebe may appear
'horned'. In winter, clear-cut cap and bill shape diagnostic.

Black-necked Grebe   *Podiceps nigricollis*

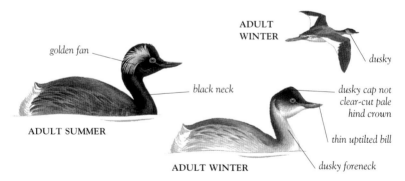

ADULT
WINTER

dusky

golden fan

black neck

*dusky cap not
clear-cut pale
hind crown*

thin uptilted bill

ADULT SUMMER

ADULT WINTER

dusky foreneck

Status: Small grebe, similar to Slavonian but head rounder
and bill thinner and uptilted. Less marine in winter.
Identification: 28–33cm (11–13in). Summer; black head
and neck broken only by 'fan' of golden plumes, rust-red
flanks. Winter; black cap becomes greyish on sides of head
with pale hind crown; compare clean-cut cap of Slavonian.
Foreneck dusky. Sits buoyantly on water, often with 'sawn-
off' tail reminiscent of Little Grebe.
Voice: A variety of harsh notes and a quiet *poo-eep*, but
less vocal than other grebes even when breeding.
Habitat: Small fresh waters. Winters near coasts.
Similar Species: See Slavonian and Little Grebes.

J F M A M J J A S O N D

Winter Grebes

All grebes, in winter, lose their summer plumes and finery and, therefore, some of their primary field marks. They do not, however, become a uniform group of six confusing species, but rather three pairs of similar species. Size, structure and head pattern remain the major criteria of identification. The pairs are:

Great Crested Grebe vs. Red-necked Grebe
Slavonian Grebe vs. Black-necked Grebe
Little Grebe vs. Pied-billed Grebe

GREAT CRESTED GREBE
White foreneck contrasts with dark hindneck and black cap does not cover eye. Pink bill.

RED-NECKED GREBE
Differs from Great Crested in having dusky, not white, foreneck; black cap terminating below eye; yellow (not pink) bill.

SLAVONIAN GREBE
Neat, medium-sized grebe. Upperparts dark grey with clear-cut black cap forming clean horizontal line with lower edge of eye. Regular shaped bill; rear end slopes to water; white foreneck.

BLACK-NECKED GREBE
Smudgy black cap extends to eye, but terminates at ear coverts leaving smudgy white wedge on rear crown. Neck grey; bill uptilted.

LITTLE GREBE
Small grebe with sawn-off white tail and stubby bill – all features shared with Pied-billed Grebe. Lacks big bill and pale eye-ring of Pied-billed.

PIED-BILLED GREBE
As Little Grebe, is small, chunky-billed and sawn off at the tail. But, bill is ivory and wedge-shaped, lacking black band of summer; eye has prominent pale ring, and lacks dark cap of Little Grebe.

Black-browed Albatross *Diomedea melanophris*

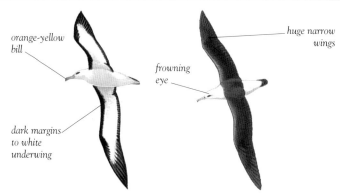

orange-yellow bill

huge narrow wings

frowning eye

dark margins to white underwing

J F M A M J J A S O N D

Status: Most likely albatross in Europe and only one to take up residence (Faeroes, Bass Rock, Hermaness). **Identification:** 89–93cm (32–36in). Huge wing-span 240cm (95in) and shape picks out albatrosses from all other seabirds. Black-browed is black above, white below with large orange-yellow bill and frowning mark over eye. Underwing is white with broad black margins front and rear. Juvenile has dusky pale centre to underwing. **Voice:** Silent at sea. **Habitat:** Breeds high on rocky islands. Otherwise at sea. **Similar Species:** Other albatrosses, but most seen probably this species.

Fulmar *Fulmarus glacialis*

short stubby bill

stiff wings

tube-nose

thick neck

Status: Thick-set seabird that glides over waves on stiffly held wings in typical shearwater fashion. Widespread. **Identification:** 44–50cm (17–20in). Pale coloration and thick-set, bull-necked appearance preclude confusion with any other stiff-wing in region. Upperparts grey; head and underparts white; short stubby bill yellow with tube-nose visible at close range. Superficial resemblance to pale gull. Gregarious at cliff-top colonies and feeding grounds. **Voice:** Harsh cackles at breeding grounds. **Habitat:** Breeds vertical cliffs, also short distances inland among walls. Winters at sea. **Similar Species:** No other grey stiff-wings in region.

J F M A M J J A S O N D

Sooty Shearwater *Puffinus griseus*

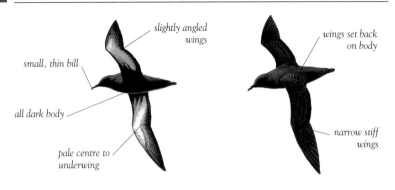

slightly angled wings

wings set back on body

small, thin bill

all dark body

narrow stiff wings

pale centre to underwing

J F M A M J J A S O N D

Status: Large, narrow-winged shearwater that is scarce summer visitor from South Atlantic.
Identification: 39–44cm (15–17in). Uniformly dark sooty coloration above and below, marked only by pale centre to underwing. Small head, thin bill, wings set well back on body. Flies fast and direct on narrow, slightly swept-back wings. Flaps more frequently than other shearwaters.
Voice: Silent at sea.
Habitat: Breeds islands. Winters at sea.
Similar Species: With good views, coloration and purposeful flight precludes confusion with other shearwaters.

Mediterranean Shearwater *Puffinus yelkouan*

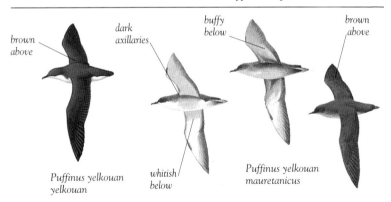

brown above

dark axillaries

buffy below

brown above

whitish below

Puffinus yelkouan yelkouan

Puffinus yelkouan mauretanicus

J F M A M J J A S O N D

Status: Manx-sized shearwater, only recently split from that bird and recognized as a separate species.
Identification: 30–38cm (11½–15in). Two distinct subspecies both with brown upperparts. Western birds P.y.*mauretanicus* buffy below, buffy wing linings and flanks. Eastern birds P.y.*yelkouan* white below,white wing linings and narrow brown axillaries. Eastern birds can be confused with Manx in poor light; western birds similar to Cory's and Sooty but smaller with faster wingbeats.
Voice: Wails and screams at breeding colonies. Silent at sea.
Habitat: Rocky islands and headlands. Winters at sea.
Similar Species: As above.

Cory's Shearwater   *Calonectris diomedea*

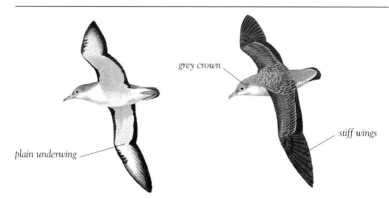

grey crown

stiff wings

plain underwing

J F M A M J J A S O N D

Status: Large, robust shearwater of Mediterranean and eastern Atlantic.
Identification: 43–48cm (17–19in). Dark brown above, white below, in Mediterranean can only be confused with much smaller Mediterranean Shearwater. In Atlantic, confusion with similar-sized Great Shearwater likely. Pale bill, pale greyish head, and clean white underwing are main features. Wings slightly bowed when gliding. Flaps and soars more than other species.
Voice: Loud, wailing coughs *kee-ogh*. Silent at sea.
Habitat: Rocky islands. Winters at sea.
Similar Species: Great Shearwater as above.

Great Shearwater   *Puffinus gravis*

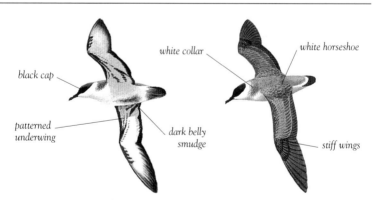

white collar

white horseshoe

black cap

patterned underwing

dark belly smudge

stiff wings

Status: Large shearwater that is summer visitor to Atlantic from breeding grounds in southern hemisphere.
Identification: 42–49cm (16½–19in). Large shearwater, which flies with long stiff-winged glides broken by short bouts of wing flapping. Dark brown above, white below. Prominent black cap contrasts with white cheeks and axillary. Narrow white horseshoe rump; dark smudge on lower belly. Dark margins to underwing, to coverts and axillaries create barred pattern.
Voice: Silent at sea.
Habitat: At sea. Breeds remote uninhabited islands.
Similar Species: See Cory's Shearwater.

J F M A M J J A S O N D

Manx Shearwater *Puffinus puffinus*

black
above

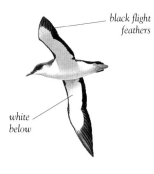

black flight
feathers

white
below

black
cap extends
below eye

J F M A M J J A S O N D

Status: Most abundant shearwater in North Atlantic and North Sea.
Identification: 30–38cm (11½–15½in). Usually seen in fast careering flight low over sea, or resting on sea awaiting cover of darkness to return to colonies. Black above extending to below eye; white below with black margins to underwing. Flashes black and white as it turns low over waves on straight, stiff wings. Mostly gregarious.
Voice: Loud wails and screams at breeding colonies.
Habitat: Uninhabited islands and bare mountain tops on larger islands in summer. At sea at other times.
Similar Species: Mediterranean and Little Shearwaters.

Little Shearwater *Puffinus assimilis*

eye shows as
black spot

tiny bill

relatively rounded
wings

J F M A M J J A S O N D

Status: Like small Manx Shearwater. Breeds on Atlantic islands; seldom ventures farther north than Portugal.
Identification: 25–30cm (10–12½in). Smaller size, shorter more rounded wings reminiscent of Puffin and fluttering flight suggests Common Sandpiper. Less gliding than Manx. Black cap does not enclose eye which stands out as result.
Voice: Silent at sea.
Habitat: Breeds on large and small islands among unfrequented rocky slopes near sea or inland. Winters at sea.
Similar Species: Manx Shearwater as above.

Wilson's Storm-petrel *Oceanites oceanicus*

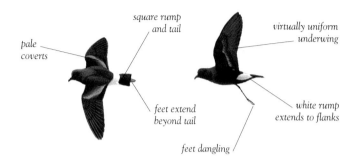

pale coverts

square rump and tail

feet extend beyond tail

virtually uniform underwing

white rump extends to flanks

feet dangling

J F M A M J J A S O N D

Status: Breeds Antarctic islands, performs huge loop migration in North Atlantic in autumn.
Identification: 17–18cm (6½in). Typical storm-petrel, with black plumage and white rump. Best features are square undivided white rump; pale wing coverts; uniform underwing; feet extend beyond tail. Patters on water's surface when feeding.
Voice: Silent at sea.
Habitat: At sea.
Similar Species: European has pale underwing bar and lacks pale upperwing coverts; Leach's has forked tail and divided rump; Madeiran has notched tail.

European Storm-petrel *Hydrobates pelagicus*

pale underwing bar

fluttering flight

square white rump

white extends to sides

square tail

dangling legs

Status: Tiny, swallow-like seabird with white rump. Most common storm-petrel in Atlantic and Mediterranean.
Identification: 15cm (6in) Black plumage broken only by square white rump and white underwing bar. Thus the only storm-petrel without pale upperwing coverts and one of only two with unforked tail. Feet do not project beyond tail. Often follows ships, picking food from wake.
Voice: When breeding utters a purr ending in a hiccough; also high-pitched squealing. Silent at sea.
Habitat: Remote, uninhabited islands. Winters at sea.
Similar Species: See Wilson's Storm-petrel for distinctions from that and other storm-petrels.

J F M A M J J A S O N D

Leach's Storm-petrel *Oceanodroma leucorhoa*

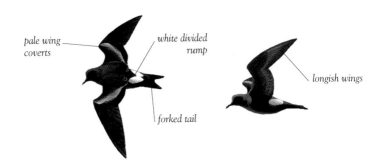

pale wing coverts

white divided rump

forked tail

longish wings

J F M A M J J A S O N D

Status: Most widespread fork-tailed storm-petrel in North Atlantic. Larger than European Storm-petrel.
Identification: 19–22cm (7½–9in). Typical storm-petrel, with divided white rump of two meeting ovals, deeply forked tail, pale upperwing coverts. Flight more shearwater-like with short glides between leisurely wing flapping. Seldom follows ships.
Voice: Croons on nest; variety of screeches at colonies.
Habitat: Uninhabited islands; winters at sea.
Similar Species: Only other fork-tailed storm-petrel with pale wing coverts is Madeiran, which is smaller, has square white rump and notched rather than deeply forked tail.

Madeiran Storm-petrel *Oceanodroma castro*

pale coverts

uniform underwing

square white rump

notched tail

J F M A M J J A S O N D

Status: Rare, recently discovered breeder that is otherwise no more than a vagrant to western seaboard.
Identification: 18–20cm (7–8in). Black storm-petrel with square white rump, pale upperwing coverts and notched tail. Most likely to be confused with Leach's, but shorter, more rounded wings give impression of smaller size. Flight even more shearwater-like. Distinguished from European Storm-petrel by pale wing coverts and lack of underwing bar.
Voice: Squeaky notes and guttural purr at nest.
Habitat: Isolated islands. Winters nearby sea.
Similar Species: Leach's Storm-petrel as above.

Northern Gannet *Morus bassanus*

dark speckled white head and forewing

thick neck and bill

white, black wingtips

JUVENILE

ADULT

FIRST SUMMER

SECOND SUMMER

THIRD SUMMER

some black tips to wing and central tail feathers

Status: Nests at a few huge colonies, mainly on remote islands. Otherwise widespread in Atlantic and (less so) in western Mediterranean.
Identification: 86–96cm (34–37in). At sea appears white and cigar-shaped with pointed head and tail. Wings pointed with large black tips. Flies low over sea on stiff, shearwater-like wings, before rising in series of flaps and starting another glide. Immatures dark brown, gradually becoming whiter.
Voice: Variety of grunts and cackles at colony.
Habitat: Offshore islands and stacks. Otherwise at sea.
Similar Species: Cape Gannet of South Africa, which has black tail, recorded in Spain: extreme caution advised.

Great Cormorant *Phalacrocorax carbo*

white face

ADULT SUMMER

FIRST WINTER

thick bill

pale belly

thick neck

white patch

white face

ADULT WINTER

Status: Widespread and common coastal bird in west and inland along major river and lake systems.
Identification: 84–89cm (33–35in). Large black, goose-like waterbird that swims low in water and frequently hangs out wings to dry. Adult glossy green-black with white face (and head in Continental birds) and round white flank patch in summer. Immature browner with pale breast and belly. Swims with uptilted head, heavy yellow bill and large head.
Voice: Croaks and grunts on breeding grounds.
Habitat: Coasts and islands, large inland waters.
Similar Species: Shag has thinner neck, smaller head and thinner bill.

Shag *Phalacrocorax aristotelis*

greenish-black

crest

no white

ADULT SUMMER

thin neck

thin bill

dark face

ADULT WINTER

buffy

FIRST WINTER

J F M A M J J A S O N D

Status: Smaller version of Great Cormorant, but confined to marine environment where frequents rocky coastlines.
Identification: 72–80cm (28–31in). Swims, dives and hangs out wings like Cormorant, but seldom flies at height. Adult glossy green-black, with short tufted crest in summer. Bill black, with yellow gape, and much thinner than Cormorant; head smaller and neck thinner. Immatures are brown above, buffy below.
Voice: Grunts and hisses at breeding grounds.
Habitat: Essentially confined to rocky coasts with cliffs and islands. Winters close inshore over similar ground.
Similar Species: See Cormorant and above.

Pygmy Cormorant *Phalacrocorax pygmeus*

brown wash

tiny bill

ADULT SPRING

long tail

ADULT

tiny bill

long tail

JUVENILE

ADULT WINTER

J F M A M J J A S O N D

Status: Smallest European cormorant confined to south-east Europe and adjacent parts of Ukraine and Russia.
Identification: 48–49cm (19in). Short stubby bill, small head and proportionately longer tail separate at all times from any other European cormorant. Adult in summer is black with brown wash over head and neck. Juvenile is dark brown above, buffy-white below and best identified on structural features. Colonial.
Voice: Harsh barking.
Habitat: Marshes, deltas, backwaters.
Similar Species: Shag could be confused, but structurally distinct as above.

White Pelican   *Pelecanus onocrotalus*

huge bill

ADULT SUMMER

contrasting flight feathers

ADULT

brown upperparts

JUVENILE

J F M A M J J A S O N D

Status: Breeds at only a few spots in our area in the Balkans.
Identification: 140–180cm (55–70in). At rest, adult is white with pinkish bill and orange-yellow pouch below; legs pinkish. From below primaries and secondaries clear-cut black contrasting with coverts and body; upper surface secondaries black washed white. Juveniles brown, gradually becoming white with age. Dalmatian Pelican has dark grey trailing edge to grey underwing, but similar pattern above.
Voice: Harsh barks.
Habitat: Large lakes and deltas with plentiful reeds.
Similar Species: Dalmatian Pelican as above.

Dalmatian Pelican   *Pelecanus crispus*

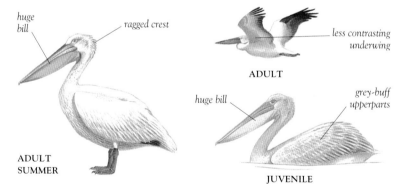

huge bill

ragged crest

ADULT SUMMER

less contrasting underwing

ADULT

huge bill

grey-buff upperparts

JUVENILE

Status: More widespread, but less numerous, than White Pelican, which inhabits same areas of south-east Europe.
Identification: 160–180cm (63–70in). Similar to White Pelican, but generally duller. Whitish with silvery-grey wash. Adult has huge bill with deep orange-red pouch in breeding season; legs dark grey. In flight upperwing shows black primaries and secondaries, like White Pelican; underwing shows dark grey trailing edge only. Juvenile much paler than juvenile White. Gregarious, soars easily.
Voice: Harsh barks.
Habitat: Lakes and deltas, also smaller waters.
Similar Species: See White Pelican and above.

J F M A M J J A S O N D

Bittern *Botaurus stellaris*

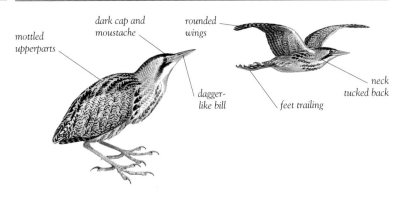

mottled upperparts

dark cap and moustache

rounded wings

dagger-like bill

feet trailing

neck tucked back

J F M A M J J A S O N D

Status: Secretive bird with highly fragmented distribution.
Identification: 70–80cm (27–31in). More often heard than seen; characteristic booming sounds like distant foghorn. Heavily camouflaged in shades of brown with black and buff mottling and barring. Dark cap and strong black moustachial streak visible when seen in open. When disturbed, points bill skywards and sways like reeds in a breeze. Mostly seen in flight with head tucked back and greenish-yellow legs trailing.
Voice: Deep booming *urrwoomp* repeated.
Habitat: Requires extensive reedbeds.
Similar Species: Vagrant American Bittern.

Little Bittern *Ixobrychus minutus*

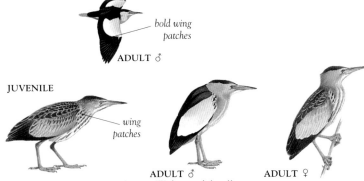

bold wing patches

ADULT ♂

JUVENILE

wing patches

ADULT ♂

ADULT ♀

J F M A M J J A S O N D

Status: Widespread, locally numerous, summer visitor to Continental European reedbeds and other marshlands.
Identification: 33–38cm (13–15½in). Male has black crown, upperparts, tail and upperwing, the last boldly marked with pinkish covert patches – the most obvious feature in flight and at rest. Adult female similar, but less contrasted with rufous-cream wing patches. Juvenile and sub-adult heavily streaked; pale wing patches still good feature.
Voice: Repeated croaking call.
Habitat: Prefers reeds, but occupies smaller stands at margins of rivers and lakes, well-vegetated swamps.
Similar Species: None in area.

Night Heron   *Nycticorax nycticorax*

black crown

thick bill

black back

black saddle

grey wings

ADULT

thick bill

ADULT   **JUVENILE**

Status: Widespread, but highly localized, summer visitor to Continental Europe. Gregarious, crepuscular.
Identification: 58–65cm (23–25in). Adult has black crown and back, with grey wings and white cheeks and underparts. Thick, chunky bill is black; legs yellow. Immatures grey-brown, spotted white above and streaked below. Always hunched, with head and neck set well into body both at rest and in flight, when cigar-shaped body diagnostic.
Voice: Harsh croaks.
Habitat: Wooded watersides when resting. Feeds at all manner of wetlands, largely at night.
Similar Species: Compare juvenile with browner Bittern.

J F M A M J J A S O N D

Squacco Heron   *Ardeola ralloides*

white wings

long bill

striped breast

ADULT SUMMER   **JUVENILE**

Status: Summer visitor to southern Europe that is generally solitary and self effacing.
Identification: 43–48cm (17–19in). A neat little heron marked rich warm buff in breeding plumage, with cascading crest of black and white plumes. Long, dagger-like bill is blue tipped black; legs orange-pink. In winter and immature plumage, upperparts grey-brown heavily streaked. White wings in flight attract attention in all plumages.
Voice: Mostly silent, but some harsh croaks.
Habitat: Small, well-vegetated, still fresh waters where it prefers margins with plentiful cover.
Similar Species: Cattle Egret also buffy in summer.

J F M A M J J A S O N D

Cattle Egret *Bubulcus ibis*

ADULT

buff plumes

dark legs

ADULT NON-BREEDING

yellow bill

jowled look

yellow-green legs

ADULT BREEDING

J F M A M J J A S O N D

Status: Confined to Iberia, Turkey and France.
Identification: 48–53cm (19–21in). Small white egret with large head and 'jowled' expression. Orange bill and legs; buffy head, back and breast plumes in summer. In winter, white with yellow bill and dark legs. Upright stance. Highly gregarious, forming large feeding flocks and densely packed colonies. Often feeds among domestic stock and follows the plough.
Voice: Silent
Habitat: Grasslands and fields often some distance from water. Breeds in tree-top colonies over or near water.
Similar Species: See Little Egret.

Little Egret *Egretta garzetta*

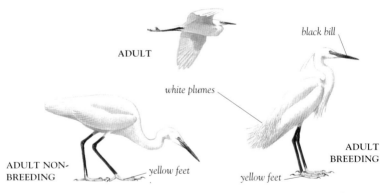

ADULT

white plumes

ADULT NON-BREEDING

yellow feet

black bill

ADULT BREEDING

yellow feet

J F M A M J J A S O N D

Status: Summer visitor to southern Europe extending northwards to central France and Hungary.
Identification: 53–58cm (21–23in). All white plumage with long, sharply pointed black bill and black legs with yellow feet. Slim elegance and gently curving neck are useful aids, where bill and feet colour cannot be easily confirmed. Beware size, especially in flight, which can be confusing with Great White Egret. Gregarious.
Voice: Silent.
Habitat: Marshes, estuaries and shorelines.
Similar Species: Larger Great White Egret has 'kinked' neck, yellow bill and yellow upper legs. See Cattle Egret.

Great White Egret   *Egretta alba*

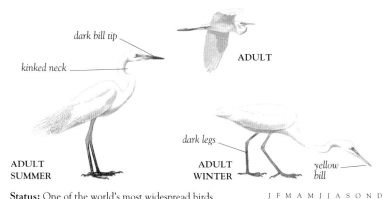

dark bill tip

kinked neck

ADULT

**ADULT
SUMMER**

**ADULT
WINTER**

dark legs

*yellow
bill*

Status: One of the world's most widespread birds.
Identification: 85–100cm (34–39in). All white heron that
is as big as Grey Heron. Long, usually 'kinked' neck; with
long, heavy yellow, or yellow-based, bill; legs dusky yellow
or, in winter, darker even black. At distance, separation
from Little Egret may cause problems, but this is always a
heavier-set, less elegant bird than that species.
Voice: Silent.
Habitat: Extensive marshes and other fresh waters with
plentiful reedbeds for breeding.
Similar Species: See Little Egret and above. Beware albino
Grey Herons.

J F M A M J J A S O N D

Grey Heron   *Ardea cinerea*

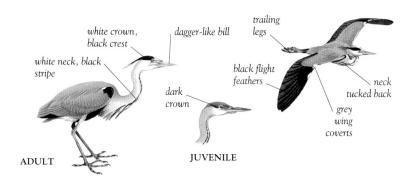

*white crown,
black crest*

dagger-like bill

*trailing
legs*

*white neck, black
stripe*

*black flight
feathers*

*neck
tucked back*

*dark
crown*

*grey
wing
coverts*

ADULT

JUVENILE

Status: Largest European heron that is variously resident,
summer visitor, passage migrant and winter visitor.
Identification: 90–100cm (35–39in). Large, grey and
white heron with long neck and dagger-like bill. Flies with
yellow-green legs trailing, with head and neck tucked into
shoulders and wings deeply bowed. Grey above and white
below; head with black crest, neck with black stripes on
front. In flight, grey coverts contrast with flight feathers.
Voice: Harsh *snark*.
Habitat: All wetlands including shorelines.
Similar Species: Purple Heron, smaller more warmly
coloured.

J F M A M J J A S O N D

Purple Heron   *Ardea purpurea*

grey coverts, brown scapulars

brown neck

black and brown head and neck

ADULT

mottled brown innerwing

JUVENILE

Status: Widespread summer visitor.
Identification: 75–85cm (29–33in). Slightly smaller than Grey Heron and significantly darker, both in flight and at rest. Head and neck rich warm brown with thin black crest and black streaking on foreneck. Back and wing coverts grey, with warm buffy tips to scapulars. Juvenile has brown wing coverts. Generally solitary and somewhat skulking.
Voice: A high-pitched *frank*, similar to Grey Heron.
Habitat: Fresh waters with strong growth of reeds and without tall trees. Marshes, backwaters.
Similar Species: See Grey Heron and above; juvenile could be confused with Bittern.

J F M A M J J A S O N D

Glossy Ibis   *Plegadis falcinellus*

purple gloss

green gloss

decurved bill

white flecks

ADULT

ADULT
SUMMER

ADULT
WINTER

neck extended

Status: Highly localized summer visitor to south-east Europe that is now only ibis in our region.
Identification: 50–65cm (20–25in). Long-legged waterbird with long decurved bill and generally dark plumage. Close approach reveals purple-glossed body and dark green-glossed wings. Legs dull green; bill horn-coloured with white line at base and around eye. At distance looks like dark, short-billed curlew. Gregarious at all times.
Voice: Mostly silent, but odd croaks.
Habitat: Shallow lakes, marshes and backwaters.
Similar Species: Bald Ibis – now extinct Turkey, but survives in Morocco and Arabia.

J F M A M J J A S O N D

Black Stork *Ciconia nigra*

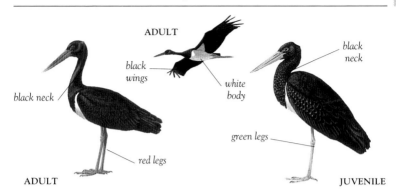

ADULT

black wings

white body

black neck

black neck

white body

black neck

green legs

red legs

ADULT

JUVENILE

J F M A M J J A S O N D

Status: Contrast to White Stork not only in coloration, but also in habits and habitats; a secretive woodland and mountain dwelling bird that never associates with man.
Identification: 90–100cm (35–39in). Whole of upperparts glossy black; neck and breast black; belly and 'armpits' white. From below, black wings contrast with white body. Heavy bill and legs red. Juvenile similarly patterned, but with green bill and legs.
Voice: More vocal, less bill clappering than White Stork.
Habitat: Old dense forests broken by wetlands. Also uplands with outcrops and caves.
Similar Species: See White Stork.

White Stork *Ciconia ciconia*

white body

white head and neck

black and white wings

J F M A M J J A S O N D

Status: Summer visitor that arrives November–December (spring) and departs July (autumn) crossing narrow straits at Gibraltar and Bosphorus.
Identification: 95–105cm (37–41in). With Black Stork, the only large black and white bird that soars with neck and legs extended. Whole of body and wing coverts (above and below) white. Flight feathers black. Large pointed bill and legs red. Gregarious, forming huge migrating flocks.
Voice: Silent, but frequently clappers bill in displays.
Habitat: Nests in tree tops and on buildings. Forages among crops, grasslands, wetlands and rubbish tips.
Similar Species: See Black Stork.

Spoonbill *Platalea leucorodia*

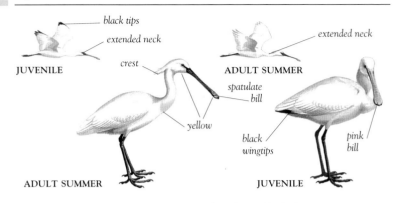

JUVENILE — black tips — extended neck — crest

ADULT SUMMER — extended neck — spatulate bill

ADULT SUMMER — yellow

JUVENILE — black wingtips — pink bill

J F M A M J J A S O N D

Status: Large, white, heron-like bird; summer visitor to eastern Europe and only two western outposts.
Identification: 80–90cm (31½–35½in). Plumage creamy-white with droopy crest and yellow wash at base of neck in breeding season. Bill long with spatulate end – black with yellow tip. Legs long and black. Flies with neck extended stork-like. Feeds with scything action in shallow water. Juvenile has black wingtips and pink bill.
Voice: Silent.
Habitat: Freshwater margins, marshes and estuaries and reedbeds for breeding. Also nests in trees.
Similar Species: Great White and Little Egrets.

Greater Flamingo *Phoenicopterus ruber*

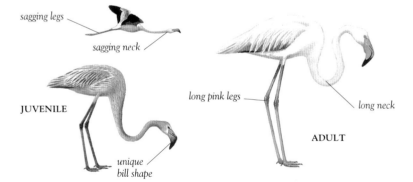

sagging legs — sagging neck

JUVENILE — unique bill shape

long pink legs — long neck

ADULT

J F M A M J J A S O N D

Status: Apart from other escaped flamingoes, can be confused with no other European species.
Identification: 125–145cm (49–57in). Large white bird flushed pink. Extremely long pink legs, equally long pinkish neck. Unique pink and black bill used upside down to filter food from shallow water. When stretched, wings show vivid pink forewing and black flight feathers. In flight, neck and legs extend fore and aft with body hung hammock-like between. Gregarious.
Voice: Goose-like *a-ha* or *ahouk*.
Habitat: Saline lagoons, lakes and estuaries.
Similar Species: Vagrant Lesser Flamingoes.

Bewick's Swan   *Cygnus columbianus*

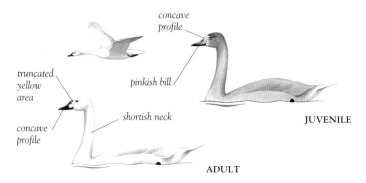

concave
profile

truncated
yellow
area

pinkish bill

concave
profile

shortish neck

JUVENILE

ADULT

J F M A M J J A S O N D

Status: Winter visitor from Siberia to long-established haunts in Britain and around North Sea.
Identification: 116–128cm (45–50in). Smallest of the three European swans; size most apparent in flight when faster wingbeats and noisy calls resemble geese. Black bill has truncated area of yellow at base. Rounded crown with concave forehead and bill profile. Neck often, but not invariably, held straight. Gregarious.
Voice: Goose-like honking flight calls.
Habitat: Breeds tundra lakes. Winters flooded grasslands, damp winter-sewn cereal fields with nearby water.
Similar Species: See Whooper Swan.

Whooper Swan   *Cygnus cygnus*

straight
profile

straight
profile

long straight
neck

pointed
yellow
area

JUVENILE

ADULT

Status: Gregarious and noisy winter visitor to temperate Europe from breeding grounds in far north.
Identification: 145–160cm (57–63in). Typical large white swan marked by yellow base to black bill. Yellow extends forward to a fine point, rather than being truncated like Bewick's – the only confusing species. Larger than that bird, with significantly longer neck and flat crown-bill profile. In flight, wings whistle. Gregarious.
Voice: Loud *whoop*, repeated among flock members.
Habitat: Breeds at high mountain and tundra lakes. Winters on grassland and crops with safe nearby water.
Similar Species: Mute Swan, Bewick's Swan as above.

J F M A M J J A S O N D

Mute Swan *Cygnus olor*

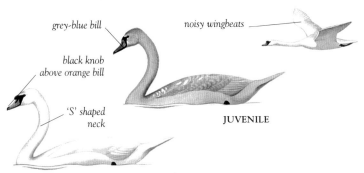

grey-blue bill

noisy wingbeats

black knob
above orange bill

'S' shaped
neck

JUVENILE

ADULT ♂

J F M A M J J A S O N D

Status: Huge, white waterbird found on variety of waters
from ponds to reservoirs, estuaries and the sea.
Identification: 152cm (60in) Adult completely white; legs
black; bill orange with large black knob at base. Juvenile
grey-buff with grey bill. Swims easily and walks with rolling
gait. At all times holds neck in gentle 'S' shape. Flies with
noisy wingbeats after laborious pattering take-off from water.
Voice: Hisses and grunts of aggression; silent in flight.
Habitat: Fresh and salt waters, fields.
Similar Species: Bewick's and Whooper Swans often form
flocks with Mute. Both have black and yellow bills and
noisy flight calls.

Greylag Goose *Anser anser*

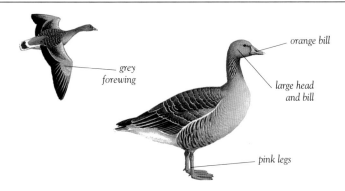

grey
forewing

orange bill

large head
and bill

pink legs

J F M A M J J A S O N D

Status: Largest and most widespread 'grey' goose; ancestor
of most domestic geese as well as common winter visitor.
Identification: 76–89cm (30–35in). Upperparts brown
finely barred; underparts buffy, barred on flanks. Large pale
head and large orange bill, both lacking any darkness, give
an 'open-faced' appearance. In eastern subspecies *A.a.
rubrirostris* bill is pink. Shows bold grey forewing in flight.
Voice: Highly vocal: deep *aahng-ung-ung*.
Habitat: From tundra swamps, through boreal marshes to
lowland lakes and other wetlands. Farmland in winter.
Similar Species: Only 'grey' goose with pale face and grey
forewings.

Bean Goose   *Anser fabalis*

uniform brown
without pale forewing

orange
bill

dark head
and neck

large head
and bill

orange
legs

J F M A M J J A S O N D

Status: Winter visitor to temperate Europe from northern Scandinavia and Arctic Russia.
Identification: 71–89cm (28–35in). Large 'grey' goose with dark head and neck. Upperparts brown barred buff. Underparts buffy finely barred white on flanks. Orange legs; orange bill with variable black base and tip. In flight has uniform brown wings with no obvious contrast between flight feathers and coverts.
Voice: Low *ung-unk*, generally less vocal than other geese.
Habitat: Breeds boreal zone lakes and marshes. Winters on fields, floods and sometimes coastal marshes.
Similar Species: Greylag and Pink-footed Geese.

Pink-footed Goose   *Anser brachyrhynchus*

small head
and bill

pink bill

dark head
and neck

grey
forewing

pink legs

Status: Small 'grey' goose with two distinct breeding populations that both winter around the North Sea.
Identification: 61–76cm (24–30in). Typical 'grey' goose brown above, buffy below with barred flanks. Small size, plus dark neck and, particularly, small dark head are the significant features. Small pink bill heavily marked black; legs pink. In flight shows bold pale grey forewing.
Voice: Vocal. High-pitched *unk-unk* and *wink-wink-wink*.
Habitat: Breeds tundra. Winters estuaries, shorelines, lakes, feeding on surrounding arable land.
Similar Species: Bean Goose lacks pale forewing and has large orange bill.

J F M A M J J A S O N D

White-fronted Goose *Anser albifrons*

Flavirostris
brown coverts
orange bill
white forehead
ADULT
darker below
pink bill
no white forehead
ADULT
barred belly
Albifrons
JUVENILE
no barring

J F M A M J J A S O N D

Status: Small, Arctic breeding, winter visitor .
Identification: 66–76cm (26–30in). Combination of small size, white base to bill, and smudgy bars on belly separate from other 'grey' geese (the last two features absent in juveniles). Bill pink in Russian subspecies *A.a.albifrons*; orange in Greenland subspecies *A.a.flavirostris*. Lack of grey forewing distinguishes from similar species except Bean Goose (Greenland birds show some grey at base of primaries).
Voice: High-pitched, musical *kow-yow* and *ryo-ryok*.
Habitat: Tundra marshes. Winters lowland pastures, bogs and winter cereals.
Similar Species: Bean Goose is larger with dark head.

Lesser White-fronted Goose *Anser erythropus*

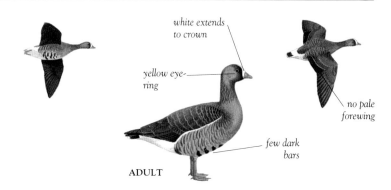

white extends to crown
yellow eye-ring
no pale forewing
few dark bars
ADULT

J F M A M J J A S O N D

Status: Decidedly scarce relative of White-fronted Goose that has declined both as a summer and winter visitor.
Identification: 53–66cm (21–26in). Smaller than White-fronted with which it usually associates. Rounded head and short neck useful in all plumages. Adult has white on forehead extending over crown to above eye; few black bars on belly; yellow eye-ring surprisingly obvious. Juveniles lack all these features; faint eye-ring.
Voice: High-pitched squeaky *kow-yow* like White-fronted.
Habitat: Breeds in alpine and tundra zones. Winters grasslands, open steppes, crops.
Similar Species: Adult White-fronted Goose.

Canada Goose *Branta canadensis*

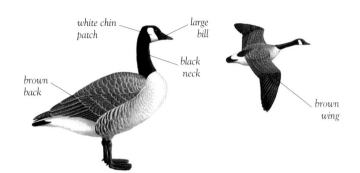

white chin
patch

large
bill

black
neck

brown
back

brown
wing

J F M A M J J A S O N D

Status: Largest of the 'black' geese, originally introduced from North America, which has prospered in Britain.
Identification: 90–100cm (35½–39in). Very large goose with long black neck and white chin patch. Upperparts brown finely barred cream; underparts creamy-buff. Neck and head (not breast) black with white patch. In flight, uniform brown wings. Generally tame.
Voice: Loud, repeated *wagh-onk*.
Habitat: Breeds at wide range of habitats from tundra to prairie. In Europe almost any pond will do.
Similar Species: Smaller Barnacle Goose has white face and grey (not brown) back.

Barnacle Goose *Branta leucopsis*

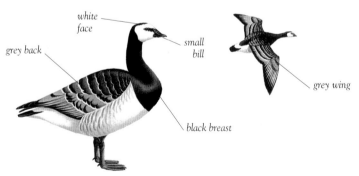

white
face

small
bill

grey back

grey wing

black breast

Status: Three distinct populations of this gregarious goose descend on Britain and North Sea coasts for the winter.
Identification: 58–69cm (23–27in). Striking, small attractive 'black' goose. Back and wings grey, neatly barred black and white. Underparts white with grey barring on flanks. Breast and neck black with white face and small black bill. In flight grey wings are lined by several prominent bars. Forms huge flocks at traditional sites.
Voice: Barking, puppy-like *yaps* and deeper growls.
Habitat: Breeds on cliffs along fjords or inland, offshore islets in tundra zone. Winters on grasslands and saltings.
Similar Species: See Brent Goose.

J F M A M J J A S O N D

Black Geese in Flight

Despite their generic name, 'Black Geese' are not black. The four species share several characteristics including short, white tails marked with black terminal bands. The pattern of a dark-necked goose with a white belly applies to three of the four, but even one of those has a subspecific dark bellied variation. In size they vary from larger than any 'grey goose' to the smallest of that group. In general, however, they are easily identifiable even at considerable distance.

CANADA GOOSE

Even larger than Greylag and marked by uniform brown wings and buff body. A long black neck is broken by a bold white chin strap. Though most European birds are large, some smaller birds do exist and the occasional very small bird may be the Alaskan subspecies *B.c.minima*, not much larger than a Mallard. These are often regarded as 'wild' North American birds.

BARNACLE GOOSE

Medium-sized goose that is the only 'black goose' that lacks uniform wings. A heavily barred pattern of black and silver transverse bars is unique among geese. The black neck forms a bold breast band with the white underparts (Canada Goose has black only on the neck) and white covers the entire face. The underwing is uniform slate grey contrasting with white belly.

BRENT GOOSE

A medium-sized goose marked by black head, neck and breast broken only by a white neck flash that is absent in juveniles and very difficult to see on adults in flight. The subspecies *B.b.hrota* from Greenland and Spitzbergen has a pale belly that contrasts with the black breast band. Siberian birds *B.b.bernicla* have dark bellies into which the black neck merges. With uniform dark wings above and below, pale-bellied Brent show a strong wing–body contrast like Barnacle Geese that is lacking in dark-bellied.

RED-BREASTED GOOSE

Though lacking the typical 'black goose' dark neck-white body pattern, this small goose appears very dark at any distance and is easily overlooked, especially among vast flocks of Brent. From below a white axillary line and narrow white breast band are useful features. At close range the head and neck pattern of black, white and chestnut is unmistakable.

Grey Geese in Flight

Grey geese of the genus *Anser* differ mainly in size and in colour of feet, bill and head. Such features are difficult to see in flight in what is a relatively uniformly plumaged group of birds that share a similar basic pattern. They do, however, show a number of features in the air that are either less apparent, or even invisible when at rest. Nevertheless, while bill and feet colour are virtually useless, head and neck coloration still play a significant part.

BEAN GOOSE
Dark neck, plus a uniform brown upperwing make this one of the darkest of grey geese in flight. Pink-footed shares a dark neck, but has prominent pale grey forewing. Greylag is equally large, shows grey forewing and lacks dark neck.

PINK-FOOTED GOOSE
Dark neck, much shorter than Bean, combined with pale grey forewing and small size make this one of the easiest of grey geese in flight. Grey-forewinged Greylag is much larger and lacks dark neck. White-fronted has less prominent grey forewing, lacks dark neck and has dark belly smudges.

GREYLAG GOOSE
Very large grey goose with large head and neck that is not dark like Bean, combined with very prominent pale grey forewing. Rump and tail band also pale grey. Only other grey-winged geese are smaller Pink-footed (dark neck) and smaller White-fronted (smudgy breast and less significantly grey wings).

LESSER WHITE-FRONTED GOOSE
Uniformly brown small goose with no grey forewing and no dark neck. Belly marked by few black smudges, not heavily smudged like White-fronted. Also shows more white on forehead than that species.

WHITE-FRONTED GOOSE
Small brown goose with no dark neck that shows grey forewing, albeit in less pronounced form than similar-sized, dark-necked Pink-footed, or much larger Greylag. Similar to Lesser White-fronted, but much more heavily smudged breast.

Brent Goose *Branta bernicla*

Bernicla

white flash

belly almost as
dark as breast

bold flash

black breast
and neck,
pale belly

pale flanks

very dark

Hrota

Nigricans

J F M A M J J A S O N D

Status: Winter visitor in large flocks to North Sea and adjacent coasts seldom far from the shoreline.
Identification: 56–61cm (22–24in). Smallest and darkest of the 'black' geese. Pale-bellied *B.b.hrota*, brown above and pale below; black head and neck terminate in clear-cut breast band. Dark-bellied *B.b.bernicla*, lacks contrast between breast and belly. Pacific Brent *B.b.nigricans* has bolder neck flash and white flanks. Juveniles show white bars across folded wing and lack neck flash.
Voice: Grumbling *krook*; very noisy in flocks.
Habitat: Tundra pools. In winter frequents coasts.
Similar Species: See Barnacle and Canada Geese.

Red-breasted Goose *Branta ruficollis*

black upper
wings

bold white
flank slash

harlequin
face pattern

very dark
below

J F M A M J J A S O N D

Status: Scarce winter visitor to eastern Europe that wanders westwards as a vagrant.
Identification: 51–58cm (20–23in). Colourful and easily identified in books and at close range, more difficult to pick out from large flocks of Barnacles or Brent at a distance. Large head, tiny bill and thick neck are good structural points. Adult has rust-red cheek, neck and breast, all outlined white; by bold white flank slash.
Voice: Shrill *kee-waa*.
Habitat: Tundra crags, gorges and river banks. Winters steppes, saline flats, grasslands, winter cereals.
Similar Species: Barnacle and Brent Geese.

Common Shelduck *Tadorna tadorna*

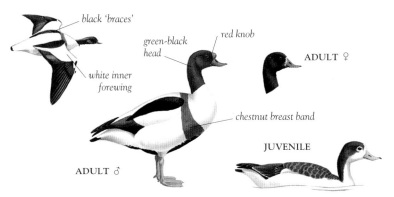

black 'braces'

white inner
forewing

green-black
head

red knob

ADULT ♀

chestnut breast band

JUVENILE

ADULT ♂

J F M A M J J A S O N D

Status: Confined to shorelines and adjacent marshes.
Identification: 58–64cm (22–25in). Head and neck dark
bottle-green; rest of plumage white with broad chestnut
breast band and black stripe along folded wing. Bill bright
red with bulbous knob at base in adult male. Female and
immature have less clear-cut markings. In flight, black
wings broken by bold white inner forewing and white body
by black 'braces'. Gregarious.
Voice: Various whistles and growls.
Habitat: Breeds among dry cover in holes near coast. Rest
of year marshes, intertidal shores, mudflats.
Similar Species: None.

Ruddy Shelduck *Tadorna ferruginea*

white head

♀

neck
ring

white inner-
wing

♂

green
speculum

♂

Status: Resident and summer visitor south-east Europe
and especially Turkey that is easily identified.
Identification: 61–67cm (24–26½in). Similar to Common
Shelduck in shape and structure, but whole plumage
chestnut-orange with pale head. Adult male has narrow
black collar; adult female has paler, almost white, head. In
flight, black wings with bold white inner forewing.
Voice: Repeated *ah-enk* and *ka-ha-ha*; rolling *korrr*.
Habitat: Lakes, rivers, marshes and even small pools,
especially saline ones.
Similar Species: See Egyptian Goose, which also shows
bold white inner forewing in flight.

J F M A M J J A S O N D

Egyptian Goose *Alopochen aegyptiacus*

dark eye patch

white innerwing

long legs

J F M A M J J A S O N D

Status: African species introduced England where feral. More like a shelduck than a goose.
Identification: 66–72cm (26–28in). Rich chestnut-pink above, paler pinky-buff below. Small pink bill with dark base and tip; characteristic dark patch around eye creates 'masked' effect. In flight wings black with bold white inner forewing. Legs long and pink. Spends much time on land and perches freely in trees.
Voice: Hissing and cackling, but usually silent.
Habitat: Freshwater parks, lakes and marshes.
Similar Species: Ruddy Shelduck shows similar flight pattern.

Mandarin Duck *Aix galericulata*

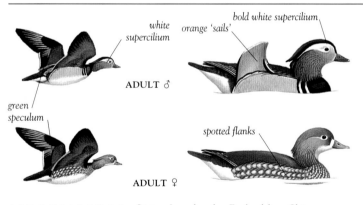

white supercilium

orange 'sails'

bold white supercilium

ADULT ♂

green speculum

spotted flanks

ADULT ♀

J F M A M J J A S O N D

Status: Introduced to England from China.
Identification: 41–47cm (16–18½in). Male has elaborate, multi-coloured plumage with dark drooping crest, white slash over eye, green nape, chestnut 'whiskers' and orange flanks. Female much duller, with grey head marked by narrow eye-ring and extended white eye-line.
Voice: Male whistles; female utters sharp *kek*.
Habitat: Small ponds and lakes surrounded by mature woodland in undisturbed estates/countryside.
Similar Species: Female may be confused with escaped female Wood Duck, which has blue speculum and bolder eye-line.

Eurasian Wigeon   *Anas penelope*

chestnut head — golden crown

white wing patch

small grey bill

ADULT ♂

ADULT ♂ ECLIPSE

warm flanks

warm brown above and below

ADULT ♂

ADULT ♀

ADULT ♀

J F M A M J J A S O N D

Status: Winters in huge flocks at favoured locations.
Identification: 43–48cm (16–19in). Male has chestnut head and neck, with golden blaze extending from forehead over crown. With white slash along flank; rear end black and white. In flight, shows white patch on innerwing; lacking in female and first winter male. Bill small, silver grey. Female cinnamon-brown with delicate rounded head and small bill. Flocks in flight show mixture of white-winged and plain-winged birds.
Voice: Characteristic whistling in flight.
Habitat: Winters coasts and floods.
Similar Species: Vagrant American Wigeon.

Gadwall   *Anas strepera*

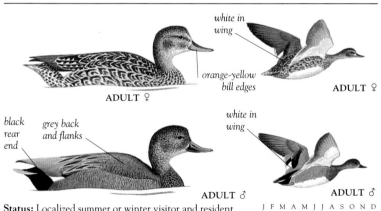

white in wing

orange-yellow bill edges

ADULT ♀

ADULT ♀

black rear end

grey back and flanks

white in wing

ADULT ♂

ADULT ♂

Status: Localized summer or winter visitor and resident easily overlooked among female Mallard.

J F M A M J J A S O N D

Identification: 48–54cm (18–21in). Nondescript grey and brown duck. Male has mottled brown head and upperparts similar to female of other surface-feeding ducks. Flanks finely barred grey. Best field mark is black rear end and white speculum. Female also shows white speculum.
Voice: Male whistles; female quacks.
Habitat: Freshwater lakes and marshes in summer. In winter large marshes and floods as well as estuaries.
Similar Species: Female Northern Pintail, Common Teal, Mallard, Northern Shoveler; lack white in wing.

Common Teal *Anas crecca*

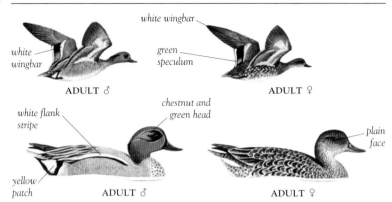

white wingbar

white wingbar

green speculum

ADULT ♂

ADULT ♀

chestnut and green head

white flank stripe

plain face

yellow patch

ADULT ♂

ADULT ♀

J F M A M J J A S O N D

Status: Small fast-flying duck that often forms compact flocks that fly in twisting, turning formation, like waders.
Identification: 34–38 cm (13–15in). Male's chestnut head has bottle-green, yellow-edged area around eye. Grey body is broken by narrow white flank slash. Black rear end encloses large yellow patch. Female buff and brown.
Voice: Male whistles; female quacks.
Habitat: Breeds from tundra lakes and woodland pools to open marshes. Winters large fresh waters, marshes, floods.
Similar Species: Female and eclipse male similar to, but smaller than other female surface-feeding ducks except Garganey, from which separated by green speculum.

Garganey *Anas querquedula*

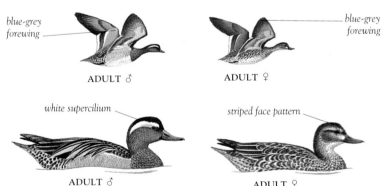

blue-grey forewing

blue-grey forewing

ADULT ♂

ADULT ♀

white supercilium

striped face pattern

ADULT ♂

ADULT ♀

J F M A M J J A S O N D

Status: Summer visitor to most of temperate Europe, but migrant only through Iberia and most of Italy.
Identification: 37–41cm (14–16in). Dainty, Teal-sized duck. Male has maroon-brown head with bold white supercilium, drooping silvery scapulars and grey underparts. Female and eclipse male are mottled brown with dark eye-stripe.
Voice: Male utters crackling rattle; female quacks.
Habitat: Summer visitor to small fresh waters, backwaters or bays of larger ones; marshes and reedbeds.
Similar Species: Female and eclipse male like female Common Teal, female White-headed and Ruddy Duck.

Mallard *Anas platyrhynchos*

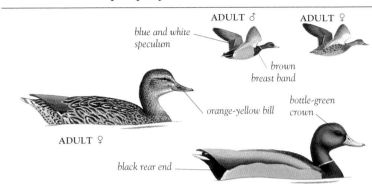

ADULT ♂   ADULT ♀

blue and white
speculum

brown
breast band

orange-yellow bill

bottle-green
crown

ADULT ♀

black rear end

ADULT ♂

J F M A M J J A S O N D

Status: Common and widespread throughout year.
Identification: 55–62cm (22–24in). Male has bottle-green head separated from chocolate-brown breast by narrow white neck ring. Black rear end with two upward-curling feathers. In flight head appears dark; dark blue speculum bordered fore and aft by white bars. Female resembles other female surface-feeding ducks; dark cap, dark eye-stripe and orange-yellow bill aid separation.
Voice: Male whistles and grunts; female loud quacks.
Habitat: Virtually any aquatic habitat.
Similar Species: Female and eclipse male show similar face pattern to much smaller Garganey.

Northern Pintail *Anas acuta*

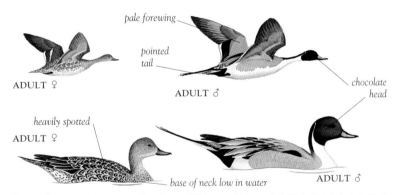

pale forewing

pointed
tail

ADULT ♀

chocolate
head

ADULT ♂

heavily spotted

ADULT ♀

base of neck low in water

ADULT ♂

Status: Summer visitor to north and east. Widespread in west in winter.
Identification: ♂ 63–70cm (25–27in); ♀ 53–59cm (21–23in). Slim, elegant duck; characteristic swimming attitude with foreparts lower in water than hindparts. Male has vertical white stripe up back of long neck. Pale rear flank patch and black rear end. Long tail pointed. Bill silver-blue. Female grey-buff – the palest surface-feeding duck.
Voice: Male growls and whistles, female quacks.
Habitat: Breeds open tundra marshes and lakes. In winter, concentrates at extensive shallow waters, estuaries.
Similar Species: Eurasian Wigeon also has pointed tail.

J F M A M J J A S O N D

Dabbling Duck in Flight

Identifying duck as they fly high and fast overhead is simply a matter of knowing what to look for. Male dabbling duck are reasonably easy at rest, while females are decidedly difficult. In flight males and females often share the same field marks. This makes females decidedly easier in flight than at rest. Crucial points to see are: the speculum (the often boldly coloured pattern on the secondaries); belly and breast colour and pattern; and tail shape.

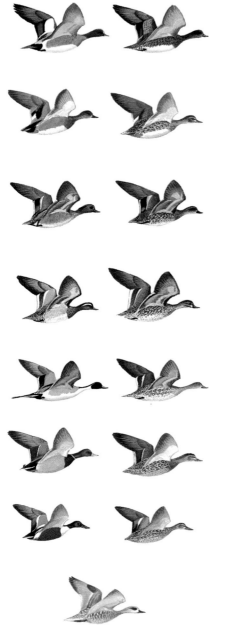

WIGEON
Flocks of Wigeon often comprise what appear to be two distinct species. Males show a bold white innerwing.

GADWALL
A dully coloured duck that shows a bold white speculum, in both male and female. Both show white bellies.

TEAL
Tiny, fast-flying duck that performs aerobatics. Both sexes have a green speculum. White line above the speculum best field mark.

GARGANEY
On size, can only be confused with Teal. Male shows pale blue innerwing and bold white supercilium.

PINTAIL
Male shows white belly and neck, with contrasting dark head. Identified in both sexes by long pointed tail, long neck.

MALLARD
White-margined blue speculum often difficult to see. Male has pale belly contrasting with dark neck.

SHOVELER
Prominent head and large bill obvious even in flight, and both sexes show pale blue innerwing.

MARBLED DUCK
Only uniformly buff duck that lacks any particular feature except dark eye patch.

Northern Shoveler . *Anas clypeata*

ADULT ♂

blue forewing

ADULT ♀

ADULT ♀

blue forewing

warm flanks

huge bill

huge bill

ADULT ♂   orange-brown belly   FIRST WINTER ♂

J F M A M J J A S O N D

Status: Summer visitor to north and east; winter visitor to south and west. Well marked in all plumages.
Identification: 47–53cm (18–21in). Feeds with broad sweeps of bill through shallow water and wet mud. Male has bottle-green head, white breast, black back, chestnut belly and flanks. Female mottled like other ducks, but bill easily separates. In flight, shows pale blue innerwing.
Voice: Male a harsh *tuk-tuk*; female quacks.
Habitat: Breeds shallow waters. Winters marshes and freshwater margins.
Similar Species: Smaller Garganey has pale blue innerwing, but no other duck has huge, spatulate bill.

Marbled Duck   *Marmaronetta angustirostris*

uniform wing

dark eye patch

spotted flanks

Status: Scarce and localized summer visitor or resident at extreme south-east and south-west.
Identification: 39–42cm (15–16in). Mottled grey-buff duck in all plumages; heavily spotted with bold white blotches creating 'marbled' effect. Bill dark. Most obvious field mark is broad, dark patch around eye.
Voice: Silent.
Habitat: Small fresh waters, or small bays and backwaters of larger ones, with plentiful emergent vegetation.
Similar Species: Many female surface-feeding duck are mottled brown and buff but none are as pale or have bold eye patch.

J F M A M J J A S O N D

Red-crested Pochard   *Netta rufina*

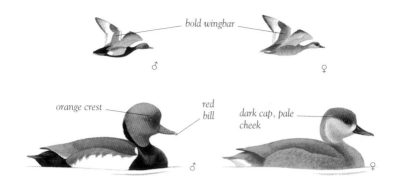

bold wingbar

♂

♀

orange crest

red bill

♂

dark cap, pale cheek

♀

J F M A M J J A S O N D

Status: Highly localized, but often numerous, summer or winter visitor through much of south and central Europe. **Identification:** 53–59cm (21–23in). Male has bold, over-large, chestnut head with paler erectile crest. In flight, shows bold white wingbar above, and white oval patches either side of black belly below. Bill bright red. Female brown above, buff below, pale cheeks and dark brown cap. **Voice:** Silent. **Habitat:** Large lakes with growth of emergent vegetation. **Similar Species:** Eurasian Wigeon and Common Pochard. Female Common Scoter has brown cap and buff cheeks like female Red-crested Pochard.

Common Pochard   *Aythya ferina*

grey wings

buff-grey wings

ADULT ♂

ADULT ♀

rusty head

wedge-shaped profile

grey back

pale eye-ring and line

ADULT ♂

ADULT ♀

J F M A M J J A S O N D

Status: Widespread breeder in relatively small numbers, but abundant winter visitor often forming huge rafts. **Identification:** 44–48cm (17–19in). Compact diving duck with characteristic wedge-shaped head. Male has grey body, chestnut head and black breast. At any distance whole of foreparts appear dark; body pale grey with dark rear end. Female greyish-brown, darker on head and neck. Highly gregarious. Flocks spend much time sleeping. **Voice:** Generally quiet; female growls in flight. **Habitat:** Steppe lakes, open and cleared areas in forest zone. In winter, large reservoirs and other fresh waters. **Similar Species:** None.

Ferruginous Duck   *Aythya nyroca*

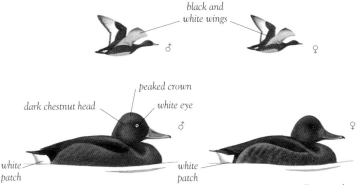

black and
white wings

peaked crown

dark chestnut head

white eye ♂

♀

white
patch

white
patch

J F M A M J J A S O N D

Status: Summer visitor, mainly to eastern Europe, that may be locally common. Scarce in western Europe.
Identification: 39–43cm (15–17in). All-dark, diving duck with rich mahogany plumage broken by prominent, clear-cut white undertail. Females and eclipse males barred paler on flanks and then resemble female Tufted Duck which may also have white undertail. Flat forehead and high peaked crown give bird distinctive head shape, and species not as difficult to pick out as some imagine.
Voice: Confiding *tuk-tuk*.
Habitat: Shallow waters with rich emergent vegetation.
Similar Species: See female Tufted Duck.

Tufted Duck   *Aythya fuligula*

white
wingbar

ADULT ♂

ADULT ♀

crest

rounded
head

hint of
crest

black back

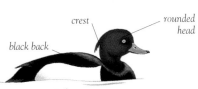

ADULT ♂

ADULT ♀

Status: Widespread breeder throughout temperate Europe. Abundant winter visitor, frequently forms large rafts.
Identification: 41–45cm (16–17in). Dainty, black and white diving duck, with round head and drooping crest. Male has all-black head, breast, back and tail; white flanks and underparts. Female sooty brown, with paler barred flanks; grey bill often has white base. In flight, shows prominent, broad, white wingbar.
Voice: Generally silent, female growls.
Habitat: Moderate depth waters but, in winter, also in sheltered bays and estuaries.
Similar Species: Goldeneye and Barrow's Goldeneye.

J F M A M J J A S O N D

Diving Ducks in Flight

RED-CRESTED POCHARD
Both sexes show the broadest and boldest white wingbar of any duck extending across whole of flight feathers. Black belly and breast of male makes this pattern particularly obvious.

POCHARD
Only duck to show broad wingbar that is grey and lacking in contrast with rest of wing. Male has dark head and neck contrasting with grey body to form breast band. Female dull grey with hint of breast band.

FERRUGINOUS DUCK
All dark duck with bold white wingbar (almost as obvious as Red-crested Pochard). Dark body (not belly) contrasts with pale underwing.

TUFTED DUCK
Dark upperwing with bold white wingbar. Male has dark head and neck contrasting with pale body and underwing. Female similar but subdued with darkish flanks.

SCAUP
Virtually the same as Tufted Duck in both male and female with bold white wingbar and contrasting dark head and white belly. Grey back of male and white face of female must be seen. Marine habitat a useful clue.

BARROW'S GOLDENEYE
Both sexes show grey back with bold white patch on innerwing contrasting with black outerwing. This is virtually identical to Goldeneye, though male's white patch is divided by black line and less obvious.

GOLDENEYE
Very similar to Barrow's Goldeneye, but white patch on innerwing is undivided and more obvious especially in male. Female virtually identical in flight. Triangular head shape separates from other species.

LONG-TAILED DUCK
Pointed tail, especially of male. Uniformly dark wing (above and below) contrasts with white belly. Male also shows black breast band. Characteristic 'head-up' shape.

Greater Scaup   *Aythya marila*

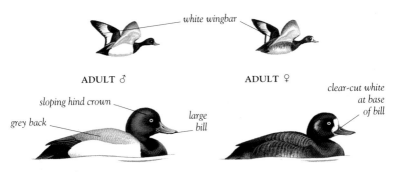

white wingbar

ADULT ♂

ADULT ♀

sloping hind crown

grey back

large bill

clear-cut white at base of bill

ADULT ♂

ADULT ♀

J F M A M J J A S O N D

Status: Marine equivalent of Tufted Duck, similarly patterned in black and white, mainly winter visitor to coastal waters, often in very large flocks.
Identification: 46–51cm (18–20in). Male has black, green-glossed head, black breast and rear end, grey back and white flanks and belly. Female has large, clear-cut white area at base of bill. In all plumages, steep forehead and backward-sloping crown create distinct head shape.
Voice: Mostly silent; female growls.
Habitat: Breeds tundra and taiga. Winters bays, estuaries.
Similar Species: See Tufted Duck, especially white-faced female.

Common Eider   *Somateria mollissima*

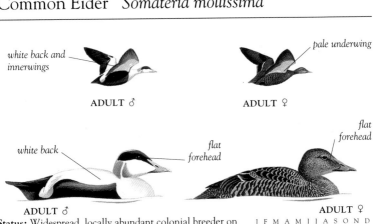

white back and innerwings

pale underwing

ADULT ♂

ADULT ♀

white back

flat forehead

flat forehead

ADULT ♂

ADULT ♀

Status: Widespread, locally abundant colonial breeder on northern coasts, that is more widespread in winter.
Identification: 55–61cm (21–24in). Large, stocky seaduck. Male white above and black below with pink tinge to white breast. Bold black mark extends over each side of crown. Female warm buff and brown, finely barred. Long, sloping forehead and longish bill form continuous line, creating wedge-shaped head with feathered bill.
Voice: Male utters dove-like cooing; female a *gok-gok-gok*.
Habitat: Rocky coasts with flat offshore islands. Winters same areas, river mouths and large estuaries.
Similar Species: Steller's and King Eiders.

J F M A M J J A S O N D

King Eider *Somateria spectabilis*

white patch

♂

♀

black body

unique head shape

bump on 'nose'

♀

♂

white patch

J F M A M J J A S O N D

Status: Winter visitor to north Norway and Iceland that is regular but rare in Scotland and vagrant elsewhere.

Identification: 47–63cm (18–25in). Adult male has black body, white breast, grey head and unique head shape with colourful face pattern. In flight, shows bold white patch on inner forewing. Female like other eiders, but pronounced bump at base of upper bill and more rufous plumage marked by broken flank bars.

Voice: Silent away from breeding grounds.

Habitat: Breeds Arctic tundra. In winter sheltered sea bays.

Similar Species: See only other eiders.

Steller's Eider *Polysticta stelleri*

white innerwing

white bordered speculum

pale underwing

♂

♀

white head

black neck-ring

pale eye-ring

♂

orange

♀

J F M A M J J A S O N D

Status: Arctic duck that creeps into Europe only northernmost Norway.

Identification: 43–48cm (17–19in). Male unique with white head marked with patches of black and green; black and white upperparts; and soft peach-coloured underparts. Female like female Eider, but steep (not sloping) forehead and pale eye-ring. Buoyant swimming posture, often with tail clear of water. In flight, male shows white inner forewing.

Voice: Occasional growling notes.

Habitat: Flat coastal tundra. Winters coasts.

Similar Species: Female resembles other female eiders.

Harlequin Duck *Histrionicus histrionicus*

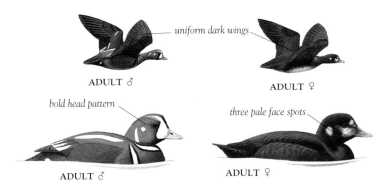

uniform dark wings

ADULT ♂

ADULT ♀

bold head pattern

three pale face spots

ADULT ♂

ADULT ♀

J F M A M J J A S O N D

Status: Iceland resident. Very rare vagrant Norway and Scotland.
Identification: 41–45cm (16–18in). Small seaduck that appears dark at any distance. Male multi-coloured, flanks dark orange-red, with head, neck and back blue-black, with patches of white. Female dusky all over save for three pale patches on sides of head. Lacks white wingbar.
Voice: Male silent; female harsh quack.
Habitat: Breeds among boulder-strewn torrents in fast-flowing rivers; winters at sea among surf over rocks.
Similar Species: See female Velvet Scoter and female Long-tailed Duck, both of which are brown with face spots.

Long-tailed Duck *Clangula hyemalis*

uniform wings

breast band

pale face patch

dark face patch

appears 'neckless'

long tail

ADULT ♂ SUMMER

ADULT ♀ SUMMER

black and white pattern

ADULT ♂ WINTER

ADULT ♀ WINTER

Status: High Arctic duck, winters at sea in the north.
Identification: ♂ 54–58cm (21–23in); ♀ 41–45cm (16–17in). Small, stocky seaduck. Large head, small bill and pointed tail; male has extended central tail feathers. Summer male has dark brown head and neck; face silvery grey. Winter male has white head with grey face patch. Female always has pale patch around eye; upperparts broadly edged buff in summer, browner in winter.
Voice: Male has yodelling calls; female quacks.
Habitat: Tundra coasts with islets, also inland tundra lakes and rivers. One of the commonest birds around sea ice.
Similar Species: None.

J F M A M J J A S O N D

Common Scoter *Melanitta nigra*

no white on head

uniform black

no white in wing

ADULT ♂

ADULT ♂

pale sides to face

ADULT ♀

ADULT ♀

J F M A M J J A S O N D

Status: Northern and tundra-breeding duck that moves to adjacent and western seaboard coasts in winter.
Identification: 46–51cm (18–20in). All black seaduck most often seen as small dark blobs bouncing among waves, or as all-dark birds flying fast and low over sea. Male black with yellow bill and black knob at base. Female brown with pale cheeks that may be picked out at considerable distance. Gregarious, flocks 10–100 strong.
Voice: Mostly silent, some croaking.
Habitat: Tundra, often some distance from water. Winters offshore, gathering in large flocks.
Similar Species: See Velvet and Surf Scoters.

Velvet Scoter *Melanitta fusca*

dark face
pale patches

ADULT ♀

white in wing

ADULT ♀

ADULT ♂

ADULT ♂

J F M A M J J A S O N D

Status: Boreal equivalent of Common Scoter. Less abundant winter visitor to north-western coasts.
Identification: 53–59cm (20–23in). Similar to Common Scoter, often forms mixed flocks. Male black with larger yellow bill. Female brown with two pale face patches. Both sexes show white in wing in flight; may also be visible at rest. Velvet Scoter may betray their presence by flapping wings, revealing white patches.
Voice: Usually silent; occasional harsh whistles.
Habitat: Boreal lakes, pools and rivers. Winters coasts.
Similar Species: Common Scoter. See also Surf Scoter.

Surf Scoter *Melanitta perspicillata*

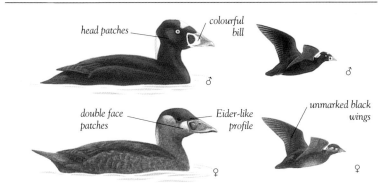

head patches — colourful bill — ♂

double face patches — Eider-like profile — ♀

unmarked black wings — ♂

♀

J F M A M J J A S O N D

Status: Rare transatlantic vagrant that is more regular than previously thought – formerly overlooked.
Identification: 45–56cm (17½–22in). Resembles other scoters and frequently associates with flocks of those more widespread birds. Male has distinctive white patches on nape, forecrown and at base of colourful bill. Shares sloping, Eider-like head shape, with female. Latter has double pale face patch like Velvet Scoter. Both sexes lack white wing patch of that bird.
Voice: Used only when mating.
Habitat: Sheltered sea bays in winter.
Similar Species: Common and Velvet Scoters as above.

Smew *Mergus albellus*

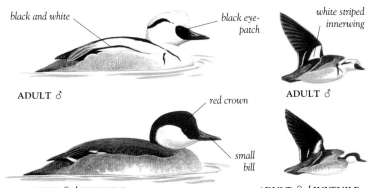

black and white — black eye-patch — white striped innerwing

ADULT ♂ **ADULT ♂**

red crown — small bill

ADULT ♀ / JUVENILE **ADULT ♀ / JUVENILE**

Status: Northern boreal zone duck, that winters southwards across Europe as far west as France.
Identification: 36–43cm (14–17in). Compact little duck. Male white with narrow black lines on crown, back and flanks. Steep forehead and hint of crest create large-headed appearance. Female and first winter male – 'redheads' – have chestnut-red crown extending to below eye.
Voice: Usually silent.
Habitat: Conifer forests with tree holes. Winters lakes, reservoirs and even small waters.
Similar Species: 'Redheads' could be confused with Slavonian Grebe in winter.

J F M A M J J A S O N D

Barrow's Goldeneye *Bucephala islandica*

steep forehead

divided white innerwing

♀

black back, white spots

white oval

♂

♂

Status: Very similar to Goldeneye, but resident Iceland, exceptional vagrant elsewhere.
Identification: 42–53cm (16–21in). Male black on head and upperparts, marked with oval (not round) white patch between eye and bill. Scapulars black with row of white spots; scapulars of Goldeneye white with row of dark lines. Overall this is 'darker' bird than Goldeneye. Steep forehead and shorter bill produce distinct head shape. Female even closer to female Goldeneye, but shares head shape.
Voice: Various grunts and growls.
Habitat: Freshwater lakes, torrents and rapids.
Similar Species: See Goldeneye above.

Goldeneye *Bucephala clangula*

brown triangular head

white flank line

white in wing

♀

bottle-green head

white striped back

white spot

white inner-wing

♂

♂

Status: Widespread diving duck that is relatively common winter visitor to much of temperate Europe. Gregarious.
Identification: 40–48cm (16–19in). Both sexes marked by peaked crown and sloping hind crown. Male has black, green-glossed head with round white patch between bill and eye; upperparts black with streaks across folded wing. Female has chocolate-brown head, white neck band and grey body. In flight, both sexes have white on innerwing.
Voice: Silent except in courtship: a rippling *rrrrt*.
Habitat: Forests with hollow trees (or nest boxes); lakes or ponds. In winter frequents fresh water and sea.
Similar Species: See Barrow's Goldeneye.

Red-breasted Merganser *Mergus serrator*

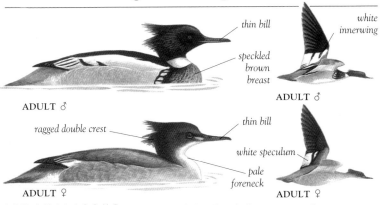

ADULT ♂

thin bill

speckled brown breast

white innerwing

ADULT ♂

ragged double crest

thin bill

white speculum

pale foreneck

ADULT ♀

ADULT ♀

J F M A M J J A S O N D

Status: North-breeding duck; winters mainly on sea.
Identification: 51–61cm (20–24in). Long, slim duck with long, thin bill. Male has dark bottle-green head with double crest extending from hind crown. Dark head and breast separated by white collar. Female has rusty head with similar double crest; foreneck and chin pale. In flight, shows black and white innerwing.
Voice: Mostly silent, but some purrs and croaks.
Habitat: Wooded and forested areas with lakes, rivers or sea nearby. Winters mainly on sea in sheltered bays.
Similar Species: Female resembles female Goosander, but has ragged, horizontal crest.

Goosander *Mergus merganser*

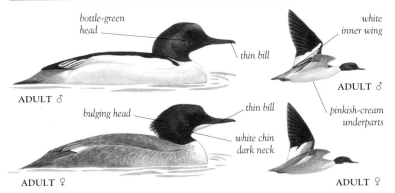

bottle-green head

thin bill

ADULT ♂

white inner wing

ADULT ♂

bulging head

thin bill

white chin dark neck

pinkish-cream underparts

ADULT ♀

ADULT ♀

Status: Largest of the 'sawbill' ducks; more freshwater orientated than Red-breasted Merganser.
Identification: 57–69cm (22–27in). Male has green-glossed, black head with rounded crest, giving head unique shape. Back black; flanks and underparts white with warm, pinkish flush. White innerwing shows in flight. Female has red head, white chin, rusty foreneck and hint of crest.
Voice: Courtship croaks and cackles; otherwise silent.
Habitat: Rivers and other inland fresh waters in mature wooded country. Winters large open waters.
Similar Species: Female Red-breasted Merganser; but female Goosander has rounded crest.

J F M A M J J A S O N D

Ruddy Duck *Oxyura jamaicensis*

cap extends to eye

long tail

uniform upperwing

blue bill
white face

ADULT ♂ SUMMER

ADULT ♂ SUMMER

tail often
hidden in
water

face stripe

ADULT ♀

ADULT ♀

J F M A M J J A S O N D

Status: North American duck introduced to south-west
England that has spread and is colonizing southwards.
Identification: 36–43cm (14–17in). Dumpy little duck of
strangely 'weight forward' appearance; stiff tail often held
cocked upright but equally often horizontal and invisible.
Male russet, with dark cap extending to eye; white face.
Brilliant blue bill. Female brown above, barred buff and
crown below; dark cap and dark line across face.
Voice: Quiet courtship grunts and hisses.
Habitat: Still freshwater ponds and lakes with emergent
vegetation.
Similar Species: White-headed Duck is only other stiff-tail.

White-headed Duck *Oxyura leucocephala*

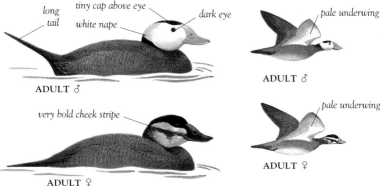

long
tail

tiny cap above eye

white nape

dark eye

pale underwing

ADULT ♂

ADULT ♂

very bold cheek stripe

pale underwing

ADULT ♀

ADULT ♀

J F M A M J J A S O N D

Status: Highly localized duck, with only seven main
breeding sites, that is seriously endangered in Europe.
Identification: 43–48cm (17–19in). Male chestnut with
white cheeks and 'weight forward' stiff-tailed appearance
similar to related Ruddy Duck. More white on head and
black cap is confined to top of crown, exposing dark eye.
Female resembles female Ruddy Duck, but bulbous bill and
dark cheek stripe much more prominent.
Voice: Female utters explosive *gek*.
Habitat: Shallow lakes and pools with emergent plants.
Similar Species: See Ruddy Duck. Hybridizes with
introduced Ruddy Duck.

Honey Buzzard *Pernis apivorus*

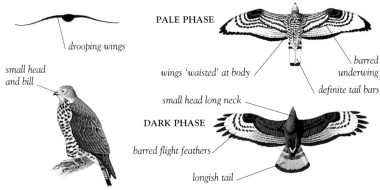

drooping wings

PALE PHASE

small head and bill

wings 'waisted' at body

barred underwing

definite tail bars

small head long neck

DARK PHASE

barred flight feathers

longish tail

J F M A M J J A S O N D

Status: Summer visitor to woodland areas less concentrated at narrow sea crossings than other migrant raptors.
Identification: 50–58cm (20–23in). Slimmer and more angular than Common Buzzard. Small head, thin neck and waisted, 'wasp-like' wings. Tail longer than Buzzard; wings droop when soaring. Plumage highly variable but carpals always dark and underwing has regularly spaced barring.
Voice: High-pitched *kee-a.*
Habitat: Large forests with clearings.
Similar Species: Small protruding head, long tail and drooping wings separate from other buzzards.

Black-shouldered Kite *Elanus caeruleus*

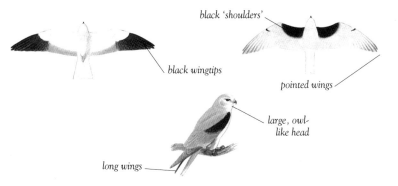

black 'shoulders'

black wingtips

pointed wings

large, owl-like head

long wings

Status: Somewhat crepuscular, rare resident Iberia.
Identification: 31–35cm (12–14in). Medium-sized grey and white raptor marked by black 'shoulder', which shows as black inner forewing in flight. Upperparts pale grey; underparts white; black on innerwing above and on wing tips below. Plumage pattern unique among European raptors. Regular hovering, buoyant flight; plus large flat head and thick neck aid identification at distance.
Voice: Mostly silent.
Habitat: Open countryside with groves.
Similar Species: Male Hen and Montagu's Harriers. Black-shouldered Kite has pointed wings.

J F M A M J J A S O N D

Black Kite   *Milvus migrans*

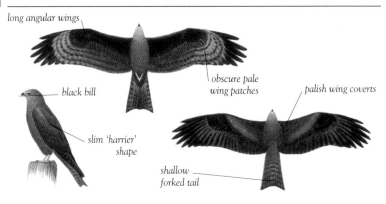

long angular wings

black bill

slim 'harrier' shape

obscure pale wing patches

palish wing coverts

shallow forked tail

J F M A M J J A S O N D

Status: Summer visitor that migrates in huge numbers through Gibraltar, Bosphorus and Cap Bon.
Identification: 53–59cm (21–23in). Dark, brownish-grey raptor with long wings and tail. Wings held bowed like Red Kite, but tail less forked and appears square-cut when partially spread. Juvenile more rufous. Slides around sky like an old Dakota aircraft.
Voice: Squealing and chattering near nest.
Habitat: Mostly near estuaries, lakes, rivers, even sea coasts; as well as towns, cities and rubbish tips.
Similar Species: Red Kite and female/young Marsh Harrier.

Red Kite   *Milvus milvus*

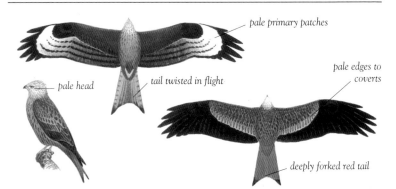

pale primary patches

pale head

tail twisted in flight

pale edges to coverts

deeply forked red tail

J F M A M J J A S O N D

Status: Resident in west; summer visitor to east. Widespread in wooded country.
Identification: 58–64cm (22–25in). Lightly built, angular raptor with long wings and tail. Rufous above and below with pale head. In flight, upperwing with rufous coverts; underwing with prominent whitish patches. Tail rufous and deeply forked, almost translucent against light. Often hangs on rising air; circles and weaves in slow, effortless flight on bowed wings with tail twisting as rudder.
Voice: Repeated *he-he-heea*.
Habitat: Wooded hillsides with grazing meadows.
Similar Species: Black Kite only slightly forked tail.

White-tailed Eagle *Haliaeetus albicilla*

broad, square wings

prominent head and bill

ADULT

short white tail

JUVENILE

wedge shaped tail

huge yellow bill

ADULT

Status: Massively built eagle resident over large areas of the eastern half of Europe, but which is highly localized as a result of persecution, though favoured areas may support several pairs. Extends eastwards across Siberia to Pacific. Siberian birds migrate, south westwards to western Europe. Reintroduced Scotland where breeds. Highly fragmented over most of Europe. Largest numbers in Norway.

J F M A M J J A S O N D

Identification: 69–91cm (27–36in). Huge, bulky eagle with enormous broad wings and very prominent head and bill. Adult mostly dark brown with tawny body and pure white tail; large pale head with very large yellow bill; and paler margins to upperwing coverts. In flight, prominent head and bill and short white tail contrast with huge, square-cut dark wings giving a distinctly 'weight-forward' appearance. Juveniles share this shape, but have dark tails or only white centres to tail feathers, depending on age. Pale head and tawny body acquired over several seasons.

Voice: Deep laughing *kok-kok-kok* in elaborate courtship flights. Far-carrying over water.

Habitat: Always associated with water, either fresh or sea; nests in trees and cliffs. From deep fjords and offshore islands to large inland lakes, reservoirs and rivers, provided that there are undisturbed areas nearby.

Similar Species: Immature similar to adult Golden and Steppe Eagles, but short, wedge-shaped tail distinguishes. Adult similar to juvenile Golden Eagle which has white tail, but with broad black terminal band. Shape distinctive in all plumages.

Lammergeier *Gypaetus barbatus*

black head and breast, paler body

wings swept back almost pointed

JUVENILE

black 'face and beard'

golden body

ADULT

very long wedge-shaped tail

ADULT

J F M A M J J A S O N D

Status: Rare and highly localized resident of a few isolated mountain ranges in southern Europe. Highly endangered.
Identification: 110–115cm (39–45in). Huge, long-winged, long-tailed vulture. Long pointed wings; long, wedge-shaped tail. Adults black, golden head and body. Immatures dark, best identified by shape and size. Soars effortlessly over high crags and gorges.
Voice: Some occasional squeals.
Habitat: Remote mountains with gorges and cliffs.
Similar Species: Immature confusable with Black Vulture in size and coloration; and with juvenile Egyptian Vulture in shape.

Egyptian Vulture *Neophron percnopterus*

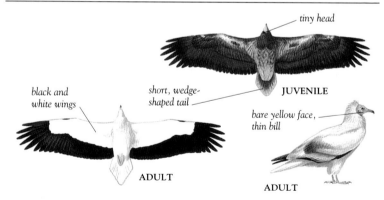

tiny head

black and white wings

short, wedge-shaped tail

JUVENILE

bare yellow face, thin bill

ADULT

ADULT

J F M A M J J A S O N D

Status: Smallest European vulture confined to Mediterranean. Numbers declining rapidly.
Identification: 60–70cm (24–27in). Has strangely cigar-shaped body and pointed wings. Adult basically white, though generally dingy; head bare and yellow, with thin bill. In the air, white with black flight feathers. Juvenile brown with paler area across wing, and bare, pale pinkish face.
Voice: Various grunts, but mostly silent.
Habitat: Open landscapes with carrion.
Similar Species: Shape like juvenile Lammergeier; flight pattern like Booted Eagle.

Griffon Vulture   *Gyps fulvus*

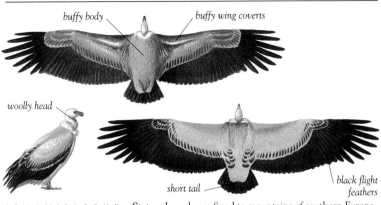

buffy body

buffy wing coverts

woolly head

short tail

black flight feathers

J F M A M J J A S O N D

Status: Largely confined to mountains of southern Europe, but will exploit wild lowlands where they exist.
Identification: 95–105cm (37–41in). Large scavenger that spends much of time soaring, usually gregariously. Both upperparts and underparts warm buff-brown marked, in adult, by white line across underwing coverts; flight feathers black. Soars on huge flat wings with small white head tucked back and short tail widely spread.
Voice: Grunts and hisses in dispute over food or space.
Habitat: Wild country with plentiful supply of carrion. Now mainly among rugged hills and mountains.
Similar Species: Only Black Vulture.

Black Vulture   *Aegypius monachus*

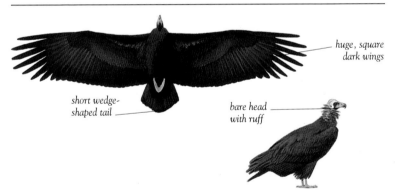

huge, square dark wings

short wedge-shaped tail

bare head with ruff

Status: Confined to extreme south-east and south-west. More widespread and numerous Turkey. Endangered.
Identification: 100–110cm (39–43in). Slightly larger than Griffon. Uniformly dark, even black, in all plumages. Adult may have warmish wash on underwing. Soars on flat wings with bare head tucked back into neck; slightly wedge-shaped tail a little more prominent than square-tipped tail of Griffon. In all plumages Griffon shows tawny on wing coverts.
Voice: Usually silent.
Habitat: Hills and mountains with extensive woodland.
Similar Species: Griffon Vulture as above.

J F M A M J J A S O N D

Marsh Harrier *Circus aeruginosus*

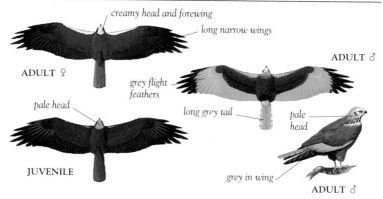

creamy head and forewing

long narrow wings

ADULT ♀

ADULT ♂

grey flight feathers

pale head

long grey tail

pale head

JUVENILE

grey in wing

ADULT ♂

J F M A M J J A S O N D

Status: Widespread resident and winter visitor in western Europe; summer visitor in east.

Identification: 48–56cm (19–22in). Largest of the harriers with slow, flap-and-glide flight creating lumbering impression. Long wings, long tail and gliding flight near ground with wings held in 'V'. Male, in flight, has grey tail and large grey area on innerwing. Female all brown with creamy head and forewing. Juvenile like female, without creamy forewing.

Voice: High-pitched *kee-a* in courtship.

Habitat: Large, lowland reedbeds and adjacent marshes.

Similar Species: Bulkier, broader-winged than other harriers.

Hen Harrier *Circus cyaneus*

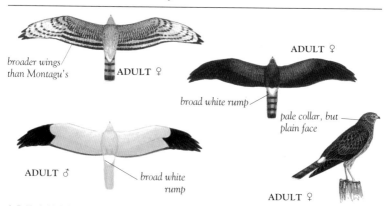

broader wings than Montagu's

ADULT ♀

ADULT ♀

broad white rump

pale collar, but plain face

ADULT ♂

broad white rump

ADULT ♀

J F M A M J J A S O N D

Status: Either summer visitor, resident or winter visitor to all parts of Europe save Iceland.

Identification: 43–51cm (17–20in). Medium-sized harrier, between Montagu's and Marsh Harrier in bulk. Male pale grey above with white rump and black wingtips; breast grey, underparts white. Female and juvenile streaked brown with bold white rump.

Voice: Cackles and squeals in courtship.

Habitat: Hillside moors, young plantations, marshes.

Similar Species: Montagu's and Pallid Harriers. Females and juveniles jointly called 'ring-tail' harriers – Hen Harrier bulkier, with larger white rump.

Pallid Harrier *Circus macrourus*

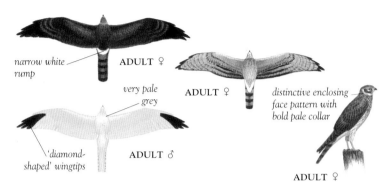

narrow white rump — **ADULT ♀**

very pale grey — **ADULT ♀**

distinctive enclosing face pattern with bold pale collar

ADULT ♂

'diamond-shaped' wingtips

ADULT ♀

J F M A M J J A S O N D

Status: Summer visitor to Russian steppes that is scarce winter visitor to south-east Europe.
Identification: 41–48cm (16–19in). Male more lightly built than Montagu's Harrier and paler grey above. Flight more buoyant and graceful. Lacks chestnut streaking on breast; black wingtips form pointed wedge. Female separated from female Montagu's by black eye-stripe and dark crescent on ear coverts enclosing pale cheek area and prominent pale collar. Juvenile has similar pale collar.
Voice: High-pitched *pree-pre-pre*.
Habitat: Dry grassy steppes, only slight adaptation to crops.
Similar Species: Montagu's and Hen Harriers.

Montagu's Harrier *Circus pygargus*

dark line across wings

ADULT ♂

no white rump

narrow wings

ADULT ♀

dark cheek crescent lacks pale collar

ADULT ♀

narrow white rump — **ADULT ♀**

ADULT ♀

Status: Summer visitor to most of temperate Europe where often abundant. Scarce Britain and absent Scandinavia.
Identification: 39–46cm (15–18in). Smaller and slimmer than Hen Harrier. Male grey above with black wingtips and black line across upperwing. Tail and rump grey. Underparts streaked chestnut. Female like female Hen Harrier but more lightly built, with narrower white rump and head with dark cheek mark.
Voice: Shrill courtship *kek-kek-kek*.
Habitat: Cereal fields and steppes.
Similar Species: Pallid and Hen Harriers especially females and juveniles.

J F M A M J J A S O N D

Identification of 'Ring-tail' Harriers

Three, of the four, European harriers are so similar in female and juvenile plumages that they are jointly called 'Ring-tail Harriers'. In these plumages Pallid, Montagu's and Hen Harriers are brown and buff birds, with long wings and tails, marked by a bold white rump – their most obvious field mark. Identification of individual species is always difficult and in some circumstances, impossible. Good views are essential though, with experience, the bulk of a Hen Harrier and its larger white rump can be quite distinctive. Most important is face pattern, distinctive in each species.

PALLID HARRIER

Structurally the lightest of the three, but with same overall pattern and narrow white rump of Montagu's. Distinguished by head markings, discernible even in flight with close approach. Dark ear covert outline bordered by pale ring extending from moustache to hind crown, complemented by bold pale supercilium and broad pale eye-ring. Summers and winters south-east Europe.

MONTAGU'S HARRIER

Heavier built than Pallid, lighter built than Hen, with narrower white rump than latter. Distinguished from Pallid by broad pale eye-ring and pale supercilium. Effectively this creates an almost uniform face broken by a bold dark 'comma'. Summer visitor only.

HEN HARRIER

Largest and most heavily built of the three, with comparatively deep chest and large white rump appearing less 'horseshoe' in shape. Face distinctly plain with only hint of paleness above and behind eye, rather than distinct eye-ring. Face surrounded by narrow, pale line, rather than broad pale band. Summers and winters west and east Europe.

Northern Goshawk   *Accipiter gentilis*

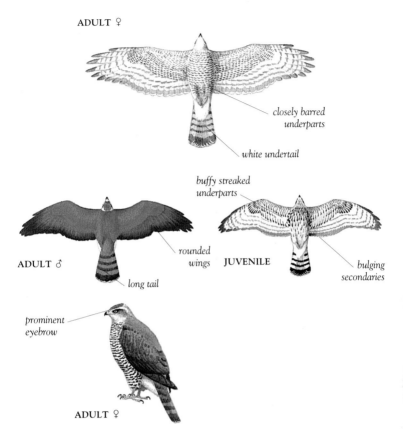

ADULT ♀

closely barred
underparts

white undertail

buffy streaked
underparts

ADULT ♂

rounded
wings

long tail

JUVENILE

bulging
secondaries

prominent
eyebrow

ADULT ♀

Status: Widespread resident virtually throughout
Europe. Some immigration from far north, but
mostly no more than local movements to non-breeding
areas in winter. Absent Portugal (where winter visitor),
Iceland, Ireland and much of Turkey. Introduced Britain
and spreading. Elsewhere widespread resident eastwards
across boreal zone of Siberia and North America.
Identification: 48–58cm (19–23in). Like an over-large
European Sparrowhawk with rounded wings and long,
barred tail. Adult grey to brownish-grey above with darker
cap and bold white supercilium. Closely barred grey below,
with prominent white undertail coverts, which are fanned
to form a 'powder-puff' in display. Female about Buzzard-

J F M A M J J A S O N D

size; much larger than male and more brownish-grey above. Juvenile brown above and
streaked brown (not barred grey) below. In flight thick, bulky body and bulging
secondaries are good features as are more ponderous wingbeats than Sparrowhawk.
Voice: Mewing *pee-oo* and chattering *kek-kek-kek* near breeding site. Otherwise
mostly silent.
Habitat: Forests and woods, especially spruce and other conifers. Also hunts over
adjacent broken countryside, but seldom far from trees. Wide range of prey, but
predominantly gamebirds, a good population of which is essential.
Similar Species: Small male may be almost same size as large female
European Sparrowhawk and should be separated with care. See features above.

European Sparrowhawk *Accipiter nisus*

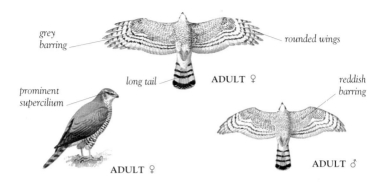

grey barring

rounded wings

long tail

ADULT ♀

reddish barring

prominent supercilium

ADULT ♀

ADULT ♂

J F M A M J J A S O N D

Status: Breeds virtually throughout our area save Iceland, northernmost Scandinavia and central European plains.
Identification: 28–38cm (11–15in). Fast-flying, agile hawk of woodlands. Grey or grey-brown above, with clear, pale supercilium in female. Male barred russet below; female barred grey. Both have long tails with at least four distinct bars. Dashing flight in pursuit of small birds. When soaring flaps rounded wings quickly for a few beats.
Voice: Loud *kek-kek-kek*.
Habitat: Wide variety of woodlands as well as copses and open country with fields and hedgerows.
Similar Species: Northern Goshawk, Levant Sparrowhawk.

Levant Sparrowhawk *Accipiter brevipes*

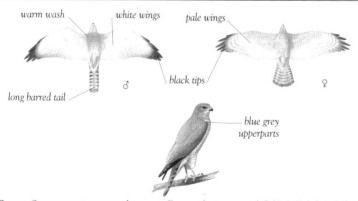

warm wash

white wings

pale wings

♂

black tips

long barred tail

♀

blue grey upperparts

Status: Summer visitor to south-eastern Europe that leaves via Bosphorus, wintering in Africa.
Identification: 32–38cm (13–15in). Similar to European Sparrowhawk, but more slender and less rounded wings. Both sexes considerably paler than European particularly on underwing in flight when both show diagnostic black wingtips. Male virtually white below with pinkish wash on body and underwing coverts.
Voice: High-pitched *keewick*.
Habitat: Deciduous forests and woods, but also copses and wind-breaks in lowlands and hill regions.
Similar Species: European Sparrowhawk, European Kestrel.

J F M A M J J A S O N D

Common Buzzard *Buteo buteo*

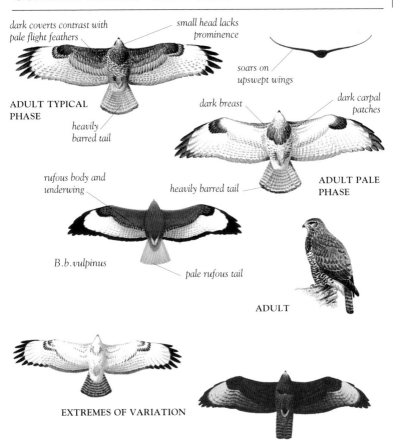

dark coverts contrast with pale flight feathers

small head lacks prominence

soars on upswept wings

ADULT TYPICAL PHASE

heavily barred tail

dark breast

dark carpal patches

rufous body and underwing

heavily barred tail

ADULT PALE PHASE

B.b.vulpinus

pale rufous tail

ADULT

EXTREMES OF VARIATION

Status: Most abundant and widespread of medium-sized raptors. Northern Palaearctic; declining.
Identification: 50–56cm (20–22in). Highly variable plumage from virtually white to almost uniformly dark with multiple intermediate phases. Broad wings; shortish, often fan-spread tail; and tiny head create characteristic flight silhouette. Soars on upswept wings held in shallow 'V' unlike other buzzards (but see Marsh Harrier). Typical birds have pale flight feathers, contrasting with dark underwing coverts, dark breast, paler belly and heavily barred tail. Pale birds always show dark carpal patches. Eastern race *B.b.vulpinus* (Steppe Buzzard) is rufous with pale, translucent pinkish tail (see Long-legged Buzzard), though some nominate birds also show a pinkish unbarred tail.
Voice: High-pitched far-carrying mewing *pee-oo*.
Habitat: Arable and grassland broken by woodland belts and larger areas of forest. Moors and heaths with rocky crags and cliffs, often marshes and estuaries in winter.
Similar Species: Beware Long-legged Buzzard in south-east, but also Rough-legged and Honey Buzzards elsewhere.

J F M A M J J A S O N D

Buzzards in Flight

The four species of European buzzard form a group of similar-sized, broad-winged hawks that are made somewhat confusing by variable plumage and, particularly, by the highly variable Common Buzzard. These variations are not sub-specific (though one is so), but occur randomly throughout the species' range. Three, of the four species, are members of the genus *Buteo* and share a common basic structure; the Honey Buzzard *Pernis* is somewhat different in shape. However, each species has a distinct flight profile with wings held flat (two species), raised or drooping, thus facilitating identification not only at great distance, but also irrespective of plumage variation.

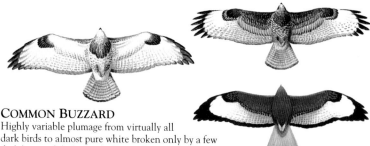

COMMON BUZZARD

Highly variable plumage from virtually all dark birds to almost pure white broken only by a few dark bars and dark carpals. Even white pale phase birds do not show the broad black terminal band of the otherwise similarly pale Rough-legged Buzzard. The eastern subspecies *B.b.vulpinus* has a rusty tail, only faintly barred, and wing coverts that vary from rich chestnut to creamy. It can thus easily be confused with Long-legged Buzzard which always shows darker carpal patches and is longer-winged. Common Buzzard soars on upswept wings.

LONG-LEGGED BUZZARD

Rich rufous underwing coverts, pronounced black carpal patches and pinkish unbarred tail separate from Common Buzzard, especially pink-tailed *B.b.vulpinus*. Juvenile Long-legged may show faint barring on tail. Soars on flat wings.

ROUGH-LEGGED BUZZARD

White underparts marked by black carpal patches and two underwing bars is normal. Variably darker, especially on underwing coverts. Dark lower belly and black-banded white tail are constants. Hovers frequently and soars on flat wings.

HONEY BUZZARD

Less broad-winged than other buzzards with prominent small head on long neck, long tail and decidedly 'waisted' wings. Varies from white multi-barred body and wings; to dark body and wing coverts contrasting with white barred flight feathers. Tail shows three distinct bands. Combination of shape and barring sufficient to identify. Soars on drooping wings.

Long-legged Buzzard   *Buteo rufinus*

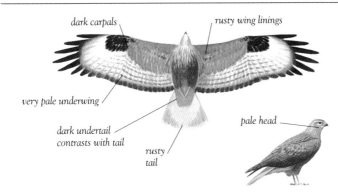

dark carpals

rusty wing linings

very pale underwing

dark undertail
contrasts with tail

rusty
tail

pale head

J F M A M J J A S O N D

Status: Summer visitor Balkans; resident and winter visitor Turkey. Vagrant elsewhere in Europe.
Identification: 50–65cm (20–25in). Similar to Common Buzzard. Adult more rufous than other buzzards. In flight, rufous wing coverts contrast with flight feathers. Unbarred pale rufous tail, paler at base and contrasting with dark undertail. Immature darker with tail bands; both important features. Eastern subspecies of Common Buzzard *B.b.vulpinus* also has rufous tail. Soars; wings in shallow 'V'.
Voice: Similar to Common Buzzard, but less vocal.
Habitat: Dry areas, semi-deserts and rocky hillsides.
Similar Species: Eastern subspecies of Common Buzzard.

Rough-legged Buzzard   *Buteo lagopus*

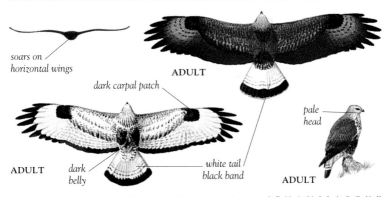

soars on
horizontal wings

ADULT

dark carpal patch

pale
head

ADULT

dark
belly

white tail
black band

ADULT

Status: Summer visitor Scandinavia and Russian tundra. Winters north and east Europe.
Identification: 50–61cm (20–24in). Similar to Common Buzzard, but less variable plumage. Flight feathers always pale; carpal patch always black and prominent. Tail white with broad black subterminal band. Dark belly patches more obvious than Common Buzzard. Always pale headed. Soars on flat wings; hangs on wind or hovers on frequently flapped wings.
Voice: Louder and deeper than Common Buzzard.
Habitat: Open tundra and tundra-like mountain areas.
Similar Species: Common Buzzard.

J F M A M J J A S O N D

Lesser Spotted Eagle *Aquila pomarina*

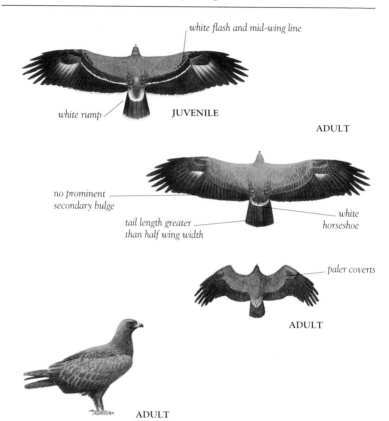

white flash and mid-wing line

white rump

JUVENILE

ADULT

no prominent secondary bulge

tail length greater than half wing width

white horseshoe

ADULT

paler coverts

ADULT

ADULT

Status: Most abundant and widespread of 'all-dark' group of east European eagles, that includes Spotted, Imperial and Steppe Eagles. Commonest eagle on passage over Bosphorus. Summer visitor to eastern Europe from Germany to Russia and Ukraine and, patchily, through Balkans and Turkey.

J F M A M J J A S O N D

Identification: 60–65cm (24–25in). Like other 'dark' eagles, passes through series of confusing plumages between juvenile and full adult, though structural differences are standard. Lesser Spotted is a well-proportioned, medium-sized eagle with narrower wings, longer tail and larger head than Spotted Eagle. Adult is dark below, with paler wing linings; above has similarly paler wing coverts, plus small white patch at base of inner primaries and narrow white 'horseshoe' rump. Juvenile similar, but with more prominent white patch on upperwing that extends in narrow line across base of secondaries. Steppe and Imperial Eagles are much larger with bigger heads and tails.

Voice: High-pitched barks, much more vociferous than Spotted Eagle.

Habitat: Wet lowland woods, often along large river systems, but also in montane forests. Hunts over dry country, with no specific wetland preference like Spotted Eagle.

Similar Species: See Spotted Eagle and above.

Eagle Flight Silhouettes

Eagles, like other birds of prey, have characteristic ways of holding their wings when soaring on warm rising air. Seen head-on these can be summarized as upswept, level and drooping. The amount of upturn of the wingtips also varies adding an extra dimension to identification.

  Such apparently minor points can not only make identification at great distance a possibility, but also serves to eliminate species from contention. A large bird of prey circling over a distant hill can be identified as a Golden Eagle, simply because no other similar-sized bird soars on upswept wings. Among European birds of prey, only Common Buzzard shares this characteristic, but that species is much smaller and lacks both the prominent head and huge, 'waisted' wings of the Eagle. Similarly, an eagle soaring on drooping wings is either a Spotted or Lesser Spotted, though it could be the much smaller, pigeon-headed Honey Buzzard. As soon as a droopy-winged eagle is seen, the breadth of wings and length of tail come into play as the second critical feature to search for as the bird circles in the air. Flight silhouette may not then specifically identify a species, but by narrowing the possibilities enables the observer to concentrate on the features that matter.

wingtips with accentuated upsweep

whole wing upswept from body

Upswept like Golden Eagle

wing tips with unnoticeable upsweep

wings appear rigid

Level with hardly any upturn to the wingtips like Imperial Eagle.

upswept wingtips unnoticeable and unimportant

distinct wing droop from body

Drooping like Lesser Spotted Eagle

upturned wing tips noticeable at all times

level wings, but not held rigidly

Level with upturned wingtips like Bonelli's Eagle

Eagles in Flight

Eagles are among the few birds that are easier to identify flying than when perched. Several species, particularly the 'all-dark' eastern eagles, are little more than a large dark bird when sitting in a tree. In flight they show more of themselves – their shape and their often obscure field marks. They are often shy birds too and identification often has to be made at considerable distance when shape and flight attitude become more important than coloration. The comparison of one species with another then takes on more importance, perhaps, more than with any other group of birds.

Short-toed Eagle: Palest of the eagles. White body and wings variably barred on body, wings and tail. Head and neck usually darker, indeed a dark-headed, pale eagle is certainly this species. Thick bull neck.

White-tailed Eagle: Juvenile is huge all dark eagle marked only by pale centres to tail feathers. Huge square wings and large prominent head are accentuated by short, wedge-shaped tail.

White-tailed Eagle: Adult has same huge, square wings and prominent head and bill as juvenile (above). But short, wedge-shaped tail is white. At some angles and in some light conditions the tail disappears, enhancing the weight-forward 'feel' of the species.

Bonelli's Eagle: Adult has lightly streaked, white body contrasting with dark wings. Close approach reveals broad black stripe along centre of each wing. Soars on flat wings with prominent head and tail.

Bonelli's Eagle: Juvenile shares perfect proportions of wing, head and tail with adult, but completely different in colour. Body and underwing coverts warm orange-buff separated from white flight feathers by broken black bar.

Lesser Spotted Eagle: Adult is all dark eagle that, at reasonable range, shows wing coverts paler than flight feathers. A well-proportioned eagle with broad wings, moderately prominent head and neck and substantial tail, which is over half of the width of the wing.

Lesser Spotted Eagle: Juvenile same shape as adult (above) and showing same wing-coverts paler than flight feathers. Under surface shows white undertail and narrow white line across wings.

Spotted Eagle: Adult is very dark eagle with hint of wing coverts being darker than flight feathers. White horseshoe-shaped rump. Wings very broad with prominent secondary bulge. Head small; short tail only a third of wing width in length.

Spotted Eagle: Juvenile shares same wing-dominant shape with adult. Narrow white underwing line separates coverts from flight feathers. This line much more obvious on upperwing, plus bars of spots across wing coverts.

Golden Eagle: Adult is very dark eagle with golden wash on crown and nape, and across upperwing coverts. Distinctive 'waisted' base to upswept wings identifies at great distance.

Golden Eagle: Large dark eagle with broad wings, prominent head and tail. Wings distinctly waisted' where they meet the body creating a 'wasp-winged' effect. Large tail often spread like a 'paddle'. Juvenile has white tail marked by broad black terminal band. Plus bold white underwing bar.

Principles of Eagle Identification

Eagles are magnificent, charismatic and difficult to identify – mostly. They differ from the smaller buzzards and larger vultures in having prominent heads and necks, and longer tails, which are often held together rather than spread. Their wings are broad, with roughly parallel sides, and end with distinctive gaps between the outer primaries. They may differ in the number of exposed primaries (fingers) at the wingtip, but these are very difficult to count in the field. Eagles pass through a confusing set of immature plumages over a period of several years before attaining adulthood. At all ages, proportions, shape and flight attitude are usually more important than plumage characters. The three varying sized birds below pick out the significant features to look for when identifying an eagle in flight.

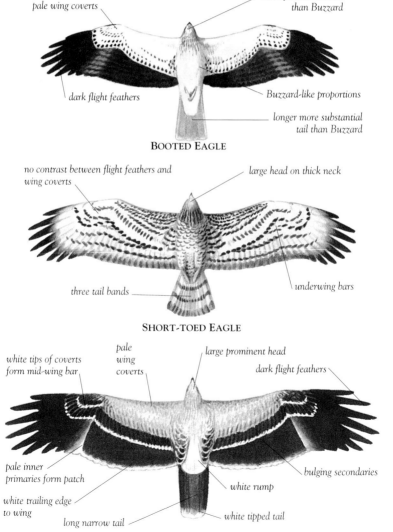

pale wing coverts

more prominent head than Buzzard

dark flight feathers

Buzzard-like proportions

longer more substantial tail than Buzzard

BOOTED EAGLE

no contrast between flight feathers and wing coverts

large head on thick neck

three tail bands

underwing bars

SHORT-TOED EAGLE

pale wing coverts

white tips of coverts form mid-wing bar

large prominent head

dark flight feathers

pale inner primaries form patch

white trailing edge to wing

long narrow tail

white rump

bulging secondaries

white tipped tail

IMPERIAL EAGLE JUVENILE

Common Buzzard Confusion

Common Buzzards are the most widespread and abundant broad-winged raptors in Europe. Not only do they soar like eagles, but their plumage is extraordinarily variable and may thus resemble several of the eagles and other birds of prey. The French name *Buse Variable* encapsulates this plumage character more succinctly than any other European language. Four examples of extreme plumage types are compared below. In each case the compared species has been drawn the same size as the Common Buzzard, though a wing-span scale has been added below.

BUZZARDS

120 cm

COMMON BUZZARD pale phase bird, with white plumage marked by bold dark carpal patches, presents similar plumage pattern to Osprey. Broader wings held in 'V' when soaring distinguish.

120 cm

COMMON BUZZARD extreme dark phase, with pale base only to primaries, resembles dark phase Booted Eagle which is similar sized. Less prominent head, dark tail and upswept wings are good features.

120 cm

COMMON BUZZARD extreme pale phase shows only rudimentary carpal patches but marked underwing bar. Distinguished from Short-toed Eagle by small head and neck and lack of multiple wingbars.

120 cm

COMMON BUZZARD typical phase has tawny wing coverts contrasting with pale flight feathers. This pattern is similar to juvenile Bonelli's Eagle.

EAGLES

157 cm

OSPREY is very similar in plumage to pale phase Common Buzzard, but small head more prominent. Wings narrow and held angled and gull-like when gliding or soaring. Much larger wing span

110 cm

BOOTED EAGLE dark phase birds may show pale patch on inner primaries. But prominent, more aquiline head and pale tail separate from dark phase Common Buzzard. Tail usually held narrow with parallel sides.

190 cm

SHORT-TOED EAGLE resembles palest of Common Buzzards, but larger head and thicker neck are usually dark. Wing shows more prominent wingbars, but some individuals are much paler than bird illustrated.

165 cm

BONELLI'S EAGLE juvenile shows similar underwing to typical Common Buzzard, but larger head and bigger tail together with much larger size identify it.

Booted Eagle: Dark phase resembles buzzard, but has definite aquiline head and longer tail. Dark wings have hint of pale patch on inner primaries; tail uniform and pale.

Booted Eagle: Pale phase has same prominent head and tail of dark birds. Black flight feathers contrast with white wing coverts and white body, making this one of the easiest of eagles to identify. Soars on flat wings.

Spanish Imperial Eagle: Adult is large straight-winged eagle with prominent large head and longish narrow tail. Crown washed pale gold, almost white; white 'braces' and obvious white leading edge to wing. Soars on flat wings.

Imperial Eagle: Large dark eagle of similar structure to Spanish Imperial. Adult has golden crown, white 'braces', but lacks white forewing of Spanish bird.

Imperial Eagle: Juvenile has broad wings, prominent head and narrow tail of adult. Tawny wing coverts contrast with black flight feathers above and below, separated by white line.

Steppe Eagle: Adult is large eagle of uniform dark plumage above and below. Lacks all features of other eagles. However, short inner primaries create a noticeable dent on rear edge of wing.

Steppe Eagle: Juvenile much easier to identify than adult. Above and below rufous-tawny wing coverts contrast with black flight feathers, separated by bold white line. White base of primaries creates bold outerwing patch (especially below).

Confusing Non-Eagle Species

Eagles are the most majestic of European birds of prey. Vultures may be larger, some of the falcons faster, but an eagle has everything that we find attractive about birds of prey. Eagles can, nevertheless, be confused with other groups of raptors, particularly by the less experienced observer.

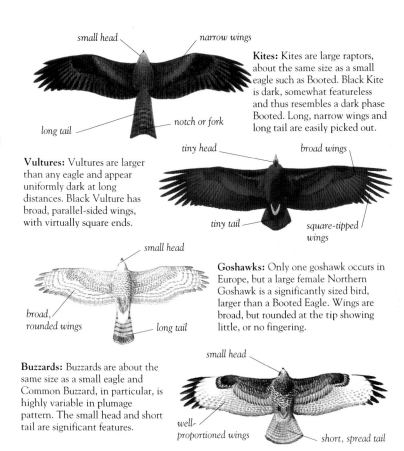

small head *narrow wings*

long tail *notch or fork*

Kites: Kites are large raptors, about the same size as a small eagle such as Booted. Black Kite is dark, somewhat featureless and thus resembles a dark phase Booted. Long, narrow wings and long tail are easily picked out.

tiny head *broad wings*

tiny tail *square-tipped wings*

Vultures: Vultures are larger than any eagle and appear uniformly dark at long distances. Black Vulture has broad, parallel-sided wings, with virtually square ends.

small head

broad, rounded wings *long tail*

Goshawks: Only one goshawk occurs in Europe, but a large female Northern Goshawk is a significantly sized bird, larger than a Booted Eagle. Wings are broad, but rounded at the tip showing little, or no fingering.

small head

well-proportioned wings *short, spread tail*

Buzzards: Buzzards are about the same size as a small eagle and Common Buzzard, in particular, is highly variable in plumage pattern. The small head and short tail are significant features.

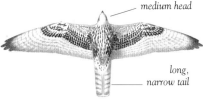

medium head

long, narrow tail

Falcons: Most falcons are relatively small, but Saker and Gyr are certainly as large as a small eagle. Saker is a generally brown bird, but its long, pointed wings and long tail preclude confusion given decent views.

Osprey: Along with the buzzards, the most confusing eagle-like species. Resembles Short-toed and Bonelli's being white below, with dark capatches. Holding its wings angled like a gull is diagnostic.

angled gull-like wings

Eagle Flight Attitudes

Eagles fly in a wide variety of different ways. They dive steeply or shallowly, they glide, and they soar. They may also flap their wings, twist wings and tail to change direction, or spread their tail to gain lift. Each type of flight produces different flight attitudes and will radically change flight geometry and shape. Four examples show how a single species (Golden Eagle) changes shape dramatically according to the flight mode adopted. As flight shape is so important to eagle identification, understanding the way flight attitude affects shape is a crucial factor.

DIVING: Innerwings are swept forward and outerwings backward, with the carpal joint virtually level with the bill. Tail is held together and may even taper.

MODIFIED DIVING: Usually used for fast travelling, losing altitude for speed, perhaps broken by wing flapping. Innerwing held less far forward and outerwing less swept back than full dive. Tail held together.

GLIDING: Less speedy and more economical method of travelling with wings well spread to maintain lift, but outerwing swept back and primaries bunched for speed. Gliding can hide structural features crucial to identification.

SOARING: Uses updraught of air or thermals to gain height for the least possible outlay of energy. The classic view of an eagle that shows all features to the best advantage. Wings and tail spread to utilise rising air. In thermals eagles will circle, offering opportunities to view both upper and lower surfaces of wings, tail and body.

Spotted Eagle *Aquila clanga*

three lines
of spots

JUVENILE

white rump

white horseshoe

secondary bulge

tail length a third
of wing width

darker coverts than
flight feathers

ADULT

ADULT

Status: Summer visitor that overlaps range of Lesser
Spotted Eagle in eastern Europe, but replaces it across
Siberia.

Identification: 65–72cm (26–28in). Easily confused with
more widespread Lesser Spotted Eagle in our region, but
also beware larger Steppe and Imperial Eagles. All-dark
eagle, 'spotted' only in juvenile plumage. Adult uniformly
dark with only hint of contrast between coverts and flight
feathers; insignificant white wing flash; and 'horseshoe' of
white on rump. Immature similar, but with white line
across base of flight feathers. Juvenile as immature, but
with three rows of white spots across wing coverts –
obvious in flight and on folded wing. Also has more prominent white wing flash and
white 'horseshoe' rump. In silhouette, shows huge, square-cut wings with prominent
secondary bulge, tiny head and short wedge-shaped tail. Scarce pale phase juvenile has
tawny wing coverts above and below and may be confused with larger juvenile Steppe
and Imperial Eagles. If contrast between wing coverts and flight feathers can be detected
in dark plumaged birds it is the reverse of Lesser Spotted, i.e. dark linings with paler flight
feathers.

Voice: A dog-like bark *kak-kak-kak*.

Habitat: Forests from boreal to edge of steppes, most commonly along rivers or beside
lakes and other wetlands. Usually associated with water at all seasons.

Similar Species: See Lesser Spotted Eagle and above.

Steppe Eagle   *Aquila nipalensis*

prominent head

rufous-tawny wing coverts

bold mid-wing line

white tipped tail

JUVENILE

hint of paleness

short inner primaries create 'dunt'

ADULT

bold white rump

bold mid-wing line

JUVENILE

ADULT

J F M A M J J A S O N D

Status: Passage migrant through central and eastern Turkey in spring and autumn, that passes around the eastern shores of the Black Sea.
Identification: 67–87cm (26½–34½in). Large eagle about same size and shape as Imperial. Adult is completely dark with broad wings and prominent head and tail. Main distinction from other dark eastern eagles is ragged appearance, subdued barring on flight feathers of wing and tail, and short inner primaries creating a clear indentation on trailing edge of wing when soaring. No more than a hint of paleness on nape, rump and upper surface of inner primaries. Juvenile similar to juvenile Imperial. Rufous-tawny (not tawny) coverts contrast with black flight feathers, but white mid-wing line, primary patch and rump all much bolder than Imperial, creating a more contrasting pattern. Sub-adults lose this pattern, but still show a narrow mid-wing line on underwing.
Voice: Mostly silent.
Habitat: Steppes; on passage may occur anywhere.
Similar Species: Imperial Eagle as above; see also Spotted and Lesser Spotted Eagles and Eagles in Eagle Flight panorama (between pages 97-97).

Spanish Imperial Eagle *Aquila adalberti*

white braces white leading edge

pale crown/ nape

white shoulders

gliding flight

ADULT

J F M A M J J A S O N D

Status: Large eagle. Endangered. Confined to Spain.
Identification: 75–83cm (30–33in). Huge eagle. Large
square-shaped wings, long parallel-sided tail and prominent
head produce classic *Aquila* silhouette. Adult very dark
brown, broken by white crown, white 'braces' and white
leading edge to innerwing. In flight, juvenile upperwing
shows contrast between tawny coverts and black flight
feathers. White line across wing; inner primaries pale wedge.
Voice: Deep barking during breeding season.
Habitat: Hillside and lowland woods.
Similar Species: Juvenile could be confused with Tawny
and wandering juvenile Imperial or Steppe Eagle.

Imperial Eagle *Aquila heliaca*

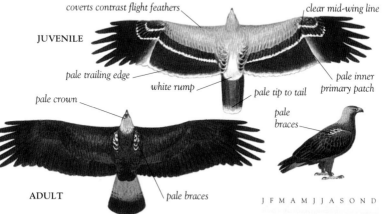

coverts contrast flight feathers

clear mid-wing line

JUVENILE

pale trailing edge

white rump

pale tip to tail

pale inner primary patch

pale crown

pale braces

ADULT

pale braces

J F M A M J J A S O N D

Status: Widespread, but scarce and declining.
Identification: 72–80cm (28½–31½in). Large, dark eagle
marked by prominent head and tail. Pale golden crown
and braces are diagnostic features. Juvenile has streaked
tawny-buff breast and shows contrast between tawny-buff
wing coverts and flight feathers; a narrow white mid-wing
line; pale inner primaries creating a pale wedge.
Voice: Deep barking around nesting area.
Habitat: Hill and lowland woods with undisturbed foraging.
Similar Species: See Steppe and Spanish Imperial eagles.

Golden Eagle   *Aquila chrysaetos*

prominent head

tawny across wings

ADULT

white wingbars

JUVENILE

white tail
black band

tawny crown
and nape

large, broad tail

ADULT

J F M A M J J A S O N D

Status: Huge, resident eagle of wilderness areas, mostly now confined to mountain regions. Circumpolar, absent Greenland and Iceland. In Europe, largely confined to mountain ranges. Strongholds with 100–400 pairs are Scotland, Norway, France, Spain and Turkey. General decline in most areas.

Identification: 76–90cm (30–35in). Adult dark brown with pale tawny crown and wing coverts. In flight, appears all dark from below. Juvenile has white tail with broad black terminal band and prominent white base to outer primaries. From below, white tail less noticeable, but bold white line extends along base of flight feathers. Flight powerful with deep wingbeats; quarters hillsides like huge harrier. Long broad wings held in shallow 'V' when soaring. In all plumages, prominent head and large, broad tail coupled with large, 'waisted' wings with prominent secondary bulge, produce characteristic shape, identifiable at great distance.

Voice: Yelping *kaa*, but less vocal than any other European eagle.

Habitat: Predominantly high mountains, though in lowland wetlands and river systems where not disturbed or persecuted by man.

Similar Species: White tail with black band of juvenile cannot be taken for any other European eagle. Adult can be confused with juvenile White-tailed. But see especially Imperial and Spanish Imperial, as well as Spotted and Lesser Spotted, all of which are predominantly dark eagles.

Booted Eagle *Hieraaetus pennatus*

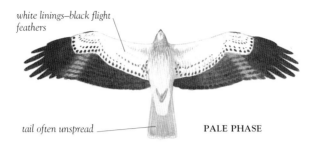

white linings–black flight feathers

tail often unspread —————— **PALE PHASE**

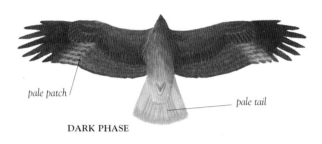

pale patch ——

—— *pale tail*

DARK PHASE

pale wing coverts ——

pale below

Status: Medium-sized raptor of typical eagle proportions. Summer visitor to south-west and south-east Europe, where found through Iberia and central France and from Hungary and Greece eastwards through Russia to southern and central Siberia. Winters savannah Africa and India.
Identification: 45–53cm (18–21in). Similar-sized to Common Buzzard, longer winged, longer tailed and with more prominent head. Frequently soars with unspread tail. Occurs in two phases: pale phase has white body and underwings contrasting with black flight feathers. White tail with broad dusky terminal band. Only differently shaped adult Egyptian Vulture has similar colour pattern. Above black flight feathers contrast with tawny wing coverts. Dark phase is dusky above and below, but with pale tail; it can be easily confused with dark Common Buzzard. Shows 'landing lights' where wings meet body, when seen head-on.
Voice: Vociferous; whistles and cackles over breeding territory.
Habitat: Lowland and hillside woodland.
Similar Species: Common Buzzard may show similar plumage patterns.

J F M A M J J A S O N D

Short-toed Eagle   *Circaetus gallicus*

large head

large, flat-faced,
owl-like head

thick neck

wings, body and
tail white with bars

dark head and
neck contrasts
with pale body

Status: Medium-sized eagle that is widespread summer visitor to much of southern and eastern Europe and which concentrates at narrow sea crossings of Gibraltar and Bosphorus on migration. Called Black-breasted Snake Eagle in Africa. Three-quarters of population in Spain where second most abundant eagle.

J F M A M J J A S O N D

Identification: 62–67cm (24–26in). From below appears a predominantly pale eagle, though marked with lines of black bars on wings and with a clear black head and neck. Only similarly pale European raptor is Osprey. In particularly pale birds bars reduced to no more than few rows of spots. White undertail with three distinct bars. Upperparts grey to grey-brown with dark flight feathers and three tail bands. Thick-set eagle with large, almost owl-like, head – an impression accentuated by darkish head and neck. Frequently hovers and wind-hangs over hillsides while searching for prey when large head and neck particularly obvious.

Voice: Generally more vociferous than other birds of prey. Male has almost oriole-like call repeated several times. Sometimes pair duet at nest site.

Habitat: Open heaths and dry, scrub-covered hillsides, groves and orchards. Nests in trees. Feeds largely on snakes and other reptiles.

Similar Species: Similarly 'pale below' Osprey has narrow, bowed gull-like wings, smaller head on thinner neck and prominent carpals. Bonelli's Eagle has pale body, but darker wings and more aquiline shape.

Bonelli's Eagle   *Hieraaetus fasciatus*

black mid-wing line

tawny body and wing linings

JUVENILE

black mid-wing line

prominent head

white body, dark wings

long tail

ADULT

white back patch

ADULT

Status: Medium-sized eagle that is scarce resident of rocky, open country in southern Europe. Population less than 1,000 pairs, half in Spain. Resident from Iberia eastwards through Italy, Greece, Turkey and Middle East to India and China. Also in east and south-west Africa where virtually black above and known as African Hawk Eagle.

Identification: 65–72cm (25½–28in). Adult slate-grey above marked by diffuse white patch on back – a diagnostic field mark. Below white body, finely streaked black, contrasts with dark wings. In mature birds bold black line extends across underwing. Juvenile tawnyginger with no contrast between body and wings, but with embryonic dark line across underwing. Immatures gradually acquire adult characteristics, including broad tail band. At a distance prominent head and long tail are extremely useful marks.

Voice: Shrill barks and grunts.

Habitat: Open, arid country with rocky outcrops, gorges and cliffs.

Similar Species: See Short-toed Eagle, which is similarly white bodied, but which lacks contrast with dark underwing and is bull-necked in appearance.

J F M A M J J A S O N D

Osprey *Pandion haliaetus*

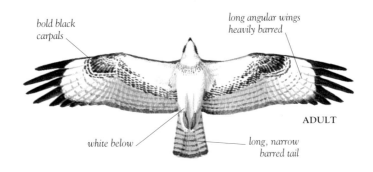

bold black carpals

long angular wings heavily barred

ADULT

white below

long, narrow barred tail

dark eye-stripe

small head and bill with crest

Status: Cosmopolitan and circumpolar. Scarce but widespread passage migrant throughout Europe that is summer visitor mainly to Scotland, Scandinavia, the southern Baltic and Russia and the Ukraine. Recolonized Scotland following extermination.

J F M A M J J A S O N D

Identification: 51–59cm (20–23in). Large, pale raptor that is sometimes mistaken for large gull. Upperparts dark brown and grey; underparts white with prominent black carpal patches, wingtips and wingbars. Flies gull-like on bowed wings. Head and nape white with prominent black eye-stripe and crested appearance. Small head and long neck apparent at all times. Catches fish in spectacular feet-first dive; often after hovering high overhead. Found by lakes in forested areas in summer, reservoirs and other large waters at other times. Hunts coasts in some areas.

Voice: A whistled *chew-chew*, but generally silent away from breeding area.

Habitat: Predominantly clear, unpolluted, fish-rich lakes in boreal zone. Also nests on sea cliffs in Mediterranean. On passage, frequents wide range of waters from lakes and reservoirs to estuaries and inshore bays and coves.

Similar Species: Could be confused with pale Common and Rough-legged Buzzards, both of which show much white and have black carpal patches. Also with Short-toed and even Bonelli's Eagles, both of which are variably white below. Osprey always shows prominent small head and bill, longish neck and flies on narrow bowed wings.

Lesser Kestrel *Falco naumanni*

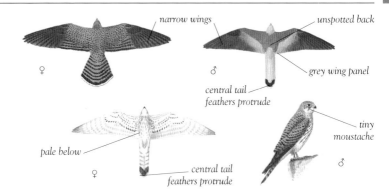

narrow wings

unspotted back

grey wing panel

central tail feathers protrude

♀

♂

tiny moustache

pale below

central tail feathers protrude

♀

♂

J F M A M J J A S O N D

Status: Gregarious little falcon that frequently breeds colonially in towns and cities. Catastrophic decline.
Identification: 29–32cm (11–12½in). In flight, buffy underparts contrast with whitish wings. Female darker and less contrasting. Male has unspotted chestnut back; pale blue head (lacking moustaches), wing coverts and tail. Both sexes have fluttering flight, hover less than Common Kestrel and two central tail feathers extended to form wedge-shaped tail and 'faulted' tail bar.
Voice: High-pitched *kee-kee-kee*.
Habitat: Open grasslands and fields; breeds buildings.
Similar Species: Common Kestrel, Red-footed Falcon.

Common Kestrel *Falco tinnunculus*

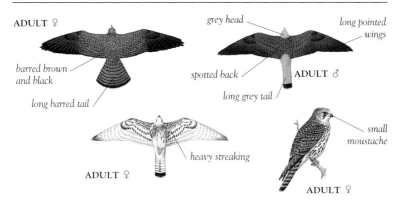

ADULT ♀

grey head

long pointed wings

barred brown and black

spotted back

ADULT ♂

long barred tail

long grey tail

small moustache

heavy streaking

ADULT ♀

ADULT ♀

Status: Widespread, common and familiar resident.
Identification: 33–36cm (13–14in). Often seen hovering. Male has grey head with thin moustachial streak; grey tail with broad black sub-terminal band. Upperparts rufous brown spotted black. Underparts tawny with streaks. Female brown with heavily barred back, dark tail bands. Long tail and shallow beats of pointed wings distinctive.
Voice: High-pitched *kee-kee-kee*.
Habitat: Open countryside, farmland, moors, heaths, coastlines, marshes and city centres. Most common and widespread bird of prey in region.
Similar Species: See Lesser Kestrel.

J F M A M J J A S O N D

Red-footed Falcon   *Falco vespertinus*

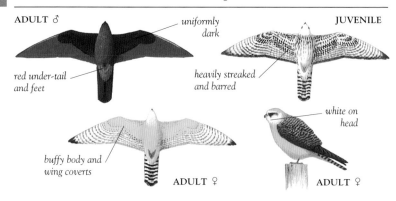

ADULT ♂

uniformly dark

JUVENILE

red under-tail and feet

heavily streaked and barred

white on head

buffy body and wing coverts

ADULT ♀

ADULT ♀

J F M A M J J A S O N D

Status: Summer visitor to eastern Europe.
Identification: 28–31cm (11–12in). Gregarious little falcon, breeds in colonies and migrates in small flocks. Perches openly, often on telegraph wires, but also hovers. Adult male dark grey marked by rufous undertail coverts and bright red eye-ring, legs and cere. Female grey above with darker barring. Underparts and wing linings warm buff; head paler, dark eye patch and 'moustache'; pale orange eye-ring. Juvenile like heavily streaked female.
Voice: Highly vocal, *kew-kew-kew*.
Habitat: Open grassland or agriculture with rookeries.
Similar Species: See Kestrel and Lesser Kestrel.

Merlin   *Falco columbarius*

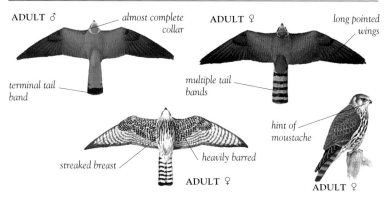

ADULT ♂

almost complete collar

ADULT ♀

long pointed wings

terminal tail band

multiple tail bands

hint of moustache

streaked breast

heavily barred

ADULT ♀

ADULT ♀

J F M A M J J A S O N D

Status: Scarce resident, summer visitor to moors and taiga zone of northern Europe. Widespread in winter elsewhere.
Identification: 27–32cm (10½–13in). Small, dark, fast-flying falcon. Male smaller; blue-grey above with dark terminal band on tail. Underparts warm buff, finely streaked black. No moustache. Female brown with multiple barred buff and brown tail. Heavily streaked below and barred across underwing. Flies low and fast.
Voice: Chattering *kik-kik-kik*, like Common Kestrel.
Habitat: Upland moors and pastures and broken taiga.
Similar Species: Hobby has longer, more angular wings.

Hobby   *Falco subbuteo*

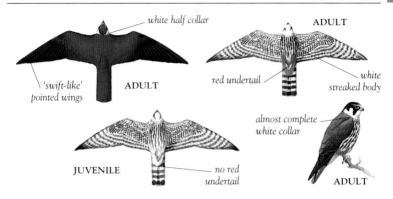

white half collar

ADULT

'swift-like' pointed wings

ADULT

red undertail

white streaked body

JUVENILE

no red undertail

almost complete white collar

ADULT

J F M A M J J A S O N D

Status: Summer visitor throughout temperate Europe that catches insects and hirundines.
Identification: 30–36cm (12–14in). Resembles Kestrel but wings longer and narrower, almost swift-like; tail shorter. Upperparts slate-grey; prominent black moustache and almost complete white 'neck ring'. Underparts streaked black on white; undertail coverts rust-red.
Voice: A repeated *kew-kew*; also high-pitched *ki-ki-ki*.
Habitat: Open lowlands with copses.
Similar Species: Merlin and Kestrel have broader wings. Pale phase Eleonora's Falcon has warm wash beneath body streaking.

Eleonora's Falcon   *Falco eleonorae*

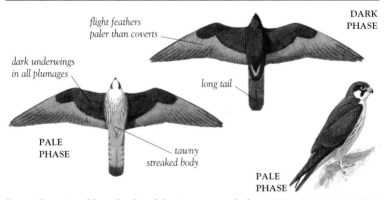

flight feathers paler than coverts

DARK PHASE

dark underwings in all plumages

long tail

PALE PHASE

tawny streaked body

PALE PHASE

Status: Gregarious falcon that breeds late in season to feed young on small migrants. Summer visitor.
Identification: 36–40cm (14–16in). Longer tail separates from Hobby. Pale and dark phases; latter cannot be confused with any other falcon in the region. Pale phase is sooty-grey above with bold moustache against white cheek; underparts tawny heavily streaked black. Dark, unbarred underwing diagnostic in all plumages.
Voice: Variable, high-pitched, repetitive calls.
Habitat: Breeds on rocky islands and cliffs. At other times often over marshes, where it hawks for large insects.
Similar Species: Beware Hobby.

J F M A M J J A S O N D

Lanner Falcon *Falco biarmicus*

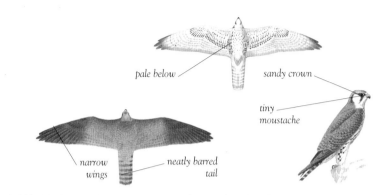

pale below

sandy crown

tiny moustache

narrow wings

neatly barred tail

J F M A M J J A S O N D

Status: Resident south and south-east Europe.
Identification: 34–50cm (13–20in). Adult paler than Peregrine with rufous cap and white cheeks marked by faint, moustachial streak. In flight, grey upperparts barred black with multiple bars on tail; underparts pale, with no contrast between wings and body. Juvenile brown, but darker body and underwing coverts contrast with pale flight feathers. Narrower wings and longer tail than Peregrine. Saker Falcon is heavier, broader-based wings.
Voice: Repeated *kee-kee-kee*.
Habitat: Bare hillsides, steppes, semi-desert.
Similar Species: Peregrine and Saker as above.

Saker Falcon *Falco cherrug*

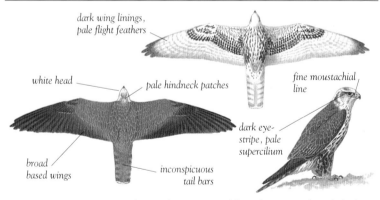

dark wing linings, pale flight feathers

white head

pale hindneck patches

fine moustachial line

dark eye-stripe, pale supercilium

broad based wings

inconspicuous tail bars

J F M A M J J A S O N D

Status: Scarce eastern falcon that is more heavily built, brown version of Peregrine. Summer visitor.
Identification: 45–55cm (18–22in). Adult brown above with narrow buffy feather margins creating 'scaled' effect. Head white with streaking, dark supercilium and fine moustachial line (often invisible). In flight, underparts white variably streaked, but usually heavier on body and wing linings, often contrasting with pale flight feathers. Tail barred below, but showing bands of white spots above.
Voice: Repeated *kee-kee-kee*.
Habitat: Open steppe, wooded hills. Often seen on pylons.
Similar Species: Peregrine and Lanner as above.

Gyr Falcon *Falco rusticolus*

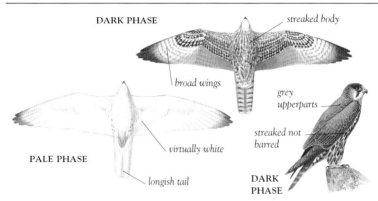

DARK PHASE

streaked body

broad wings

grey upperparts

streaked not barred

DARK PHASE

PALE PHASE

virtually white

longish tail

J F M A M J J A S O N D

Status: Huge, pale falcon that occasionally strays from Arctic breeding grounds. Circumpolar.
Identification: 50–62cm (20–24in). Birds from northern part of range virtually white, marked only by a few black crescents on upperparts and tail. More southerly birds heavily blotched and streaked to create dark grey impression. Intermediate birds occur. Lacks prominent moustachial streak. Much larger and more heavily built than any other falcon; broad wings very obvious.
Voice: Deep *kee-kee-kee*.
Habitat: Bare mountainsides, cliffs, tundra.
Similar Species: Saker and Peregrine may be confused.

Peregrine Falcon *Falco peregrinus*

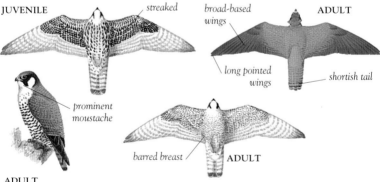

JUVENILE

streaked

broad-based wings

ADULT

long pointed wings

shortish tail

prominent moustache

barred breast

ADULT

ADULT

Status: Scarce but increasing resident, or summer, or winter visitor throughout Europe.
Identification: 38–48cm (15–19in). Large robust falcon with shortish tail and long, broad-based, pointed wings; immense speed and power. Upperparts slate-grey; barred tail. White face with bold black moustaches. Underparts and underwing finely barred. Juvenile brown with heavily streaked body.
Voice: Loud *kek-kek-kek*.
Habitat: Coasts and mountains with cliffs or gorges, also estuaries.
Similar Species: See Saker, Lanner and Gyr Falcons.

J F M A M J J A S O N D

Caspian Snowcock *Tetraogallus caspius*

black facial stripe

broad white eye stripe

white throat

spotted breast

broad white wingbar

J F M A M J J A S O N D

Status: Highly localized and scarce resident of high mountains of central and eastern Turkey.
Identification: 58–62cm (23–24½in). Large, mountain dwelling, Ptarmigan-like bird, cryptically coloured in shades of grey, buff and brown that shows broad white wingbar in flight. White widening eye-stripe, spotted breast. Difficult to locate and best sought at dawn.
Voice: Penetrating whistle.
Habitat: Rocky areas above tree line, but below snow line. Ascends to open screes at dawn.
Similar Species: Caucasian Snowcock nearly reaches easternmost Turkey and could yet be discovered there.

Hazel Grouse *Bonasa bonasia*

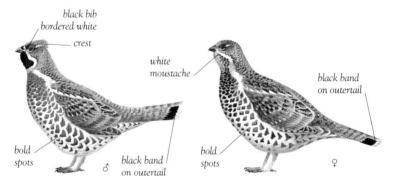

black bib bordered white

crest

white moustache

black band on outertail

bold spots

black band on outertail

♂

bold spots

♀

J F M A M J J A S O N D

Status: Secretive and highly elusive resident of conifer and mixed forests eastwards from eastern France.
Identification: 35–37cm (14–14½in). Well-camouflaged gamebird. Male grey above with rich mottling and boldly spotted white underparts. Black bib bordered white. In flight, shows broken black tail band. Female similar, but lacks black bib. Juvenile paler, more rusty. Loud wing-beating display and whistled call best signs of presence.
Voice: Repeated whistles.
Habitat: Conifer forests with understorey of birch and alder.
Similar Species: See female Black Grouse.

Willow Grouse / Red Grouse *Lagopus lagopus*

chestnut

rufous

♀ **Red Grouse**

♂ **Red Grouse**

white lores

♂ **Willow Grouse** WINTER

white wings

white legs

white legs

♀ **Willow Grouse SUMMER**

♂ **Willow Grouse SUMMER**

Status: Hardy, resident gamebird of north and west Britain and Scandinavia. Red Grouse is the bird of grouse-moor fame in Britain. Circumpolar, called Willow Ptarmigan in North America. Absent Greenland and Iceland. From northern and western Britain and Ireland, through Scandinavia southwards to the Baltic states eastwards through northern Russia and central Siberia. Leaves extreme northern tundra, but only short distances.
Identification: 33–39cm (13–19in). Two distinct subspecies that, until relatively recently, were regarded as distinct species. Willow Grouse *L.l.lagopus* is found in Scandinavia; Red Grouse *L.l.scoticus* in Britain and Ireland. Red Grouse is dark reddish brown, heavily spotted and barred black. Male has considerably richer coloration than female, with bolder red comb above eye. Generally seen when flushed from heather; flies away strongly before gliding back to cover on bowed wings. Willow Grouse differs in having white wings throughout the year and completely white plumage in winter. At this season closely resembles Ptarmigan, but lacks black on lores. An intermediate subspecies *L.l.variegatus* of western Norway has black marks on white wings, retains part brown plumage in winter.
Voice: Characteristic *go-back, go-back, go-back, go-back, back-back-back*.
Habitat: Willow Grouse frequents tundra, moors, bogs and other dwarf, berry-bearing vegetation with willow and birch. Red Grouse virtually exclusively heather moors.
Similar Species: See Ptarmigan.

J F M A M J J A S O N D

Ptarmigan *Lagopus mutus*

red comb

greyish-brown

ADULT ♀ WINTER

dark lores

white belly

white wing

ADULT ♂ SUMMER

ADULT ♂ WINTER

J F M A M J J A S O N D

Status: Close relative of Red-Willow Grouse that lives at higher altitudes and latitudes but is similarly resident.
Identification: 33–36cm (13–14in). Mottled greys and browns camouflage against scant vegetation and broken rocks of high mountain tops. In winter, whole plumage white; in summer, only wings white. Even intermediate white and grey patchy birds difficult to see. Male has red comb in summer; black mark on lores in winter.
Voice: Cackling *aar-aar-ka-ka-ka*.
Habitat: Bare, stony mountain tops and high Arctic tundra.
Similar Species: Always greyer than Willow Grouse.

Capercaillie *Tetrao urogallus*

white bill

red comb

ADULT ♀

orange breast

ragged beard

rounded tail

ADULT ♂

huge, wedge-shaped tail

J F M A M J J A S O N D

Status: Largest of grouse, resident in conifer forests of mountains and boreal zone.
Identification: ♂ 82–90cm (32–35in); ♀ 58–64cm (22–25in). Huge Turkey-like male; black with brown back and wings; long tail fanned in display. Large head with ragged 'beard'; red wattle above eye; white bill. Female smaller, barred shades of brown with orange breast and rounded tail.
Voice: Crowing *ko-ko-kok*; series of clicks ending in pop.
Habitat: Confined to extensive conifer forests with adjacent open areas of dwarf, berry-bearing shrubs.
Similar Species: Black Grouse has lyre-shaped tail.

Black Grouse   *Tetrao tetrix*

red comb

ADULT ♀

wingbar

dark, barred
breast

tail shape

white in
wing

ADULT ♂

white
undertail

lyre-
shaped tail

notched tail

J F M A M J J A S O N D

Status: Resident temperate mountains and boreal zone.
Identification: ♂ 51–56cm (20–22in); ♀ 40–44cm
(15–17in). Best seen at lekking grounds in early morning
or evening. Gregarious. Male black, with longish lyre-
shaped tail, erected in display to show bold white
undertail. Large red comb above eye, bold white wingbar
in flight. Female barred brown and black above, black and
buff below. Tail shows notch in flight.
Voice: A *roo-koo* repeated at *lek*; a sneezed *chew-oosh*.
Habitat: Margins of boreal forest with scattered trees.
Similar Species: See Caucasian Black Grouse, which does
not overlap range; also larger Capercaillie.

Caucasian Black Grouse   *Tetrao mlokosiewiczi*

white at
bend of
wing

♂

♂

black undertail

extended
downcurved tail

♀

Status: Resident mountain forests extreme north-eastern
Turkey.
Identification: 38–52cm (15–20½in). Smaller bodied, but
longer tailed version of Black Grouse; ranges do not
overlap. Male black with red comb over eye. Tail long,
forked and decurved at tip lacks white undertail. Female
mottled and barred brown, black and chestnut with white
throat and lacks white wingbar.
Voice: Virtually silent.
Habitat: Exclusively montane forests with open clearings
and open areas above tree line.
Similar Species: Black Grouse as above.

J F M A M J J A S O N D

Chukar Partridge *Alectoris chukar*

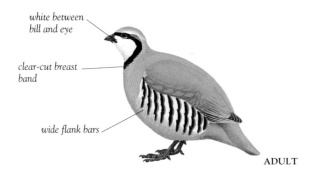

white between bill and eye

clear-cut breast band

wide flank bars

ADULT

J F M A M J J A S O N D

Status: Replaces very similar Red-legged and Rock Partridges eastwards from north-eastern Greece.
Identification: 33–36cm (13–14in). From Red-legged Partridge, Chukar best distinguished by 'clean-cut' appearance – lacks black spotting on breast and has fewer, bolder, broader and more distinct flank stripes on creamy not grey background. From Rock by less numerous and wider flank bars and lack of black between bill and eye.
Voice: Guttural *chook-ar, chook-ar*.
Habitat: Bare, rocky hillsides, but also agricultural land.
Similar Species: As above, but note different call from Rock Partridge.

Rock Partridge *Alectoris graeca*

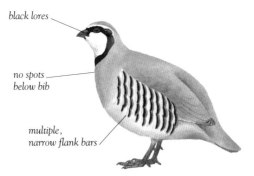

black lores

no spots below bib

multiple, narrow flank bars

ADULT

J F M A M J J A S O N D

Status: Replaces Red-legged Partridge in south-eastern Europe, itself replaced farther east by Chukar Partridge.
Identification: 32–35cm (13–14in). Buff-grey upperparts, white bib bordered by bold black facial disc, and multi-barred flanks are common features of the 'red-legged partridge' group. Rock Partridge lacks neck spots of Red-legged. Distinguished from Chukar (with care) by finer and more numerous flank bars.
Voice: Distinctive *whit-whit-whit*, and other whistled calls, more varied than Chukar.
Habitat: Dry rocky mountain slopes with scant vegetation.
Similar Species: Chukar as above.

Red-legged Partridge *Alectoris rufa*

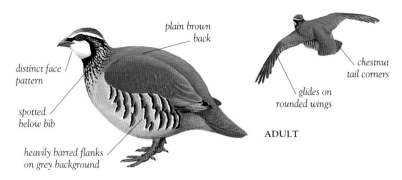

plain brown back

distinct face pattern

spotted below bib

heavily barred flanks on grey background

chestnut tail corners

glides on rounded wings

ADULT

J F M A M J J A S O N D

Status: Resident partridge of south-western Europe that just overlaps range of similar Rock Partridge.
Identification: 33–36cm (13–14in). Rotund, stocky bird. Distinctive facial pattern consists of black eye-stripe extending across ear coverts and neck to join broad, speckled breast band and enclose creamy chin and throat. Blue flanks (creamy in confusing species) barred black and chestnut. Gregarious, found in small flocks. Flies low over ground and glides on bowed wings.
Voice: Loud *chuk-chuk-chukar-chukar*.
Habitat: Open areas with dry, bare ground; grasslands.
Similar Species: See Rock and Chukar Partridges.

Grey Partridge *Perdix perdix*

streaked back

orange face

grey breast

chestnut horseshoe

chestnut tail corners

♂

Status: Resident gamebird throughout temperate Europe that is largely absent Iberia and Mediterranean.
Identification: 29–32cm (11–13in). Generally gregarious, occurring in coveys; flies low over ground on bowed wings. Pale, washed-out coloration appears buffy at any distance. Closer approach reveals pale orange face, grey breast, brown bars on flanks and bold chestnut horseshoe on belly – reduced to chestnut smudge in female. Streaked upperparts.
Voice: Decelerating *krikrikri-kri-krikri*; rusty-hinge *kirr-ik*.
Habitat: Grasslands, but has adapted to arable.
Similar Species: Streaked upperparts, orange face, chestnut horseshoe on belly separate from other partridges.

J F M A M J J A S O N D

Barbary Partridge *Alectoris barbara*

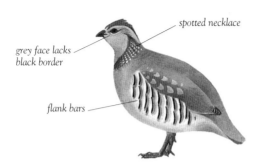

grey face lacks
black border

spotted necklace

flank bars

ADULT

J F M A M J J A S O N D

Status: The common partridge of North Africa where resident from Mauritania to Libya. Introduced to Gibraltar, where about 50 pairs. Resident Sardinia, but origins unknown.
Identification: 32–34cm (12½–13in). Similar to Red-legged Partridge, with similar though paler coloration and pattern of bars on flanks. Main differences are in head pattern which is grey with bib margins chestnut spotted white. Overall a paler, washed-out Red-legged.
Voice: Repeated *kutch-uk*.
Habitat: Rocky slopes with dwarf vegetation.
Similar Species: See above.

See-see Partridge *Ammoperdix griseogularis*

supercilium

yellow
bill

white ear
coverts

grey
throat

flank bars

barred
underparts

yellow legs

♀

♂

J F M A M J J A S O N D

Status: Small partridge of arid hills and semi-desert that occurs only in south-eastern Turkey.
Identification: 22–25cm (8½–10in). Considerably smaller than true partridges, but larger than Quail. Male rufous with series of black and chestnut flank bars. Grey throat, white ear patch and neat yellow bill create distinctive head pattern. Female barred buffy with pale supercilium. Yellow legs.
Voice: Far-carrying *whoo-it* repeated frequently betrays presence before bird is seen.
Habitat: Semi-desert; arid hillsides and sometimes dunes.
Similar Species: Extralimital Sand Partridge.

Golden Pheasant   *Chrysolophus pictus*

yellow crown

brownish eye-patch

gold and black fan

red underparts

♂

brown legs

♀

J F M A M J J A S O N D

Status: Exotic pheasant, introduced from South-east Asia, still confined to few areas of Britain.
Identification: ♂ 89–109cm (35–43in); ♀ 61–71cm (24–28in). Male highly colourful and unmistakable with bright red underparts, golden crown and rump and long tail. Female heavily barred rust and buff. Secretive. Hybridizes with Lady Amherst's.
Voice: Harsh *chak*.
Habitat: Dense rhododendrons mixed with conifers.
Similar Species: Female resembles female Common Pheasant but is more rufous above. Also like female Lady Amherst's but has brownish, not blue, eye patch and legs.

Lady Amherst's Pheasant   *Chrysolophus amherstiae*

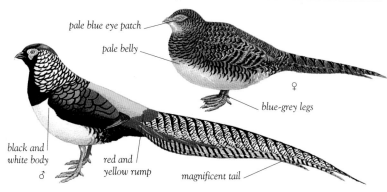

pale blue eye patch

pale belly

♀

blue-grey legs

black and white body

♂

red and yellow rump

magnificent tail

Status: Introduced pheasant found only in southern England outside mountains of Burma and south-west China.
Identification: ♂ 115–150cm (45–59in); ♀ 58–68cm (23–27in). Male magnificent in black and white with orange rump, red uppertail coverts and extremely long black and white marbled tail. Female barred black and chestnut. Secretive; confined to conifer woods with dense undergrowth and rhododendron scrub.
Voice: A *su-ik-ik-ik*.
Habitat: Dense young woodland, especially conifers, with thick brambles or rhododendrons.
Similar Species: See female Golden Pheasant.

J F M A M J J A S O N D

Common Pheasant *Phasianus colchicus*

red
wattle

bottle-green
head and
neck

white neck ring

variants

♀

♂

J F M A M J J A S O N D

Status: Widespread resident throughout temperate
Europe, locally abundant where reared for sport.
Identification: ♂ 75–90cm (30–35in); ♀ 52–64cm
(20–25in). Plumage of male highly variable but always has
red eye-wattle and green head. Female buffy; heavily
speckled black above and on flanks. Generally found in
small groups. When disturbed, often runs or flies to cover;
takes off powerfully and glides on bowed wings, often low.
Voice: Far-carrying *kok…kok-kok*.
Habitat: Open fields and heaths broken by woods,
Similar Species: Female can be confused with females of
Golden and Lady Amherst's Pheasants.

Black Francolin *Francolinus francolinus*

white ear patch

black face

upright stance
with long neck

barred
breast

black
underparts

♂

♀

J F M A M J J A S O N D

Status: Resident gamebird Cyprus and southern Turkey.
Identification: 33–36cm (13–14in). Larger than typical
partridges with more upright stance and longer neck. Loud
rhythmic calling in spring aids identification and location.
Male black on head and underparts, speckled and barred
white on flanks, with difficult-to-see chestnut neck ring.
Female more partridge-like in colour, with clearly barred
breast unlike any other similar species in our area.
Voice: A loud harsh *kek-keery-kek*, repeated monotonously
by male from mound or post in spring.
Habitat: Dry river beds and cultivation.
Similar Species: None.

Little Button-quail *Turnix sylvatica*

dark outerwing

orange breast patch

bold flank spots

J F M A M J J A S O N D

Status: Extremely rare resident southern Spain where not seen every year. Formerly called Andalusian Hemipode.
Identification: 15–16cm (6in). Tiny, secretive ground-dwelling bird with orange breast and boldly spotted flanks. In flight, dark outerwing contrasts with paler, warmer innerwing and body. Only confusable with more widespread Common Quail.
Voice: Low hooting call *whoooo*, repeated, sounds like distant quavering fog horn.
Habitat: Dry open brush and grassland where runs for cover when disturbed.
Similar Species: Common Quail.

Common Quail *Coturnix coturnix*

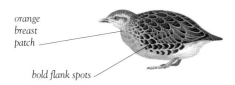

cigar-shaped body

long angled uniform wings

prominent head pattern

ADULT ♂

ADULT ♀

Status: Declining summer visitor temperate Europe.
Identification: 17–18.5cm (6–7in). Small, fast-flying, gamebird; more often heard than seen. Ventriloquial call makes location difficult. Good views of bird on ground exceptional. When flushed combination of stocky body and long pointed wings is unique. Upperparts brown, streaked and barred; underparts warm buffy orange. Pattern of bold creamy supercilium and dark facial streaks more pronounced in male than female.
Voice: Distinctive *wet-me-lip* repeated.
Habitat: Open grasslands also winter cereals.
Similar Species: Little Button-quail.

J F M A M J J A S O N D

Water Rail   *Rallus aquaticus*

long red bill

white undertail

plain grey

trailing legs

barred flanks

pinkish legs

J F M A M J J A S O N D

Status: Widespread, marsh-dwelling, waterbird resident throughout western Europe; summer visitor in the east.
Identification: 27–29cm (10½–11½in). Highly secretive, Moorhen-like with long, red bill. In winter, may emerge in open. Upperparts dark brown, heavily streaked black; sides of head, throat and breast metallic grey. Flanks and belly barred black and white. Long legs and toes and short rounded wings. Short cocked tail frequently flicked, showing white undertail coverts.
Voice: Repeated *kip-kip-kip*. Pig-like squeals.
Habitat: Freshwater marshes with dense vegetation.
Similar Species: Only rail with long bill.

Spotted Crake   *Porzana porzana*

creamy undertail

yellow bill, red base

barred flanks

spotted breast

no primary projection

spots and bars

yellow-green legs

yellow-green legs

ADULT SUMMER

JUVENILE

J F M A M J J A S O N D

Status: Highly elusive summer visitor.
Identification: 22–24cm (8½–9½in). Decidedly skulking. Upperparts brown, heavily streaked black; face grey with dark mark through lores. Underparts grey. Resembles small, short-billed Water Rail but prominent white spots on sides of breast and brown, black and white bars on flanks less clear-cut and zebra-like than Water Rail. Undertail coverts creamy. Bill yellow with red base; legs green.
Voice: Usually noted by call summer evenings. Far-carrying *quip-quip-quip* like tap dripping into half-empty barrel.
Habitat: Shallow, freshwater marshes or floods.
Similar Species: Beware brief views of smaller crakes.

Little Crake *Porzana parva*

long primary projection

red base to bill

red base to bill

under tail barring

unbarred flanks

grey flanks

green legs

ADULT ♀

ADULT ♂

J F M A M J J A S O N D

Status: Localized, summer visitor more common in the east.
Identification: 18–20cm (7–8in). Summer male blue-grey below, with white bars beneath tail. Female similar, but creamy-white below. Like juvenile, both sexes become creamy-buff in winter. Little Crake always paler below than Spotted Crake, with darker, bottle-green legs. Rarer Baillon's Crake has flanks and undertail barred black on white. Neither shows primary projection of Little Crake.
Voice: A *quck-quck-quck* accelerating into a trill.
Habitat: Freshwater marshes with tall vegetation.
Similar Species: Only short-billed crake with long primary projection.

Baillon's Crake *Porzana pusilla*

tiny primary projection

♂

barred black and white

pure-green bill

flanks barred black and white

legs often brownish

heavily barred flanks

JUVENILE

Status: Decidedly scarce summer visitor temperate Europe.
Identification: 17–18.5cm (7in). Tiny secretive crake brown above, liberally streaked black, spotted and streaked white. Underparts dark grey with black and white barring on flanks and undertail. Legs and feet olive–brown, bill green. Colour of legs, feet and bill and definite black and white barring on rear flanks separate from Little Crake. Primaries only just project beyond folded tertials.
Voice: Easily confused with Little Crake, but faster creaking *trill trrr-trrr*, repeated.
Habitat: Freshwater marshes with sedges and rushes.
Similar Species: Little Crake as above.

J F M A M J J A S O N D

Corn Crake   *Crex crex*

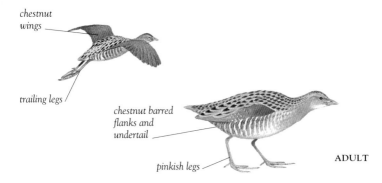

chestnut wings

trailing legs

chestnut barred flanks and undertail

pinkish legs

ADULT

J F M A M J J A S O N D

Status: Secretive summer visitor that has declined with agricultural change.
Identification: 25–28in (10–11in). More often heard than seen. When flushed, bold, chestnut wings and trailing legs diagnostic. Upperparts have black feather-centres edged with buffy brown, producing 'scalloped' effect. In summer, male has pale grey face and upper breast; less grey in winter. Underparts buff, barred chestnut.
Voice: A grating, endlessly repeated *crek-crek*.
Habitat: Hay and cereal fields, also other grasslands with low (not close-cropped) ground cover.
Similar Species: None occupying dry habitats.

Juvenile Crakes

Crakes are difficult enough to see let alone identify. If this is true of adult males, it applies more so to juveniles. All are more heavily barred on underparts than females, but the extent of barring is of little help. Bill and leg colour are also similar. Primary projection and relatively subtle plumage features must be sought.

Baillon's Crake
Heavily barred black and white flanks similar to, but more pronounced than Little Crake. Primaries covered (little or no primary projection) by chestnut margined tertials.

Little Crake
Less heavily barred flanks than Baillon's. Prominent primary projection; creamy margined tertials bunched to form prominent pale patch on wing.

Spotted Crake
Longer and darker than others with white spots on grey-brown neck and breast. Bold barring on flanks. Bill dark with yellowish base.

Moorhen   *Gallinula chloropus*

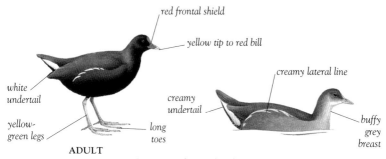

red frontal shield

yellow tip to red bill

creamy lateral line

white undertail

creamy undertail

yellow-green legs

long toes

ADULT

buffy grey breast

J F M A M J J A S O N D

Status: Widespread and common resident, though only a summer visitor to eastern Europe. Seldom in flocks.
Identification: 31–35cm (12–14in). Most often seen walking waterside banks with jerking, chicken-like movements of head. On land, long legs and toes obvious, as is white, cocked tail. In adult, white lateral line separates dark grey underparts from dark brown wings. Juvenile brown with whitish chin and foreneck; lateral line creamy; bill and legs dullish green. Swims well.
Voice: Loud *currick*; high-pitched *kik-kik-kik-kik*.
Habitat: Wide variety of aquatic habitats. Tolerant of man.
Similar Species: Common Coot.

Purple Gallinule   *Porphyrio porphyrio*

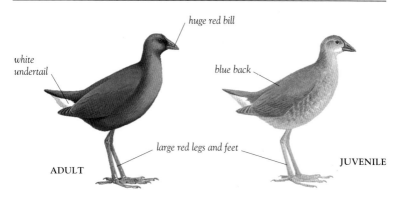

huge red bill

white undertail

blue back

large red legs and feet

ADULT

JUVENILE

Status: A widespread Old World species resident in only three small areas of Europe.
Identification: 45–50cm (18–20in). Large blue waterbird with large conical red bill and huge red legs and feet. Undertail coverts white. Spends much of time among dense emergent vegetation where slow-moving rather than secretive. Swims openly from one stand of sedges to the next. Like a giant blue Moorhen.
Voice: Various snoring and trumpeting notes.
Habitat: Small fresh waters with sedges.
Similar Species: Extremely rare Allen's Gallinule and American Purple Gallinule.

J F M A M J J A S O N D

Common Coot *Fulica atra*

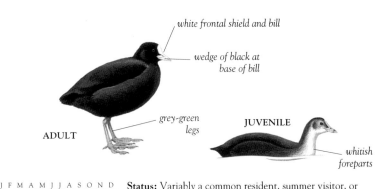

white frontal shield and bill

wedge of black at base of bill

grey-green legs

ADULT

JUVENILE

whitish foreparts

J F M A M J J A S O N D

Status: Variably a common resident, summer visitor, or abundant winter visitor to major regions of Europe.
Identification: 36–40cm (14–16in). Bulky, sooty-black waterbird distinguished by white bill and frontal shield. Juvenile brownish with whitish face and foreneck; lacks frontal shield. Swims buoyantly; dives for food; also up-ends. Often feeds on splashy grasslands. Evades danger by running over water surface rather than flying. Flies strongly on broad, rounded wings with long legs trailing.
Voice: Explosive *kook* or *teuk*.
Habitat: Highly adaptable to huge variety of waters.
Similar Species: See Red-knobbed Coot.

Crested Coot *Fulica cristata*

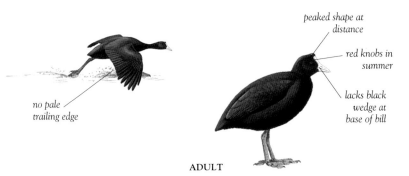

peaked shape at distance

red knobs in summer

lacks black wedge at base of bill

no pale trailing edge

ADULT

J F M A M J J A S O N D

Status: An African species that has a single outpost in Europe in southern Spain. Resident.
Identification: 38–42cm (15–16in). Virtually identical to Common Coot. Uniform black with white bill and frontal shield. Juvenile darker than juvenile Common Coot. At a distance, knobs on crown create 'peaked' appearance. Lack of black wedge at base of bill confirmed by close approach, diagnostic in winter when red knobs disappear.
Voice: Explosive *klukuk* differs from Common Coot.
Habitat: Lakes and ponds; keeps to cover more than Common Coot.
Similar Species: Common Coot as above.

Common Crane   *Grus grus*

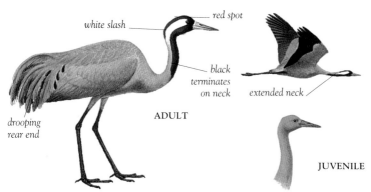

white slash
red spot
black terminates on neck
extended neck
drooping rear end
ADULT
JUVENILE

J F M A M J J A S O N D

Status: Breeds from Scandinavia and Baltic eastwards. Migrates along well-defined south-westerly and south-easterly routes.
Identification: 106–118cm (42–46in). Long-legged, long-necked bird of marshes and fields. Very tall, mostly grey, with distinct pattern of black and white on head and neck, and a spot of red on crown. Uppertail coverts cascade over tail. Frequently flies goose-like in 'V' formations.
Voice: Loud trumpeting and braying in flight, courtship.
Habitat: Breeds northern lakes and marshes in boreal forest and taiga margins. Winters marshes and fields.
Similar Species: See Demoiselle Crane.

Demoiselle Crane   *Anthropoides virgo*

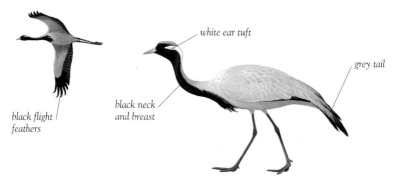

white ear tuft
grey tail
black neck and breast
black flight feathers

Status: Summer visitor to eastern Turkey and Black Sea region of Ukraine that occasionally wanders westwards into Europe.
Identification: 90–100cm (40in). Small version of Common Crane marked by black head and cascade of black plumes on foreneck and breast. Tail grey, not black. In air black flight feathers contrast with grey coverts.
Voice: Trumpeting and rolling calls like Common Crane, but higher pitched.
Habitat: Steppes and similar open grasslands, salt flats and low brush country, usually near water.
Similar Species: Common Crane.

J F M A M J J A S O N D

Little Bustard *Tetrax tetrax*

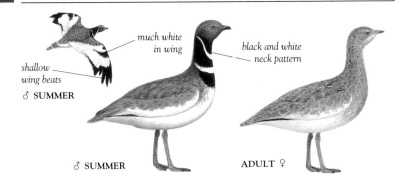

much white
in wing

black and white
neck pattern

shallow
wing beats

♂ SUMMER

♂ SUMMER

ADULT ♀

J F M A M J J A S O N D

Status: Resident various regions of southern Europe and summer visitor to France. Locally quite common.
Identification: 41–45cm (16–18in). Both sexes brown above, variously streaked and mottled with black and white below. Summer male shows bold pattern of black and white on neck that is particularly obvious in display. In both sexes, majority of flight feathers white. In flight, resembles large duck, but with fast, fluttery wingbeats.
Voice: Abrupt *prrt*.
Habitat: Steppes and grasslands, pastures and large arable fields. Also among grass in olive and cork groves.
Similar Species: None.

Stone-Curlew *Burhinus oedicnemus*

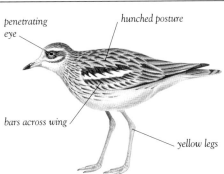

penetrating
eye

hunched posture

bold stripes
along wing

bars across wing

yellow legs

J F M A M J J A S O N D

Status: Resident Iberia, summer visitor elsewhere in Europe as far north as Britain. Dry, stony ground essential.
Identification: 38–43cm (15–17in). Large, plover-like bird most active at dawn and dusk. When disturbed, prefers to run rather than fly. Buffy brown streaked with black above and on breast; wings have bold horizontal white bar with black border. Complex face pattern of brown and white stripes. Long, yellow legs and penetrating yellow eye. Cryptic camouflage. In flight, bold black and white pattern.
Voice: Rippling *coor-lee*, sounds like tin whistle.
Habitat: Stony. sparsely vegetated ground.
Similar Species: Female Little Bustard more stoutly built.

Great Bustard   *Otis tarda*

much white in wing ♂

white neck often puffed up and conspicuous

thick legs ♀

tail raised in display

♂

thick legs

Status: Huge, turkey-like bird of steppes and open grasslands, confined to Eurasia, and suffering serious decline owing to ever-changing agricultural practices in major haunts. Resident Iberia and from eastern Germany southwards through central European plains to Romania, Crimea and Turkey. Active conservation started in Spain, Austria and Hungary, but special measures required urgently.

Identification: ♂ 95–105cm (37–41in); ♀ 75–85cm (29½–33½in). Large, bulky, walking bird generally found in small flocks. Both sexes have grey head and neck; chestnut back, wings and tail delicately barred with crescents of black and white. Strong, longish legs grey. In flight, most of wing white with black flight feathers. Male, larger than female, has bold white moustaches and, by raising tail and turning wings inside-out in display, becomes a white and buff ball, obvious at great distances. Even when not displaying, male frequently raises tail and resembles a galleon sailing across a sea of grass. Generally gregarious throughout the year, with males forming flocks during the nesting season.

J F M A M J J A S O N D

Voice: Generally silent, but utters a low bark.

Habitat: Grasslands and steppes, but also now utilizes pastures, large arable fields and crops and even groves near open grasslands. In Iberia, rolling countryside with rocky outcrops.

Similar Species: Houbara Bustard is smaller with dark neck line; extremely rare vagrant from south and east.

Oystercatcher *Haematopus ostralegus*

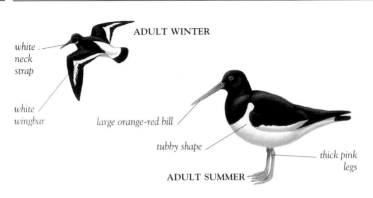

ADULT WINTER

white neck strap

white wingbar

large orange-red bill

tubby shape

thick pink legs

ADULT SUMMER

J F M A M J J A S O N D

Status: Widespread, resident, coastal bird in north and west. Summer visitor inland in east. Huge flocks in winter.
Identification: 41–45cm (16–18in). Large, tubby, strikingly black and white bird with long, thick, orange-red bill and long, pink legs. Eye red with bright orange-red eye-ring. In winter, adult has brownish wash over black upperparts and white half collar. Juvenile as adult winter but browner above with only rudimentary half collar. Rocky and sandy shores; often gathers in large flocks.
Voice: Loud penetrating *kleep*; also characteristic piping.
Habitat: Wide variety of marine habitats.
Similar Species: None.

Black-winged Stilt *Himantopus himantopus*

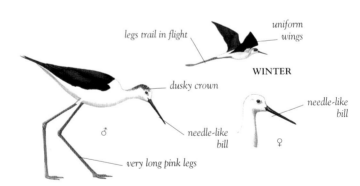

legs trail in flight

uniform wings

WINTER

dusky crown

needle-like bill

♂

needle-like bill

♀

very long pink legs

J F M A M J J A S O N D

Status: Summer visitor, mainly to southern Europe, that is primarily a coastal species.
Identification: 36–40cm (14–16in). Extremely long-legged black and white wader, marked by long neck, delicately rounded head, and needle-thin straight pointed bill. Pink legs extend almost length of body beyond tail in flight. Whole body white in female, male has dusky hind crown, nape and rear neck. Wings black above, and below. Juvenile dull version of adult. Generally gregarious.
Voice: Shrill *kee-uk* repeated.
Habitat: Shallow, open waters often saline.
Similar Species: Avocet and Oystercatcher.

Avocet *Recurvirostra avosetta*

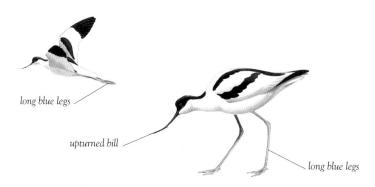

long blue legs

upturned bill

long blue legs

J F M A M J J A S O N D

Status: Mainly summer visitor that has prospered after generations of persecution.
Identification: 41–45cm (16–18in). Large, elegant, black and white wader with long legs and distinctly upcurved bill. At rest, black areas form a white-filled oval pattern on wings. Seen mostly on coasts and marshes. Feeds head-down with regular side-to-side scything movements of bill. Generally in small groups; sometimes in much larger winter flocks. Often noisy.
Voice: Loud *kloo-et*.
Habitat: Shallow lagoons and marshes, often near coast.
Similar Species: Black-winged Stilt, Oystercatcher.

Cream-coloured Courser *Cursorius cursor*

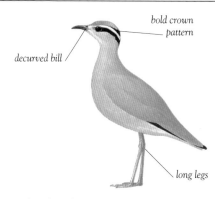

bold crown pattern

decurved bill

long legs

legs trail

black outerwing

Status: May breed south-east Turkey; vagrant north and west.
Identification: 19–21cm (7½–8½in). Long-legged desert-running species. Creamy buff plumage with marked black, white and blue crown pattern that forms a 'V' on back of head and is particularly obvious from behind as bird runs away. Short, decurved bill. Flight almost tern-like with whole of underwings black. Upperwings buff with black primaries.
Voice: Piping whistling; hard *praak*.
Habitat: Stony deserts; vagrants on shorelines.
Similar Species: None.

J F M A M J J A S O N D

Collared Pratincole   *Glareola pratincola*

black and white
trailing edge

dark flight
feathers contrast
with pale coverts

chestnut
underwing
difficult to see

ADULT SUMMER

J F M A M J J A S O N D

Status: Gregarious summer visitor to Mediterranean, mainly to south-west and south-east.
Identification: 24–27cm (9½–10½in). Dumpy, short-legged bird with stubby bill that looks somewhat plover-like at rest; transformed in the air to long-winged tern-like bird. Adult brown above, buffy on breast and white below. Large eye shows narrow white ring, and chin is warm orange-yellow, bordered black.
Voice: Tern-like *kirrick*.
Habitat: From dry steppes and semi-desert to open lagoons.
Similar Species: Black-winged Pratincole lacks white trailing edge to innerwing.

Black-winged Pratincole   *Glareola nordmanni*

dark mantle

long
wings

no white
trailing edge

J F M A M J J A S O N D

Status: Summer visitor north and west Black Sea; vagrant westwards.
Identification: 24–27cm (9½–10½in). Very similar to Collared Pratincole, with creamy 'face' patch enclosed by black line. Darker upperwing coverts create less contrast with black flight feathers than that species. Lack of white trailing edge to secondaries diagnostic. Black underwing difficult to see.
Voice: Tern-like *kirrick*, lower than Collared.
Habitat: Dried out wetlands.
Similar Species: Collared Pratincole as above.

Little Ringed Plover *Charadrius dubius*

yellow eye-ring

white crown bar

no prominent wingbar

black bill

yellowish legs

ADULT

JUVENILE

J F M A M J J A S O N D

Status: Summer visitor except far north.
Identification: 14–16cm (5–6in). Smaller, slimmer and longer winged than Ringed Plover. Similar round-headed appearance, short bill and typical 'run-stop' plover behaviour. Adult has black band across crown bordered by white line; yellow eye-ring. In flight, lacks wingbar. Juvenile similar.
Voice: Short, down-slurred *peu*.
Habitat: Shingle margins of freshwaters; opportunistic.
Similar Species: Ringed Plover has orange bill. Kentish Plover always sandy. See Identification of Juvenile Plovers page 133.

Ringed Plover *Charadrius hiaticula*

orange bill, black tip

bold wingbar

brown back

orange-yellow legs

breast band often incomplete

yellowish legs

ADULT

JUVENILE

Status: Widespread summer visitor to northern coastlines and tundra. Flocks in winter at estuaries.
Identification: 18–20cm (7–8in). Typical plover rotund shape with rounded head and short bill. Orange bill and legs, banded head, in adult; broad white wingbar in flight. Juvenile has brown head with bold supercilium (lacking in Little Ringed Plover) and smudgy, incomplete breast band. Bill black; legs yellowish.
Voice: Melodic *tu-lee*.
Habitat: Coastal and river beaches.
Similar Species: See Identification of Juvenile Plovers page 133.

J F M A M J J A S O N D

Kentish Plover *Charadrius alexandrinus*

sandy cap

wingbar

buffy

dark smudge

marks at side of breast

buffy back

ADULT ♂ SUMMER

black legs

black legs

JUVENILE

ADULT ♀

J F M A M J J A S O N D

Status: Mainly a summer visitor to most of European range.
Identification: 15–17cm (6–6½in). Smaller than Ringed Plover with black smudges at sides of breast; bill and legs black. In summer, male has black breast patches and head markings; crown sandy. Winter male, female and juvenile have buffy brown breast patches and head markings; juvenile has only faintest smudge either side of breast.
Voice: Quiet *wit-wit-wit*; melodic *choo-wit*.
Habitat: Saline coastal flats, estuaries and saltpans.
Similar Species: Ringed, Little Ringed (page 131) and GreaterSand Plover. See page 133.

Greater Sand Plover *Charadrius leschenaultii*

longish heavy bill

rufous breast band

dark breast smudge

very long legs

ADULT SUMMER

FIRST WINTER

Status: Summer visitor central and eastern Turkey, vagrant westwards.
Identification: 22–24cm (9–9½in). Summer plumage with rich rufous-orange breast band confusable only with rare Lesser Sand Plover. Winter and juvenile lack orange and are featureless plovers with faint, buffy breast band like Kentish Plover. Longer legs and longer, heavier bill separate from both confusing species.
Voice: Rippling, repeated *treep*.
Habitat: Sandy shores, bare salt lake margins.
Similar Species: Kentish and Lesser Sand Plovers as above.

J F M A M J J A S O N D

Identification of Juvenile Plovers

Juvenile 'ringed-plovers' should be separated with care and certainly without having to flush them to confirm presence or absence of wingbars. Relative length of wing and leg, leg colour and habitats as well as size, are useful criteria. Head markings are crucial.

RINGED

Narrow white forehead, bold supercilium, virtually complete breast band, and an even curve to dark ear coverts.

KENTISH

Bold white forehead extends to broad white, tapering supercilium that terminates just behind eye. Breast band incomplete, often no more than a smudge at the bend of the wing. Sandy coloration much paler than Ringed or Little Ringed.

DOTTEREL

Dark cap and forehead, long broad supercilia that meet at nape creating capped effect especially from behind. Pale breast band on heavily speckled background.

LITTLE RINGED

Lacks white forehead (which develops in first winter) and supercilium. Shows almost complete breast band; faint, but discernible, eye-ring; and dark on ear coverts extends lower and is angled rather than smoothly curved.

GREATER SAND

White forehead narrows over eye and extends as narrow supercilium. Breast band incomplete. Large black bill proportionally much longer and heavier than other species.

American Golden Plover *Pluvialis dominica*

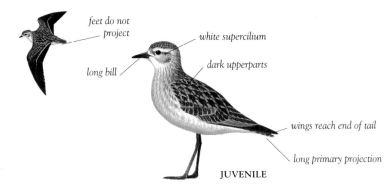

feet do not project

white supercilium

long bill

dark upperparts

wings reach end of tail

long primary projection

JUVENILE

J F M A M J J A S O N D

Status: Transatlantic vagrant, mainly to Britain, with up to ten each autumn. Probably previously overlooked.
Identification: 24–28cm (9½–11in). Very similar to Golden and Pacific Golden Plovers. Distinguished from Golden by being smaller and slimmer, by longer legs, longer wings, shorter neck, more pronounced white supercilium, and by grey underwing. Upperparts more greyish and underparts more buffy than Golden. First winter has barring on flanks. Great care needed.
Voice: *Klee-ee* with emphasis on first syllable.
Habitat: Grasslands, marshes, mudbanks. Breeds tundra.
Similar Species: Golden Plover, Pacific Golden Plover.

Pacific Golden Plover *Pluvialis fulva*

buffy supercilium

longish, heavy bill

fine wingbar

feet project

well-marked breast and flanks with yellow wash

long legs

J F M A M J J A S O N D

Status: Rare vagrant to Britain and Holland, easily confused with Golden and American Golden Plovers.
Identification: 23–26cm (9–10in). Once regarded as conspecific with European and American Golden Plovers. Very similar, but with heavier and longer bill and longer legs, which project beyond tail in flight. Smaller and slimmer than European with clearer supercilium, white at base of upper mandible, and grey (not white) underwing. Generally more yellow and buff than American.
Voice: *Cher-it* like Spotted Redshank.
Habitat: Grassland, marshes, mudbanks.
Similar Species: See above.

European Golden Plover *Pluvialis apricaria*

narrow wingbar

white underwing

ADULT WINTER

ADULT NORTHERN SUMMER

more black on face

little streaking on buffy breast

black belly

ADULT WINTER

ADULT SOUTHERN SUMMER

J F M A M J J A S O N D

Status: Breeds northern uplands and tundra; winters open grasslands of south and west.
Identification: 27–29cm (10½–11½in). Medium-sized plover with typically rotund body, round head, short bill and long legs. Upperparts spangled black and gold. In winter, underparts whitish with buffy breast markings. Northern subspecies has more black on belly, breast and black face.
Voice: A whistled *tlui*.
Habitat: Upland moors and tundra in summer. In winter flooded grasslands and open fields. Seldom on estuaries.
Similar Species: Grey Plover. See also smaller, longer-legged American and Pacific Golden Plovers.

Dotterel *Charadrius morinellus*

supercilia meet at nape

no wingbar

bold supercilium

ADULT

indistinct band

breast band

yellow legs

ADULT ♀ SUMMER

JUVENILE

Status: Summer visitor to mountains and tundra of northern Europe. Passage migrant to bare grasslands.
Identification: 22cm (8½in). Small rotund plover, easily overlooked. Summer adults have distinctive grey breast and chestnut underparts separated by white band. Prominent white supercilia meet on nape. In winter and juvenile plumages, becomes greyish; marked only by white supercilium and indistinct breast band.
Voice: Quiet *peep-peep* in flight; *titi-ri-titti-ri* repeated.
Habitat: Bare mountain tops, plateaus, tundra.
Similar Species: Juvenile Greater Sand and Sociable Plovers have yellow, not dark, legs.

J F M A M J J A S O N D

Grey Plover *Pluvialis squatarola*

WINTER

black and
pale grey

black axillaries (armpits)

black face
and belly

ADULT SUMMER

little
streaking on
white breast

WINTER

J F M A M J J A S O N D

Status: High Arctic breeder that is common winter visitor
– passage migrant to southern and western Europe.
Identification: 28–31cm (11–12in). Similar to Golden
Plover, but larger. Upperparts spangled grey and black. In
winter, underparts white with grey speckling on breast. In
summer, belly, breast and face black, with white margins
on sides of breast and head. In flight, shows wingbar, white
rump and black axillaries. Legs extend just beyond tail.
Voice: Plaintive whistled *tlee-oo-ee*.
Habitat: Open tundra near rivers or lakes. In winter and
on passage frequents estuaries, open mudflats.
Similar Species: See European Golden Plover as above.

Spur-winged Plover *Hoplopterus spinosus*

black and white
below

brown back contrasts
with black wings

black cap,
white cheek

J F M A M J J A S O N D

Status: Chunky, well-marked plover that spread westwards
through the Balkans since 1950s, but which remains scarce.
Identification: 25–27cm (10–11in). Long-legged plover;
fawn-brown above with black cap separated by white
cheeks from black throat streak terminating in bold black
breast. Bill and legs dark. In flight, primaries black
separated from fawn-buff wing coverts and back by broad
white band; underwing black with white linings; tail
broadly tipped black.
Voice: Screeching *did-e-do-it*, also a sharp *kik*.
Habitat: Shallow coastal lagoons, brackish but not saline.
Similar Species: None.

Sociable Plover   *Chettusia gregaria*

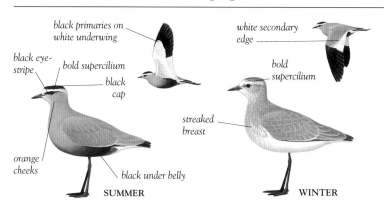

black primaries on white underwing

white secondary edge

black eye-stripe

bold supercilium

black cap

bold supercilium

streaked breast

orange cheeks

black under belly

SUMMER

WINTER

J F M A M J J A S O N D

Status: Rare vagrant from southern Russia to most of Europe: Britain in autumn, Continent in spring.
Identification: 27–30cm (10½–12in). Adult summer is grey-buff marked by black crown, black eye-stripe, and black and chestnut belly band absent in winter. Juvenile has pale margins to upperparts creating scaly look; breast streaked becoming neat lines of chevrons. In all plumages upperwing shows all white secondaries; white underwing contrasts with black primaries.
Voice: Short whistle.
Habitat: Steppes and grasslands on passage and in winter.
Similar Species: First-winter Dotterel.

Lapwing   *Vanellus vanellus*

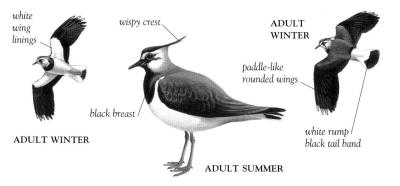

white wing linings

wispy crest

ADULT WINTER

paddle-like rounded wings

black breast

ADULT WINTER

white rump
black tail band

ADULT SUMMER

Status: Widespread, often common resident, summer visitor, passage migrant and winter visitor through Europe.
Identification: 29–32cm (11½–12½in). Looks black and white at any distance; distinctive crest. Head white with intricate pattern of black markings; throat black, widening into black breast band. In winter, throat and upper breast become white. In flight, shows black paddle-like, rounded wings.
Voice: Plaintive *pee-wit*.
Habitat: Damp grasslands and plough, marshes, upland moors with wetlands, estuaries, saltings, lakesides.
Similar Species: None.

J F M A M J J A S O N D

Knot *Calidris canutus*

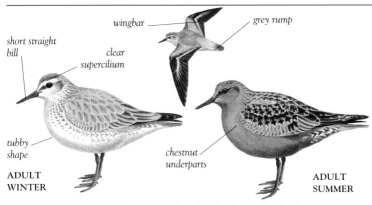

wingbar

grey rump

short straight bill

clear supercilium

tubby shape

chestnut underparts

ADULT WINTER

ADULT SUMMER

J F M A M J J A S O N D

Status: Abundant, but highly localized, winter visitor to a few particularly favoured estuaries.
Identification: 24–27cm (9½–10½in). Medium-sized, stocky shorebird similar to Dunlin, but considerably larger, with shorter bill and legs. In winter, upperparts grey; underparts white, speckled breast and flanks; well-marked supercilium. In summer, mantle spangled black and chestnut; underparts chestnut. Faint wingbar and distinctive white rump.
Voice: Low *knut*.
Habitat: Breeds high Arctic tundra. Winters intertidal zones.
Similar Species: Winter Dunlin, but Knot is larger.

Sanderling *Calidris alba*

bold wingbar

short bill

pale grey upperparts

heavily streaked breast

black at bend of wing

ADULT WINTER

ADULT SUMMER

J F M A M J J A S O N D

Status: Common winter visitor to open shorelines where small flocks run in and out with the waves.
Identification: 19–22cm (7½–8½in). Palest of the shorebirds with light grey upperparts and white below; prominent black mark at bend of wing. In summer, head, breast and back spangled black and chestnut and may be confused with stints away from shoreline.
Voice: A repeated piping *quit-quit*.
Habitat: Breeds high Arctic tundra. Winters coasts.
Similar Species: No other wader runs up and down beach with the waves or is so pale in winter plumage.

Semipalmated Sandpiper *Calidris pusilla*

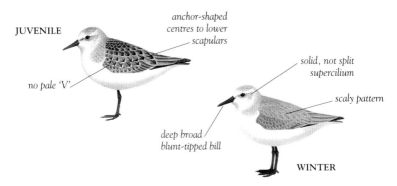

JUVENILE

anchor-shaped centres to lower scapulars

no pale 'V'

deep broad blunt-tipped bill

solid, not split supercilium

scaly pattern

WINTER

J F M A M J J A S O N D

Status: Rare transatlantic autumn vagrant easily confused with Little Stint.
Identification: 14–16cm (5½–6in). Tiny, stint-like sandpiper with dark legs and webbing between outer toes, though this is often hidden by sticky mud. Broad-based, blunt, almost bulbous-tipped bill is major feature. Juvenile lacks double white 'V' on mantle and split supercilium of Little Stint. Anchor-shaped centres to lower scapulars quite distinct from Little Stint, but shared with other rare stints and peep.
Voice: Low *chrup*.
Habitat: Marshes, other wetland margins.
Similar Species: Little Stint as above.

Little Stint *Calidris minuta*

rufous back

narrow wingbar

short bill

black legs

double white 'V' on back

grey upperparts

ADULT SUMMER

JUVENILE

a little breast streaking

ADULT WINTER

Status: Scarce summer visitor to northernmost Norway. Passage migrant and winter visitor elsewhere.
Identification: 14–15cm (5½in). In winter, grey above, white below. In summer, crown and upperparts warm brown with black feather centres and brown speckling at sides of breast. Juvenile brown with black feather centres, double white 'V' on back.
Voice: Sharp *tyit*.
Habitat: Tundra coasts and islands in summer. In winter and on passage on estuaries and backwaters.
Similar Species: The 'standard' small sandpiper. See Stints and Peeps panorama (between pages 144-145).

J F M A M J J A S O N D

Temminck's Stint   *Calidris temminckii*

narrow wingbar

white outertail

olive-grey back

uniform greyish

grey streaked breast

short, thin bill

yellow-green legs

ADULT SUMMER

JUVENILE

J F M A M J J A S O N D

Status: Not uncommon summer visitor to Scandinavian fjells and tundra. Scarce winter visitor and on passage.
Identification: 13–15cm (5–6in). Greyer, more uniformly marked than Little Stint. Winter adult and juvenile grey above, white below with grey breast. Short green legs and picking feeding action recall Common Sandpiper rather than Dunlin.
Voice: High-pitched *trr-trr*.
Habitat: Breeds tundra. Otherwise freshwater margins.
Similar Species: See Little Stint. Stints and Peeps panorama (between pages 144-145).

White-rumped Sandpiper   *Calidris fuscicollis*

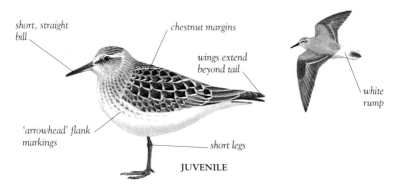

short, straight bill

chestnut margins

wings extend beyond tail

white rump

'arrowhead' flank markings

short legs

JUVENILE

J F M A M J J A S O N D

Status: Rare, but regular, transatlantic vagrant mainly to Ireland and south-east England.
Identification: 16-18cm (6-7in). Small, Dunlin-like shorebird, with short legs and long wings producing attenuated shape. Straight bill about length of head. Juvenile upperparts broadly edged rufous on back and white on wings. Broad supercilium, on rounded head. White flanks show distinctive dark 'arrowheads'. Wings extend beyond tail. Bold white rump and outertail in flight.
Voice: Quiet *jeet*.
Habitat: Small quiet pools.
Similar Species: Baird's Sandpiper.

Baird's Sandpiper *Calidris bairdii*

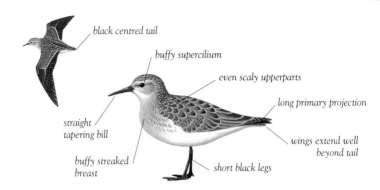

black centred tail

buffy supercilium

even scaly upperparts

long primary projection

straight tapering bill

wings extend well beyond tail

buffy streaked breast

short black legs

J F M A M J J A S O N D

Status: Vagrant from North America mainly to Britain and Ireland: about six records per annum.
Identification: 14–17cm (6in). Falls roughly between Little Stint and Dunlin in size, but short straight tapering bill gives more stint-like feel. Buffy margins to feathers of upperparts create an even pattern not found in any other wader. Long wings extend well beyond tail. Buffy supercilium and breast; unmarked flanks. Short legs accentuate low-to-the-ground impression.
Voice: Soft *krrt*.
Habitat: Pools and marshes, but also grasslands.
Similar Species: Common and White-rumped Sandpipers.

Pectoral Sandpiper *Calidris melanotos*

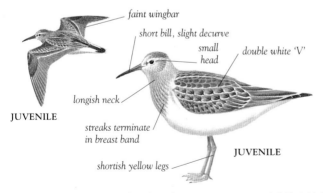

faint wingbar

short bill, slight decurve

small head

double white 'V'

longish neck

JUVENILE

streaks terminate in breast band

JUVENILE

shortish yellow legs

Status: Most numerous regular of North American shorebird in Europe, particularly in autumn.
Identification: 17–21cm (7–8in). About same size as Dunlin, but with shorter bill and shorter yellow legs. Upperparts brownish, 'scalloped' like Ruff, with double white 'V' on back. Breast uniformly streaked, terminating with pectoral band. Head small; neck slender.
Voice: A clear-cut *kreet*.
Habitat: Breeds tundra marshes and rivers. On passage and in winter frequents freshwater marshes and pools.
Similar Species: Rarer Sharp-tailed Sandpiper is Siberian equivalent.

J F M A M J J A S O N D

Curlew Sandpiper *Calidris ferruginea*

long neck, rounded head

decurved bill

ADULT WINTER

JUVENILE

square white rump

ADULT SUMMER

longish legs

buffy unstreaked breast

JUVENILE

J F M A M J J A S O N D

Status: Double passage migrant.
Identification: 18–20cm (7–8in). Shape distinctive; long legs, long neck, decurved bill; more elegant than hunched-up Dunlin. White rump diagnostic. Juvenile migrants with buff feather margins giving scaled appearance and buff wash over unstreaked breast. Adults grey above, white below. In spring, chestnut head and body.
Voice: Flight call *churrip*.
Habitat: Breeds tundra; otherwise freshwater marshes, estuaries. Autumn.
Similar Species: Slim lines and elegance separate from Dunlin.

Purple Sandpiper *Calidris maritima*

narrow wingbar

WINTER

brown feather margins

uniform grey back

orange-red base to bill

spotted breast

ADULT WINTER

orange-yellow legs

ADULT SUMMER

J F M A M J J A S O N D

Status: Summer visitor, resident and winter visitor to north-west Europe. Seldom far from rocky shores.
Identification: 20–22cm (8–9in). Stockily-built, short-legged wader with bill about same length as head; base of bill orange-red. Few distinguishing features apart from shape and general dark coloration. In winter, head and breast dark grey with white eye-ring and throat. Upperparts black with dark grey feather margins. Belly white with dark spots. In summer, back and wings dark.
Voice: Mostly silent; occasional *weet-weet*.
Habitat: Rocky shores and islands at all times.
Similar Species: No other European wader is so dark.

Dunlin *Calidris alpina*

streaked
breast

buff feather
margins

spots
on belly

JUVENILE

WINTER

white
wingbar

white
tail
patches

**ADULT
WINTER**

longish bill
slight decurve

black belly

**ADULT
SUMMER**

J F M A M J J A S O N D

Status: Most widespread and abundant wader virtually
throughout the whole of Europe.
Identification: 16–19cm (6½–7½in). Dumpy hunched-up
wader that feeds busily. In winter, upperparts grey;
underparts white with streaked breast. In summer, shows
black belly patch. Autumn adults retain partial black belly.
Juvenile with black spots on flanks.
Voice: Rasped *schreep* with distinctly nasal quality.
Habitat: Breeds tundra, moors and lowland
marshes.Winters coasts.
Similar Species: The small wader from which all others
have to be distinguished.

Broad-billed Sandpiper *Limicola falcinellus*

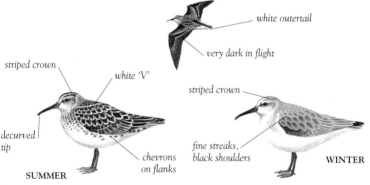

white outertail

very dark in flight

striped crown

white 'V'

decurved
tip

chevrons
on flanks

SUMMER

striped crown

fine streaks,
black shoulders

WINTER

Status: Uncommon summer visitor to Scandinavia that
passes through eastern Europe in small numbers.
Identification: 16–17cm (6½in). Slightly smaller than
Dunlin and reminiscent of Jack Snipe. Legs distinctly
short and bill distinctly long, with definite turned-down
tip, combine to produce elongated effect. Upperparts
broadly edged brown with pale double inverted 'V'. Breast
streaked, with chevrons on flanks. Dark eye-stripe, pale
supercilium and dark cap divided by lateral crown.
Voice: A trilling *tir-eek*.
Habitat: Breeds bogs. On passage uses fresh marshes.
Similar Species: Beware Dunlin and Jack Snipe.

J F M A M J J A S O N D

Sandpipers in Flight

Sandpipers may be fast-flying highly aerobatic birds, but in flight they are often easier to identify than at rest. Flight also offers the chance of confirmation of an identification made on the ground. Wing and tail patterns are the crucial features, but the projection (or not) of the legs and/or feet beyond the tip of the tail may clinch a diagnosis.

KNOT
Medium-sized chunky wader with shortish bill. Grey (lightly barred) rump and fine, narrow, white wingbar combine to create more uniform upperparts than any similar species. Overall a chunky, little- marked, greyish wader.

SANDERLING
Pale grey, small wader with shortish bill. Bold white wingbar (more so than any other shorebird) contrasts with black wings. This feature makes rump pattern of grey, white margined, black-tipped tail irrelevant.

LITTLE STINT
Tiny wader with short bill; size particularly apparent when seen in flight with other species. White wingbar and white margins to rump similar to Dunlin, but not Temminck's Stint. Juveniles show white 'V' on back.

TEMMINCK'S STINT
Similar to Little Stint with white wingbar, but black flight feathers contrast with grey back. White tail margins, lacking in Little Stint.

PURPLE SANDPIPER
Larger than Dunlin and always much darker, especially on head and breast. Narrow white wingbar only just extends to primaries. Double white ovals on rump.

CURLEW SANDPIPER
Dunlin-sized wader with longish, decurved bill. Shows white wing bar and bold white rump, the only regular sandpiper with this feature. Feet show at tail tip.

DUNLIN
Standard wader and base for all sandpiper identification; longish, slightly decurved bill. Bold white wingbar and double white ovals on rump.

BROAD-BILLED SANDPIPER
Dunlin-sized dark wader with narrow white wingbar and white outertail. Not identified in flight with certainty.

Principles of Stint and Peep Identification

Identification of this group of tiny waders depends on a close examination of plumage and structural characters. A single character is seldom sufficient for 100 per cent certainty so noting as many as possible of the points described is essential.

SIZE

The first and most important factor is to decide that the bird is indeed a stint or peep. These are the smallest of the waders, but size is not always apparent, or easily determined. If another wader species is present then a direct comparison, with birds alongside one another should establish that a stint or peep is on view. Dunlin, the most abundant shorebird, makes a perfect comparison, for even this small bird (smaller than a Common Starling) towers above a stint or peep (smaller than a House Sparrow). When found by itself, or in company with other stints or peep, size may still be apparent by comparison with vegetation, or an inert object such as a tin can, for example. The bird's daintiness and speed of movement are other features.

A good clue is the length of bill. Stints and peep have short, straight, bills that are about the same length as the head, or twice the loral distance, at best. Only the much larger Sanderling or Knot shows such a feature. So a small, short-billed wader is a stint or peep.

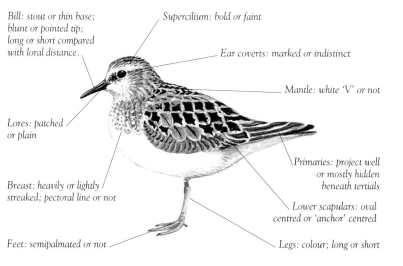

Bill: stout or thin base; blunt or pointed tip; long or short compared with loral distance.

Supercilium: bold or faint

Ear coverts: marked or indistinct

Mantle: white 'V' or not

Lores: patched or plain

Primaries: project well or mostly hidden beneath tertials

Breast: heavily or lightly streaked; pectoral line or not

Lower scapulars: oval centred or 'anchor' centred

Feet: semipalmated or not

Legs: colour; long or short

LEGS

Although leg length varies between the species it also varies according to posture and activity, though Temminck's Stint is always short-legged. Leg colour, however, is a constant and stints and peep can be divided into dark-legged and pale-legged species. Sadly, even pale-legged birds wade around in sticky, dark mud and can thus appear dark-legged. However, a pale-legged bird is Temminck's or Long-toed Stint, or Least Sandpiper. Always bear in mind that the common bird in Europe is Temminck's Stint and that all pale-legged stints or peep are this species until proved otherwise. All dark-legged stints or peep are Little Stint until shown to be one of the much, much rarer species.

views, careful examination and a search for the finest of points. A European birder confronted with a flock of Little Stints should examine each individual with the greatest of care (particularly autumn/winter adults) before concluding that all are indeed Little Stints and not the rarity of a lifetime.

Stints and peep can be divided into 'black-legged' and 'yellow-legged', though sticky mud can make all 'black-legged' some of the time. Two have small webs between the toes (often similarly hidden), thereafter attention to plumage detail is the only means of separation. With several species a close and prolonged feather by feather examination is essential.

Least Sandpiper: Yellow-legged American peep. Short-legged, short-billed, low-slung peep. Upperparts with dark centres and pale margins to feathers creates 'scaly' look, unlike Temminck's uniform coloration. Breast streaked with spots, not washed, and narrow white 'V' on back.

Semipalmated Sandpiper: Black-legged juvenile American peep. Chunky with short, thick, blunt-tipped bill; clear unsplit supercilium; and semipalmated feet. Lower scapulars have distinct anchor-shaped centres. No white 'V's on back.

Semipalmated Sandpiper: Winter as juvenile, but greyer. Structural features such as bill shape, semipalmated feet and lack of primary projection more significant.

Long-toed Stint: Yellow-legged Asian stint. Long legs (and toes) combined with long, thin bill create different shape to Temminck's and Least. Chestnut cap isolated by long, bold supercilium, with narrow secondary line above, and white forehead. Narrow white 'V' on back.

Stints and Peep

The stints and other tiny sandpipers of the genus *Calidris* are all long-distance migrants. Many travel from their Arctic breeding grounds as far south as land exists, making lengthy crossings of the world's oceans. Along the way it takes only a small navigational error, the result perhaps of a clouded sky or storm, to place them hundreds of even thousands of miles off-route. Their land-fall, if noticed, is greeted with delight by any birder fortunate enough to find one and skilful enough to identify it.

These are highly confusing little birds known collectively as 'stints' in the Old World and 'peep' in the New World. Their identification requires close

Western Sandpiper: Black-legged American peep. Longer legs and bill, plus slim elongated build create less chunky 'feel' than Little Stint or Semipalmated Sandpiper – the most likely confusion species. Look for chestnut scapulars; longish, decurved and fine-tipped bill; and Dunlin-like 'feel' of Western.

Little Stint: Black-legged juvenile. The common European stint and base for group identification. Short, fine-tipped bill, long primary projection, split supercilium, warm rufous-buff coloration marked by bold white double 'V' on back.

Little Stint: In autumn adult/winter, differs from juvenile by lack of white double 'V' on back and, therefore, more likely to be confused with other species. Look for oval centres to lower scapulars compared with Red-necked and Semipalmated.

Little Stint: Summer plumage adult is warm brown on 'face', with diffuse brown streaking on breast and sides of neck. Autumn adult shows mixture of this and grey winter plumage and, lacking white 'V's on back, can easily be mistaken for rarer species.

Two of the dark-legged peep, Semipalmated and Western Sandpipers, have short webs between their toes. But, once again, sticky mud clinging to the feet may create a semi-webbed appearance. Despite this, it is surprisingly easy to see this feature accurately (if looked for) with a close approach and/or use of a telescope. The secret is patience.

MANTLE
Most rare stints and peep occur in autumn and are in juvenile plumage. At this time all juvenile Little Stints show a pronounced double white 'V' on the mantle, a feature shared with only one other dark-legged Stint, the Red-necked. Pale-legged Least Sandpiper also shows a white 'V' on the mantle, but this bird and Red-necked Stint are much less boldly marked in this way than Little Stint.

Several species also show a contrast between the mantle and the wing coverts. Red-necked Stint and Western Sandpiper both have chestnut mantles and buffy-grey wing coverts creating a 'warm-backed' appearance. In the latter, in late autumn, this actually becomes a narrow chestnut band along the upper scapulars.

BILL
The length and shape of the bill is often critical to an accurate identification. Most stints and peep have shortish, pointed bills, but close examination shows some to be longer (Western Sandpiper) than others; some thicker based and blunt-tipped (Semipalmated Sandpiper); some decidedly thin and pointed (Long-toed Stint); and some decurved (Western Sandpiper). As with every other aspect of stint and peep identification, these are fine points that need care and concentration in picking out.

FACE PATTERN
Though all stints and peep show a supercilium, eye-stripe and ear covert marking, the prominence of each varies from species to species. Differences between the American peep is a prime case in point. Semipalmated and Western Sandpipers have the heaviest bills of any stint or peep, are dark-legged and have semipalmated feet. While both show prominent supercilia and loral patches, these are much bolder in Western than in Semipalmated. Similarly, among pale-legged birds, Long-toed Stint has long supercilia that meet at the nape to create a capped appearance, unlike any other stint or peep. Strangely enough, even the long toes of this species may be apparent in the field.

SCAPULAR PATTERN
Imagine a Sparrow-sized bird busily bustling around feeding in sticky mud and then imagine trying to pick out the pattern of a single feather. Impossible? Often! But not always! The feathers of the lower scapulars are generally pale-edged. But while some have dark centres, others show distinctive anchor-shaped marks. Red-necked Stint and Semipalmated and Western Sandpipers show 'anchor' marks. Little Stint does not. Find an 'anchor' marked bird and you have found a dark-legged rarity.

Dark-legged Stints and Peep

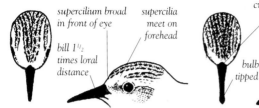

Little Stint: Bill short and relatively thin, lacking bulbous or blunt tip. Supercilium (split over the eye) isolates dark ear coverts. Dark loral patch.

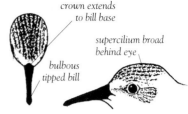

Semipalmated Sandpiper: Bill short, but with stout base and blunt, or even bulbous tip. Long-billed individuals may show slight decurve. Supercilium pale and straight, loral patch can be quite prominent.

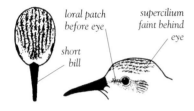

Red-necked Stint: Bill short and thin, like Little Stint. Supercilium and ear coverts not as prominent as that bird, but similarly shows dark loral patch.

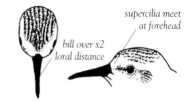

Western Sandpiper: Bill relatively long and slightly decurved with fine, not blunt, tip. Supercilium broad in front of bill with faint eye-stripe rather than bold dark loral patch. Ear coverts with hint of chestnut.

Pale-legged Stints and Peep

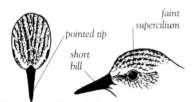

Temminck's Stint: Bill thin, short and tapered. Supercilium never prominent. Plain faced lacking bold cap and loral patch, with unmarked ear coverts.

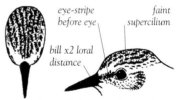

Least Sandpiper: Bill thin and tapered, but slightly longer than Temminck's. Supercilium and ear coverts both prominently marked, and dark loral patch.

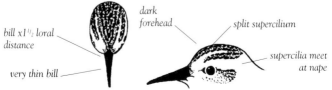

Long-toed Stint: Bill long and thin. Supercilium bold and clearly divided enclosing small crown cap. Ear coverts prominent, but lacks loral patch.

Stints and Peep in Flight

white double 'V'

white rump with black centre

Little Stint:
Black centre to divided white rump extends through greyish tail band. Shows narrow white wingbar across inner wing that widens over base of primaries. Juvenile is a warm biscuit colour above, marked by bold white double 'V' on back, a feature that separates this species from all other autumn stints and peep – even in flight.

white wingbar across whole wing

narrow white wingbar

white outer tail and rump

Temminck's Stint:
Dark centres to white rump and white tail create a clear white outer tail pattern, more like Common Sandpiper than any other stint or peep. Clear, but narrow, white wingbar contrasts with dark flight feathers and paler, uniform mantle.

dark flight feathers with paler uniform mantle

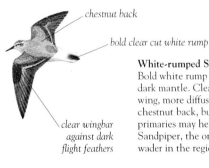

chestnut back

bold clear cut white rump

White-rumped Sandpiper:
Bold white rump contrasts with black tail and dark mantle. Clear white wingbar across inner wing, more diffuse across primaries. Pattern of chestnut back, buffy wing coverts and dark primaries may help to distinguish from Curlew Sandpiper, the only other small, white-rumped wader in the region.

clear wingbar against dark flight feathers

scaly upperparts

dark centre to rump and tail

Baird's Sandpiper:
Black centre to white rump and dark grey tail is similar to many other small sandpipers. Pale wingbar extends across whole of wing. Dark flight feathers with neat pale margins to feathers of back and wing coverts create a scaly look.

clear pale wingbar extends across whole body

Ruff   *Philomachus pugnax*

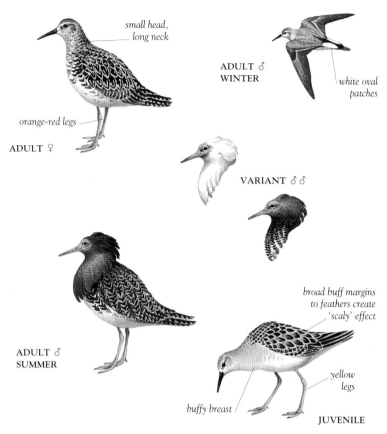

small head,
long neck

**ADULT ♂
WINTER**

white oval
patches

orange-red legs

ADULT ♀

VARIANT ♂ ♂

broad buff margins
to feathers create
'scaly' effect

**ADULT ♂
SUMMER**

yellow
legs

buffy breast

JUVENILE

Status: Somewhat localized summer visitor, but abundant double passage migrant and increasing winter visitor.
Identification: ♂ 27–31cm (10½–12in); ♀ 22–25cm (9–10in). One of the most confusing of all waders to the beginner, yet one of the easiest once its characteristics are known. Male (Ruff) much larger than female (Reeve). Such size difference apparent, but only obvious, in the field when both sexes seen together. Red legs and brown plumage leads inexperienced directly to Common Redshank at best, Spotted Redshank at worst. Buff-breasted juvenile regularly misidentified as vagrant Buff-breasted Sandpiper by aspiring twitchers. Yellow legs lead to other transatlantic vagrants. In all plumages combination

J F M A M J J A S O N D

of medium length straight bill, small head and long neck, and bulky body are unique. Male in summer, even on passage, boasts elaborate multi-coloured plumes on head and neck and has wattled, bare red face that cannot be confused. Females, juveniles and males at other times have back always scalloped with buff margins to brown feathers. Breeding female has scaly barred breast. Juvenile with warm buff breast extending only to white belly and yellowish-green legs. Buff-breasted Sandpiper has completely buff underparts, larger head and shorter neck.
Voice: A *chuck-uck* in flight.
Habitat: Wide variety of marshlands from wet meadows in temperate Europe to marshes and deltas of sub-tundra zone.
Similar Species: See above.

Jack Snipe *Lymnocryptes minimus*

ADULT

striped crown

medium bill

dark
wedge-shaped
tail, no white

ADULT

J F M A M J J A S O N D

Status: Small version of Common Snipe; summer visitor
to north, scarce winter visitor to south and west.
Identification: 18–20cm (7–8in). Cryptically coloured like
Snipe, but much more elusive, keeping well hidden in
cover; shorter bill diagnostic. Usually seen when flushed;
flies when in danger of being trodden on. Silent take-off
and brief, low, straight flight with no towering or zig-
zagging. No white on tail margins.
Voice: Usually silent.
Habitat: Wet, tussocky ground in summer. In winter
flooded grasslands and marshes.
Similar Species: Common Snipe is larger, with longer bill.

Common Snipe *Gallinago gallinago*

striped crown

very long
bill

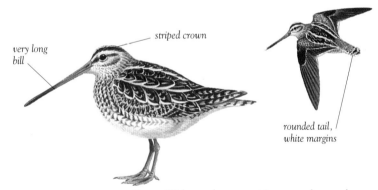

rounded tail,
white margins

J F M A M J J A S O N D

Status: Widespread summer visitor to northern and
eastern Europe, winter visitor elsewhere though localized.
Identification: 25–27cm (9½–10½in). Mottled brown and
black above with two bold, buff stripes on back forming 'V'.
Distinctively striped crown. Tends to keep to cover but also
feeds quite openly when not alarmed. If disturbed, flies off
with pronounced zig-zagging, often towering into the air.
Voice: Harsh *scarp*; repeated *chirper-chirper*; aerial bleating
of outertail feathers, called 'drumming'.
Habitat: Marshlands with tussocks or clumps of
vegetation.
Similar Species: See Jack Snipe and Great Snipe.

Great Snipe   *Gallinago media*

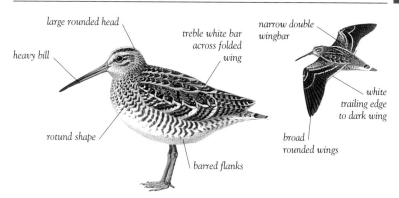

large rounded head

heavy bill

treble white bar
across folded
wing

narrow double
wingbar

rotund shape

barred flanks

white
trailing edge
to dark wing

broad
rounded wings

J F M A M J J A S O N D

Status: Scarce summer visitor to north-east Europe. Scarce on passage through eastern Mediterranean.
Identification: 27–29cm (11in). Looks like Snipe, flies like Woodcock. Cryptically camouflaged plumage. Similar size to Common Snipe, but much stouter with larger head, more-rounded wings and shorter bill. Barred underparts reminiscent of Woodcock. Flies low, straight and briefly, not erratically towering like Snipe. White outertail feathers.
Voice: Croaking sounds, but generally silent.
Habitat: Moist grasslands and taiga. Also woodland with muddy patches.
Similar Species: Common Snipe as above.

Woodcock   *Scolopax rusticola*

long bill

barred
crown

barred
back

rounded
wings

rotund
shape

Status: Chunky woodland-dwelling wader that breeds throughout temperate Europe and winters in south and west.
Identification: 32–36cm (12–14in). Bulky, snipe-like wader of moist, open woodland. Well camouflaged by brown and buff bars creating a 'dead leaves' effect. Hardly ever seen on ground but occasional bird may be flushed from nest. In flight, bulky shape, long down-pointed bill and broad rounded wings diagnostic. Mainly nocturnal. Territorial display flight (roding) at dawn and dusk.
Voice: Shrill *tssick* flight note in roding display flight.
Habitat: Throughout year in damp woodlands.
Similar Species: Common Snipe and Great Snipe.

J F M A M J J A S O N D

Black-tailed Godwit *Limosa limosa*

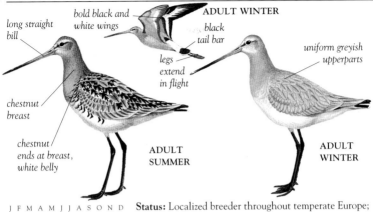

long straight bill

bold black and white wings

ADULT WINTER

black tail bar

legs extend in flight

uniform greyish upperparts

chestnut breast

chestnut ends at breast, white belly

ADULT SUMMER

ADULT WINTER

J F M A M J J A S O N D

Status: Localized breeder throughout temperate Europe; double passage migrant and winter visitor.
Identification: 38–43cm (14½–16½in). In summer, adult has chestnut head, neck and breast. Back spangled black and chestnut; wings grey. In winter, grey back and wings with no prominent streaking. Juvenile brown and buff; upperparts 'scalloped'. In flight, shows black band at tip of white tail and broad white wingbar across black wings.
Voice: Loud *reeka-reeka-reeka*.
Habitat: Breeds winter-flooded grasslands, Winters floods, marshes and estuaries.
Similar Species: Bar-tailed Godwit is smaller.

Bar-tailed Godwit *Limosa lapponica*

long bill, slightly uptilted

no wingbar

streaked back

ADULT WINTER

ADULT WINTER

chestnut on whole of underparts

ADULT SUMMER

J F M A M J J A S O N D

Status: Double passage migrant and locally abundant winter visitor from Siberian breeding grounds.
Identification: 36–40cm (14–16in). In summer, males have chestnut underparts extending to undertail. Back spangled black and chestnut; wings grey. In winter, upperparts buffy grey, heavily streaked black. Juvenile streaked buff and black. In flight, uniformly greyish, white 'V' extending upwards from rump; feet barely extended beyond tail.
Voice: An occasional low *kirrick-kirrick*.
Habitat: High peat bogs and marshy tundra in breeding season. In winter essentially coastal.
Similar Species: Larger Black-tailed Godwit.

Whimbrel   *Numenius phaeopus*

bold supercilium — striped crown

bill
decurved
towards tip

white 'V'
extends
up back

J F M A M J J A S O N D

Status: Breeds north otherwise passage migrant; winter
visitor far south.
Identification: 39–43cm (15–17in). Smaller size than
Curlew is deceptive. Best mark is central crown-stripe,
pale bordered black; pale supercilium. Bill decurved
towards tip rather than completely curved like Curlew;
also considerably shorter. In flight, shows white 'V' up
back; feet protrude just beyond tail.
Voice: A rapidly whistled *whi-whi-whi-whi-whi-whi-whi*.
Habitat: Breeds upland moors, tundra and northern edge
of boreal zone. Winter and on passage largely coastal.
Similar Species: Eurasian and Slender-billed Curlews.

Slender-billed Curlew   *Numenius tenuirostris*

white 'V' extends up back

faint supercilium

no crown stripes

decurved
bill with
thin tip

dark
lores

streaked on
white background

spots, not
chevrons, on
flanks

Status: Passes through Mediterranean on route between
Siberia and Morocco. Europe's most endangered bird.
Identification: 36–41cm (14–16in). Similar to Eurasian
Curlew and Whimbrel, about same size as the latter. Lacks
crown stripes; bill is decidedly thinner tipped. Faint
supercilium and dark loral stripe. Streaked breast white;
flank spots round. Juvenile has streaked not spotted (or
chevroned) flanks.
Voice: Like high-pitched Eurasian Curlew *coor-lee*.
Habitat: Breeds lowland peat bogs of southern taiga.
Winters coastal marshes and lagoons.
Similar Species: Whimbrel and Eurasian Curlew as above.

J F M A M J J A S O N D

Eurasian Curlew   *Numenius arquata*

white 'V' extends up back

no crown-stripes

very long, curved bill

J F M A M J J A S O N D

Status: Widespread, breeds in temperate and northern Europe. Winter visitor and on passage in south and west.
Identification: 51–61cm (20–24in). Large shorebird with long legs and very long, decurved bill. Upperparts brown with buffy feather margins; underparts heavily streaked brown on neck and breast. In flight, shows uniform wings and white 'V' extending up rump. Generally gregarious.
Voice: Drawn-out *coor-lee*; bubbling call in summer.
Habitat: Wet moorland and rough grazing among hills with peat bogs and heather-clad hillsides. Also lowland marshes and tussocky fields among steppes and near coasts.
Similar Species: Whimbrel, Slender-billed Curlew.

Buff-breasted Sandpiper   *Tryngites subruficollis*

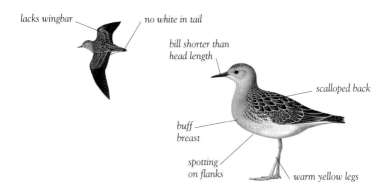

lacks wingbar

no white in tail

bill shorter than head length

scalloped back

buff breast

spotting on flanks

warm yellow legs

J F M A M J J A S O N D

Status: Rare, but regular transatlantic vagrant in autumn.
Identification: 18–20cm (7–8in). Neatly proportioned, upright-stanced wader. Warm coloration eliminates most confusion species. Upperparts brown neatly fringed buff to create scalloped effect. Underparts warm buff (white belly) neatly spotted sides of breast and nape. Legs warm yellow. Only female juvenile Ruff has comparable coloration, but has dark eye-stripe, smaller head, longer neck and less spotted breast.
Voice: Silent away from breeding grounds.
Habitat: Short-cropped undisturbed grasslands.
Similar Species: Small juvenile Ruff as above.

Spotted Redshank   *Tringa erythropus*

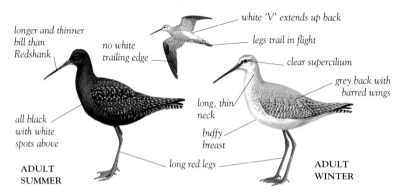

longer and thinner bill than Redshank

no white trailing edge

white 'V' extends up back

legs trail in flight

clear supercilium

grey back with barred wings

all black with white spots above

long, thin neck

buffy breast

long red legs

ADULT SUMMER

ADULT WINTER

J F M A M J J A S O N D

Status: Breeds far north; regular double passage migrant; winters in small numbers.
Identification: 29–32cm (11–12½in). In summer, adult black above and below, white spangling on wings and back. In winter, upperparts grey; wing feathers spotted black with white margins; clear supercilium. Juveniles with brown upperparts finely spotted black and white.
Voice: Explosive *choo-it*.
Habitat: Open tundra and taiga hillsides. On passage and in winter on lagoons and marshes.
Similar Species: Long legs and bill, and lack of wingbar separate from Common Redshank.

Common Redshank   *Tringa totanus*

shorter bill than Spotted Redshank

white trailing edge

brown back

red legs

red legs

ADULT SUMMER

ADULT WINTER

Status: Common summer visitor to large areas of north and east Europe. Winter visitor and passage migrant.
Identification: 26–30cm (10–12in). Neatly proportioned wader marked by long red legs. Upperparts brown, paler and more uniform in winter. Underparts white with heavy streaking, particularly in summer. Legs and base of bill bright red. In flight, shows broad white trailing edge to wing. Usually gregarious concentrating in large flocks.
Voice: Harsh *twook-twook*. Melodic *tew-u-u*.
Habitat: Wet grasslands, well-vegetated marshes plus coasts in winter.
Similar Species: Spotted Redshank; red-legged Ruff.

J F M A M J J A S O N D

Marsh Sandpiper *Tringa stagnatilis*

white 'V' high up back

legs project

plain wings

needle-like bill

spotted effect

plain white face

pale grey

SUMMER

very long greenish legs

WINTER

J F M A M J J A S O N D

Status: Summer visitor Russia and migrant eastern Europe.
Identification: 22–24cm (9in). Upperparts grey, spangled black in summer, more uniformly pale in winter. Underparts white, heavily spotted only in summer adult. Rump white extends in 'V' up back, legs extending beyond tail in flight. Bill thin, needle-like, straight, about twice length of head. Picks food from surface rather than probes.
Voice: A *tu* or *tchoo*, plus a hard *chik*.
Habitat: Freshwater margins, marshes, sewage pools.
Similar Species: Only superficially like Greenshank. See Wilson's Phalarope, beware transatlantic Lesser Yellowlegs.

Greenshank *Tringa nebularia*

grey and black back

grey, uptilted bill

no white on wing

white extends in 'V' up back

legs trail in flight

grey back

ADULT SUMMER

green legs

ADULT WINTER

J F M A M J J A S O N D

Status: Summer visitor to north and scarce winter visitor in west and south. Common double passage migrant.
Identification: 29–32cm (11–12½in). Long-legged, long-billed, grey wader that appears dark, slatey at a distance. Upperparts grey, streaked black in summer. Underparts mainly white, speckled grey in summer. Long green legs and long grey slightly upturned bill. Wings grey, white rump extends in 'V' up back; feet extend beyond tail.
Voice: Loud *tu-tu-tu*.
Habitat: Open moors, with pools. In winter, wide variety of wetlands.
Similar Species: None, but see Marsh Sandpiper.

Green Sandpiper *Tringa ochropus*

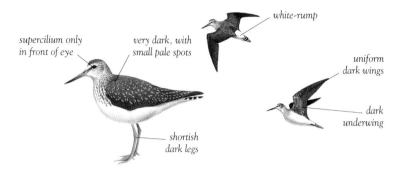

supercilium only in front of eye

very dark, with small pale spots

white-rump

uniform dark wings

dark underwing

shortish dark legs

J F M A M J J A S O N D

Status: Breeds in north; winters in south and west. Widespread, but not numerous, passage migrant elsewhere.
Identification: 22–24cm (8½–9in). Medium-sized wader, dark slate-grey above and white below; always appears black and white at any distance and in flight. Speckled on breast; short white supercilium. In flight, shows dark wings and back, white rump. Bobs head and tail.
Voice: Rising *tluit-weet-wit*.
Habitat: Nests in trees in disused nests of other birds. In winter and on passage along dykes and ditches.
Similar Species: Wood Sandpiper is paler and more heavily speckled white with longer and paler legs.

Wood Sandpiper *Tringa glareola*

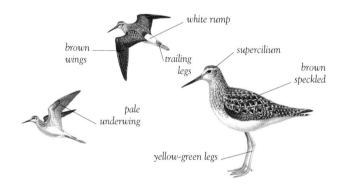

white rump

brown wings

trailing legs

supercilium

brown speckled

pale underwing

yellow-green legs

Status: Summer visitor to north and east, widespread and common passage migrant.
Identification: 19–21cm (7–8in). Similar to Green Sandpiper but always browner above with heavily speckled plumage and more pronounced supercilium. Slimmer build and longer, paler legs produce a more elegant impression. In flight, shows white rump, barred tail, trailing legs, uniform wing.
Voice: A flat *chi-chi-chi*.
Habitat: Wide variety of fresh waters in summer. In winter and on passage on open marshes and lakes
Similar Species: See Green Sandpiper and above.

J F M A M J J A S O N D

Winter 'Shanks' in Flight

'Shanks' are longer-legged, more elegant, generally more solitary waders of the genus *Tringa*. Some are named from their 'shank' colour, while others are called sandpiper as are some of the *Calidris*. Wingbars and tail patterns are as important as with that genus and the feet extend beyond the tip of the tail in all species, the length of leg that shows varies and is an important aid to identification.

SPOTTED REDSHANK
Medium-sized, grey wader with white speckled flight feathers forming a hint (no more) of a pale trailing edge to the wing. Legs extend well beyond tail tip which is lightly barred. White rump extends up back in 'V' shape.

REDSHANK
Medium-sized, brown wader with broad white trailing edge to wing diagnostic. Only tips of feet extend beyond tail and white 'V' up back less prominent than other, similar-sized 'shanks'.

MARSH SANDPIPER
Medium-sized to small wader with plain grey wings and huge white 'V' extending up back. Legs project well beyond tail, more than any similar species.

GREENSHANK
Medium-sized, grey wader with uniform grey wings. White 'V' extends up back and legs extend beyond tail, but neither feature as marked in Marsh Sandpiper. Heavier, uptilted bill a useful feature.

GREEN SANDPIPER
Small, dark wader with unmarked, almost black wings. Square white rump and three or four distinct tail bands. Feet just visible beyond tail tip. Wood Sandpiper can also appear very dark winged in flight.

WOOD SANDPIPER
Small wader with unmarked dark wings. Square white rump with multi-barred tail. Feet extend prominently beyond tail. These features more important than darkness (or otherwise) of wings and back.

Common Sandpiper *Actitis hypoleucos*

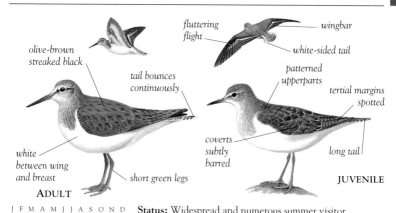

fluttering flight

wingbar

white-sided tail

olive-brown streaked black

patterned upperparts

tail bounces continuously

tertial margins spotted

coverts subtly barred

white between wing and breast

short green legs

long tail

ADULT

JUVENILE

J F M A M J J A S O N D

Status: Widespread and numerous summer visitor.
Identification: 18–21cm (7–8in). Brown streaking at sides of breast terminates in line above bend of wing; white wedge between the two. Clear-cut eye-stripe and supercilium. Short green legs accentuate long body; folded wings do not reach tip of tail. Continual bobbing motion. Flickering, shallow wingbeats, low over water.
Voice: Whistled *hee-dee-dee-dee*.
Habitat: Breeds tumbling streams with plentiful rocks; winters freshwaters and coasts.
Similar Species: See Spotted Sandpiper. Wood Sandpiper and Green Sandpiper also 'bob' but not continually.

Spotted Sandpiper *Actitis macularia*

plain back

coverts neatly barred buff and black

spotted underparts

short tail

ADULT SUMMER

yellowish legs

tertials with unspotted margins

JUVENILE

Status: Increasingly frequent vagrant from North America mainly to Britain and Ireland.
Identification: 18–20cm (7–7½in). Very similar to Common Sandpiper, but adult in summer has underparts boldly spotted black. In winter has less prominent white breast wedges, unstreaked throat and central breast. Juvenile more uniform back than Common Sandpiper; wing coverts more heavily barred black and buff. Tertials lack spotting on margins. Wings reach tip of tail.
Voice: *Tweet-weet-weet*.
Habitat: Mainly fresh waters on passage.
Similar Species: Common Sandpiper as above.

J F M A M J J A S O N D

Terek Sandpiper *Xenus cinereus*

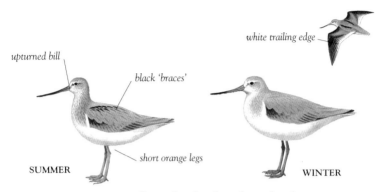

white trailing edge

upturned bill

black 'braces'

short orange legs

SUMMER

WINTER

J F M A M J J A S O N D

Status: Rare breeder in far north and scarce passage migrant through eastern Europe and Mediterranean.
Identification: 22–24cm (9in). Upperparts greyish-brown marked by black flecks on scapulars in breeding plumage. Underparts white with buffy wash on sides of neck and breast, particularly in juvenile. Shortish orange-yellow legs produce long-bodied, low-slung effect that is heightened by long, red-based, upturned bill.
Voice: Whistled *wik-wik*.
Habitat: Mainly boreal zone. On passage and in winter on mudflats and estuaries.
Similar Species: None.

Turnstone *Arenaria interpres*

complex pattern of bars and stripes

complex head and face pattern

rich chestnut

remnant face pattern

greyish

ADULT SUMMER

short legs orange

ADULT WINTER

J F M A M J J A S O N D

Status: Stocky, short-legged that turns stones (as well as anything else).
Identification: 22–24cm (8–9in). In summer, upperparts rich chestnut marked with black and buff. Head and neck white with intricate black markings extending to broad black breast band. In winter, same pattern but in shades of grey. In flight, wingbar and wing patch combined with white rump and double tail bands are unmistakable.
Voice: Distinctive chattering *tukatuk* repeated.
Habitat: Coastal islands of tundra in summer. At other times, coasts – rocky, or broken with sea defences.
Similar Species: None.

Wilson's Phalarope *Phalaropus tricolor*

lacks wingbar

white rump

ADULT WINTER

face pattern

yellow legs summer/black legs winter

♀ SUMMER

shortish legs

needle-like bill

pale grey

FIRST WINTER

J F M A M J J A S O N D

Status: Increasingly regular transatlantic vagrant mainly to Britain and Ireland.
Identification: 22–24cm (8½–9½in). Larger than other two phalaropes and swims less frequently. May be confused with Marsh Sandpiper. Bill long and needle-like as in that species, but legs shorter and black, yellow in autumn. Paler grey above than any similar species. Lacks wingbar, but shows white rump.
Voice: Usually silent, but utters a few croaks.
Habitat: Fresh and brackish marshes; occasionally estuaries.
Similar Species: Other phalaropes, Marsh Sandpiper.

Red-necked Phalarope *Phalaropus lobatus*

wingbar

grey and black back

red neck

dark crown and eye patch

ADULT WINTER

needle-like bill

bold buff 'V's on back

JUVENILE

ADULT ♀ SUMMER

Status: Delicate wader; spends most of its life swimming – Arctic marshes in summer; open oceans in winter.
Identification: 17–19cm (6½–7in). In breeding season, female has grey crown, nape, lower breast and back; the last marked by two buffy 'V's. Chin white, neck and upper breast orange-red. Male duller. In winter, grey above and white below; small dark comma extends behind eye. Juvenile has two buff 'V's on back and dark crown. Very fine bill is longer than head.
Voice: Quiet *tyit*.
Habitat: Mostly tundra pools. Winters at sea.
Similar Species: Compare Grey Phalarope.

J F M A M J J A S O N D

Grey Phalarope *Phalaropus fulicarius*

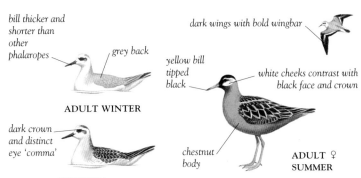

bill thicker and shorter than other phalaropes

grey back

ADULT WINTER

dark wings with bold wingbar

yellow bill tipped black

white cheeks contrast with black face and crown

dark crown and distinct eye 'comma'

chestnut body

ADULT ♀ SUMMER

JUVENILE

J F M A M J J A S O N D

Status: Small wader that swims buoyantly on fresh water and at sea. Circumpolar.

Identification: 19–21cm (7–8in). More bulky and stronger built than other phalaropes with shorter, stouter bill. Similar swimming style. In summer, black crown and 'face' contrast with white cheeks. Neck and whole of underparts warm rust; upperparts show double buffy 'V' on tortoiseshell patterned back. Bill yellow, tipped black; legs yellow. In winter, pale grey; head marked by black 'comma'.

Voice: High-pitched *twit*.

Habitat: Fresh water and shorelines; winters at sea.

Similar Species: Red-necked and Wilson's Phalaropes.

Winter Phalaropes in Flight

Phalaropes are small, pale grey waders, which swim buoyantly and easily. Grey and Red-necked spend winter at sea, the vagrant Wilson's is more marsh orientated. In autumn, all three may use marshes. Separation is based on darkness of upperparts, length of bill and presence or absence of wingbars.

WILSON'S PHALAROPE
Lacks wingbar and entire wings and back uniformly grey; white rump. Feet project beyond grey tail.

RED-NECKED PHALAROPE
Very dark, slatey-grey wader, with bold white wingbar and pale 'V' on back. White ovals on rump.

GREY PHALAROPE
Grey wader, with bold white wingbar across black wings contrasting with pale grey coverts and back. White ovals on rump.

Pomarine Skua *Stercorarius pomarinus*

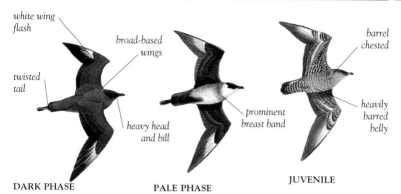

white wing flash

broad-based wings

twisted tail

heavy head and bill

DARK PHASE

prominent breast band

PALE PHASE

barrel chested

heavily barred belly

JUVENILE

Status: Scarce, double passage migrant, most often seen during extended seawatches, or wind-blown after storms.
Identification: 43–53cm (16–21in). Like Arctic Skua, occurs in two phases – light and dark. Both show white wing flashes, but pale phase has smudgy breast band. Spring adults easily separated from Arctic by broad twisted central feathers extending well beyond rest of tail. Pomarine always heavier and more bulky bodied than Arctic. Juvenile always more heavily barred on belly.
Voice: A *yowk* or *geck* on breeding grounds; silent at sea.
Habitat: Low-lying tundra. In winter and on passage at sea.
Similar Species: Confusable only with Arctic Skua.

Arctic Skua *Stercorarius parasiticus*

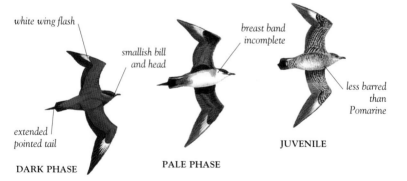

white wing flash

smallish bill and head

breast band incomplete

less barred than Pomarine

extended pointed tail

DARK PHASE

PALE PHASE

JUVENILE

Status: Summer visitor to northern Europe and double passage migrant farther south. Most commonly seen skua.
Identification: 38–48cm (15–19in). Fast, highly agile, dashing flight. Occurs in two phases – light and dark – both of which show white wing flashes. Pale phase has dark cap and upperparts; underparts with indistinct breast band. Spring adults have two central tail feathers extended; absent in juveniles and (usually) autumn adults.
Voice: High *kee-ow*; silent at sea.
Habitat: Coastal tundra. Winters at sea.
Similar Species: Lighter and more agile than Pomarine Skua. Heavier and less tern-like than Long-tailed Skua.

J F M A M J J A S O N D

Long-tailed Skua *Stercorarius longicaudus*

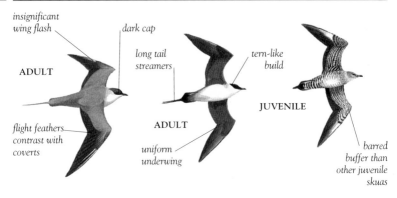

insignificant wing flash

dark cap

long tail streamers

tern-like build

ADULT

flight feathers contrast with coverts

ADULT

uniform underwing

JUVENILE

barred buffer than other juvenile skuas

J F M A M J J A S O N D

Status: Rarest of skuas. Less piratical than others.
Identification: 56–61cm (22–24in). Overall length due to extended central tail feathers in summer, usually lacking in autumn and sub-adult. Upperparts greyish, not brown; underparts pure white. Dark cap more contrasting than in other pale phase skuas; wing flashes absent or tiny and inconspicuous. Rare dark phase known only from Greenland, but probably overlooked.
Voice: Strident *kreek*. Silent at sea.
Habitat: Sub-Arctic fjells, Arctic tundra. Winters at sea.
Similar Species: Small size, light build and absence of wing flashes separates from Arctic and other skuas.

Great Skua *Stercorarius skua*

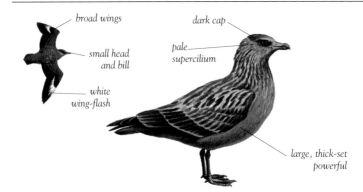

broad wings

small head and bill

white wing-flash

dark cap

pale supercilium

large, thick-set powerful

Status: Largest, most fearsome of the skuas. Scarce European North Atlantic.
Identification: 56–61cm (22–24in). Uniformly dark brownish plumage and bold white wing flashes. Wings much broader than other skuas and flight less agile. Smaller head and bill than large gulls, and easier, dashing flight, especially in pursuit of other seabirds. Not really confusable with any other European species.
Voice: Harsh *uk-uk-uk*; nasal *skeerr*.
Habitat: Uplands near seabird colonies. Winters at sea.
Similar Species: Closely related South Polar and Antarctic Skuas may wander northwards.

J F M A M J J A S O N D

Great Black-headed Gull   *Larus ichthyaetus*

pale mid-wing panel

clear tail band

clear tail band

black tipped inner-wing

black and white wingtips

SECOND WINTER

ADULT

FIRST WINTER

black outer primaries and black tipped inner primaries

sloping forehead

clear black head

large, black-banded bill

ADULT SUMMER

Status: Large, black-headed gull almost same size as Great Black-back, scarce migrant through eastern Mediterranean. Vagrant westwards. Fragmented range from southern Ukraine eastwards through Siberia to northern China.
Identification: 57–61cm (23in). Adult is huge pale-winged gull as Herring Gull, but with prominent white wingtips bordered by bold subterminal black line. Underwing whitish. Black head in summer with yellow bill marked by black line. First- and second-year birds, and adult in winter, show smudgy black around eye and on hind crown with prominent broken white eye-ring. Second years have brown spotting on hindneck, more extensive black on primaries, and black tail band. First years show broad central wing panel. All have heavy bill and sloping forehead.
Voice: Crow-like *kraa*.
Habitat: Lakes, rivers and deltas in dry steppe country often with salt or brackish water nearby. Winters coasts, shorelines, harbours, large rivers.
Similar Species: Smudgy head and white eye-ring recall Mediterranean Gull, but much larger with black at wingtips.

J F M A M J J A S O N D

Mediterranean Gull *Larus melanocephalus*

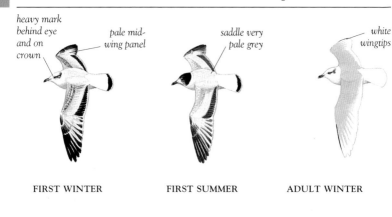

heavy mark behind eye and on crown

pale mid-wing panel

FIRST WINTER

saddle very pale grey

FIRST SUMMER

white wingtips

ADULT WINTER

black head, broken white eye-ring

droopy red bill

red legs

white wingtips

ADULT SUMMER

Status: Scarce virtually throughout fragmented range. Tendency to spread through Continental Europe, but largest numbers in Black Sea.

Identification: 37–40cm (14½–16in). Very pale gull with heavy, droopy, red bill and red legs. Adult in summer has black, not brown, head with prominent broken white eye-ring. Back and wings very pale grey, with white primaries and white underwing that combine to produce an exceptionally pale gull comparable with 'white-winged' Glaucous and Iceland Gulls. In winter, black head replaced by dark smudge behind eye and streaked hind crown. Uniform white primaries and underwing of adult facilitate identification at considerable range. Juvenile more like Common than Black-headed Gull, but marked by paler central wing panel. First winter and first summer plumages maintain this feature and are more like Ring-billed Gull with mid-wing panel, dark trailing band to secondaries and palish inner primaries. Main distinction is Mediterranean's lack of spots on tail above a black terminal band and on nape and sides of head. Second summer birds are virtually full adult, but may show a few black spots on primary tips.

Voice: Distinctive, plaintive *kee-ow* in flight. Other calls at breeding grounds.

Habitat: Breeds on islands among coastal marshes, often in single species colonies, but also with other species. In winter mostly coastal.

Similar Species: See Common and Ring-billed Gulls.

J F M A M J J A S O N D

Little Gull *Larus minutus*

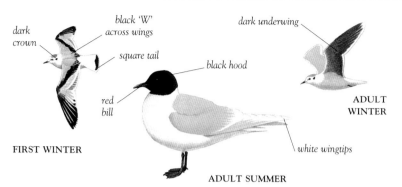

dark crown

black 'W' across wings

square tail

red bill

FIRST WINTER

dark underwing

ADULT WINTER

black hood

white wingtips

ADULT SUMMER

J F M A M J J A S O N D

Status: Summer visitor to eastern Baltic; smaller numbers North Sea. Elsewhere passage migrant and winter visitors.
Identification: 27–29cm (10½–11½in). Small tern-like gull that picks insects from water like a marsh tern. Adult has pale grey wings lacking black tips; underwing dark grey. In summer, head black, tiny bill red. In winter, has dark hind crown and spot behind eye. Juvenile and first winter birds have inverted black 'W' across upperwings in flight.
Voice: Repeated *ka-ee* and low *ka-ka-ka*.
Habitat: Freshwater marshes often alongside shoreline. Mainly coastal outside breeding season.
Similar Species: See Ross's Gull.

Bonaparte's Gull *Larus philadelphia*

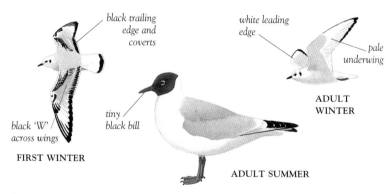

black trailing edge and coverts

white leading edge

pale underwing

ADULT WINTER

tiny black bill

black 'W' across wings

FIRST WINTER

ADULT SUMMER

Status: Rare vagrant to eastern Atlantic coasts from North America.
Identification: 30–32cm (12–13in). Bears strong resemblance to small Black-headed Gull. Pale grey above, marked by white forewing and black trailing edge. Black spot behind eye in winter. Major difference from Black-headed is white underwing. First winter with incomplete black 'W' across back.
Voice: Nasal *tea-rr*.
Habitat: Marshes and lakes; winters coasts at harbours, mudflats and offshore kelp beds and at sea.
Similar Species: Black-headed and Little Gulls as above.

J F M A M J J A S O N D

Black-headed Gull   *Larus ridibundus*

hint of white in forewing

pale grey back

FIRST WINTER

chocolate hood

red bill

red legs

ADULT SUMMER

dark outer underwing

white forewing

ADULT WINTER

J F M A M J J A S O N D

Status: Widespread and common colonial breeder; abundant winter visitor and passage migrant.
Identification: 35–38cm (13½–15in). Distinguished by white outer primaries creating a white forewing. Outer underwing dark. Adult in summer has chocolate hood, red bill and red legs. In winter, hood reduced to spot behind eye. First-winter birds have pale grey backs with brown markings across wings. Gregarious at all times.
Voice: Repeated *kuk-kuk*; angry *kee-ar*.
Habitat: Breeds islands, marshes and lakes. Very adaptable.
Similar Species: See Mediterranean, Little and especially Slender-billed Gull, which also has bold white forewing.

Slender-billed Gull   *Larus genei*

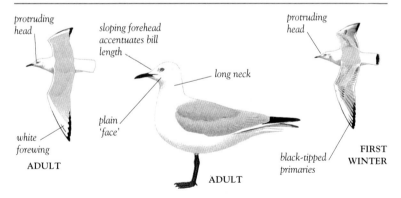

protruding head

white forewing

ADULT

sloping forehead accentuates bill length

plain 'face'

long neck

ADULT

protruding head

black-tipped primaries

FIRST WINTER

J F M A M J J A S O N D

Status: Highly fragmented breeding distribution through Mediterranean eastwards. Decidedly rare elsewhere.
Identification: 41–45cm (16–18in). Easily confused with Black-headed Gull, with major field mark of white forewing. Slightly larger with more extensive black trailing edge to primaries. Head lacks dark markings in all plumages, except juvenile. Bill long, red, sharply pointed; length accentuated by sloping, forehead. Neck long, giving bird curious, weight-forward, look in flight.
Voice: Nasal yelping.
Habitat: Saline marshes. Coastal outside breeding season.
Similar Species: Black-headed Gull as above.

Audouin's Gull *Larus audouinii*

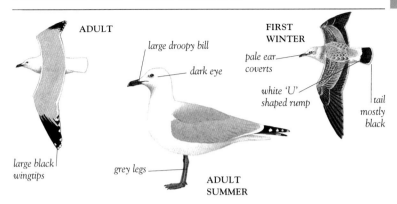

ADULT

large droopy bill

dark eye

large black wingtips

grey legs

ADULT SUMMER

FIRST WINTER

pale ear coverts

white 'U' shaped rump

tail mostly black

J F M A M J J A S O N D

Status: Confined to Mediterranean, wanders only as far as Atlantic shores of Spain, Morocco and West Africa.
Identification: 48–52cm (19–20½in). Long, flattish head; thick droopy bill; and slim pointed wings. Adult grey above with extensive black wingtips and tiny white mirrors. Forehead slopes markedly, peaking behind eye. Legs slate-grey. Immatures brown with uniform grey-buff crown and breast, and white face and crown.
Voice: Donkey-like braying.
Habitat: Sea coasts with rocky islands. Outside breeding season frequents sheltered bays.
Similar Species: Beware juvenile Mediterranean Gull.

Ring-billed Gull *Larus delawarensis*

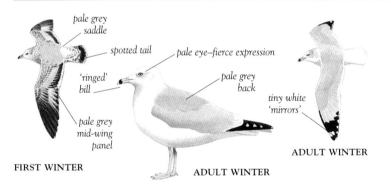

pale grey saddle

spotted tail

'ringed' bill

pale grey mid-wing panel

FIRST WINTER

pale eye–fierce expression

pale grey back

ADULT WINTER

tiny white 'mirrors'

ADULT WINTER

Status: Replaces Common Gull in eastern North America. Regular and increasing, mainly England.
Identification: 46–51cm (18–20in). Similar to Common Gull, but larger, with paler grey upperparts and heavier bill with dark band. Heavier bill and head, darkish 'frown' over eye and pale iris (in second summer and older) create fierce expression. Juveniles spotted on tail, breast and flanks. First summer birds yellow legs and bill and pale grey saddle.
Voice: Loud mewing.
Habitat: Breeds coastal islands and marshes and inland lakes. In Europe, mostly coastal.
Similar Species: Common and Mediterranean Gulls.

J F M A M J J A S O N D

Common Gull *Larus canus*

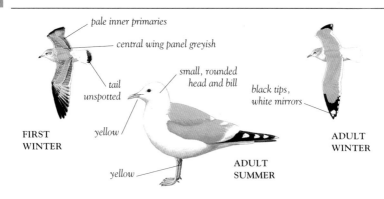

pale inner primaries

central wing panel greyish

tail unspotted

small, rounded head and bill

black tips, white mirrors

yellow

FIRST WINTER

yellow

ADULT WINTER

yellow

ADULT SUMMER

J F M A M J J A S O N D

Status: Northern breeding gull that is abundant winter visitor to Baltic and North Sea and adjacent inland areas.
Identification: 38–43cm (14–16½in). Grey upperparts with black wingtips and white 'mirrors' create similar pattern to Herring Gull, but head and bill significantly smaller, giving more gentle look. Thin, yellow bill lacks red spot. Juvenile and first winter birds show dark trailing edge to secondaries and pale mid-wing panel.
Voice: High *kee-aa* and mewing calls.
Habitat: Breeds rocky islands and inland moors.
Similar Species: See first winter Mediterranean Gull and especially all ages of Ring-billed Gull.

Lesser Black-backed Gull *Larus fuscus*

SECOND WINTER

narrow pale feather margins

lacks pale inner primaries

more marked trailing edge than Herring

yellow bill, red spot

all dark back

dark primaries and trailing edge

ADULT WINTER

yellow legs

ADULT SUMMER

FIRST WINTER

J F M A M J J A S O N D

Status: Summer visitor, passage migrant, winter visitor.
Identification: 51–56cm (20–22in). Large dark-backed gull with yellow legs and yellow bill with red spot. Scandinavian subspecies, *L.f.fuscus*, nearly as black on back. British and Iceland birds *L.f.graellsii* slightly paler. Slate-grey 'saddle' by second summer. Juvenile with dark upperparts and unbroken dark trailing edge to wing.
Voice: Variety of low calls including *kyow-kyow* and *kee-aa*.
Habitat: Breeds flat-topped islands, upland bogs, moors. Outside breeding season widespread inland and coasts.
Similar Species: Great Black-backed Gull much larger. See immature Herring and Yellow-legged Gulls.

Herring Gull *Larus argentatus*

pale grey
(saddle)
back

streaked
head

black tips,
white mirrors

pale inner
primaries

ADULT WINTER

**SECOND
WINTER**

dark
trailing
edge

**FIRST
WINTER**

yellow bill,
red spot

pink legs

ADULT SUMMER

Status: Common and familiar large gull of northern and western Europe. Widespread resident and winter visitor.
Identification: 53–59cm (21–23½in). Grey back; grey wings with black tips and white 'mirrors'. Large yellow bill with red spot; flesh-coloured legs. In winter, head variably streaked black. Immatures must be separated with care from Lesser Black-backed Gulls of same age. Juvenile Herring Gulls have wider pale margins to upperparts and pale inner primaries that break up hindwing pattern. First-summer birds invariably have pale creamy upperparts, much paler than Lesser Black-backed. Second-winter birds have pale grey 'saddles'. Adult Yellow-legged Gulls marked as named. Sub-adults difficult, but first winter Yellow-legged has pronounced mid-wing panel.
Voice: Loud ringing *kyow-kyow*; also laughing *kau-kau-kau-kau*.
Habitat: Coastal cliffs, islands and seaside town roofs. Also inland moors and lowland marshes and dunes. Winters mainly along coasts especially harbours and sewage outfalls, but inland at rubbish tips and reservoirs. Highly adaptable and successful.
Similar Species: The taxonomy of the 'Herring Gull' complex has led to the recent splitting off of Yellow-legged and Armenian Gulls (see page 168). There will be further debate on the species within this group of species.

J F M A M J J A S O N D

Yellow-legged Gull *Larus cachinnans*

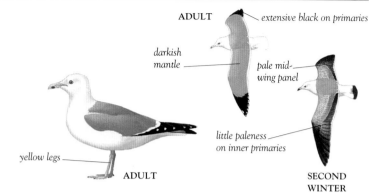

ADULT

extensive black on primaries

darkish mantle

pale mid-wing panel

little paleness on inner primaries

SECOND WINTER

yellow legs

ADULT

J F M A M J J A S O N D

Status: Resident Atlantic Iberia and Mediterranean and recently 'split' from Herring Gull.
Identification: 55–67cm (21½–26½in). Very similar to Herring Gull, but with yellow legs. Adult darker than Herring with more black on wing tips. First summer and second winter have more prominent mid-wing panel, more black on primaries and less prominent pale inner primaries than Herring Gull. The standard 'Herring Gull' throughout the Mediterranean region.
Voice: As Herring Gull.
Habitat: As Herring Gull.
Similar Species: As above.

Armenian Gull *Larus armenicus*

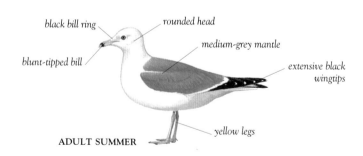

black bill ring

rounded head

medium-grey mantle

blunt-tipped bill

extensive black wingtips

yellow legs

ADULT SUMMER

J F M A M J J A S O N D

Status: Formerly regarded as subspecies of Herring Gull, found only in Armenia and in adjacent area of eastern Turkey.
Identification: 53–59cm (20–23in). Closely resembles slightly larger Yellow-legged Gull, but darker grey with more rounded head. Yellow legs. Bill yellow with black band in front of red spot on lower mandible, but not invariably present.
Voice: Similar to Herring Gull.
Habitat: Mountain lakes with islands and marshes. In winter with other gulls in same region.
Similar Species: Yellow-legged Gull as above.

Iceland Gull *Larus glaucoides*

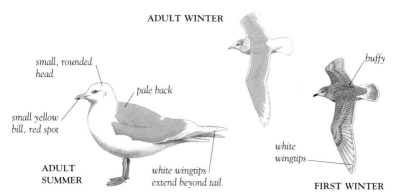

ADULT WINTER

small, rounded head

pale back

small yellow bill, red spot

buffy

white wingtips

ADULT SUMMER

white wingtips extend beyond tail

FIRST WINTER

J F M A M J J A S O N D

Status: Scarce winter visitor to Iceland, Britain and Norway.
Identification: 51–57cm (20–22in). Adult has very pale grey back and wings with white primaries. First-year birds are buffy; second-year birds are pale creamy above and below – both have white primaries. Smaller, more rounded head, coupled with smaller bill and more benign expression are most reliable means of separating this bird from larger and more abundant Glaucous Gull.
Voice: Shrill *kyow*.
Habitat: Breeds on high cliffs. In winter, edge of pack ice.
Similar Species: Glaucous Gull as above.

Glaucous Gull *Larus hyperboreus*

ADULT WINTER

buffy

large head fierce eye

shorter wings than Iceland

large yellow bill, red spot

white wingtips

FIRST WINTER

ADULT SUMMER

Status: High Arctic breeding species that is a regular winter visitor to northern coasts.
Identification: 58–69cm (22–27in). Large, pale grey-backed gull – almost as large as Great Black-backed. Can be confused with rarer Iceland Gull but bill much longer and more powerful and head flatter with fiercer expression. Pink legs and yellow bill with red spot. Immatures all have white primaries.
Voice: Loud *kyow* similar to other large gulls.
Habitat: Mainly Arctic cliffs or cliff tops depending on competition from related species. Winters coasts.
Similar Species: Iceland Gull as above.

J F M A M J J A S O N D

Great Black-backed Gull   *Larus marinus*

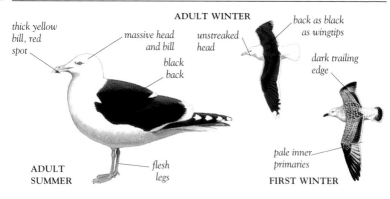

ADULT WINTER

thick yellow bill, red spot

massive head and bill

black back

unstreaked head

back as black as wingtips

dark trailing edge

ADULT SUMMER

flesh legs

pale inner primaries

FIRST WINTER

J F M A M J J A S O N D

Status: Massive gull, essentially maritime in habits.
Identification: 63–69cm (25–27in). Sheer size picks out in any gull flock. Adult has black back and wings, huge head and large, deep bill. Immatures much more contrasted than Herring and Lesser Black-backed Gulls. Shows dark trailing edge to secondaries as Lesser Black-backed, but pale inner primaries as Herring.
Voice: Harsh *owk*; also confiding *uk-uk-uk*.
Habitat: Breeds coasts, cliffs. Winters mainly at sea and along coasts, sometimes inland.
Similar Species: Adult and immature Lesser Black-backed and immature Herring Gulls.

Immature 'W' Winged Gulls

Four gulls in first-winter plumage show, to a variable extent, a distinct 'W' across the open wings. All are small and all, save Little Gull, are distinctly marine in habitat. All show a black band at tail tip, though tail shape varies. Underwing colour is another useful feature.

LITTLE GULL
Black 'W' on grey wings extends across back. Small black patch behind eye and dark crown. Dark underwing.

SABINE'S GULL
Black on outer primaries meets brown coverts to give 'W' impression, heightened by white infilling of inner primaries and secondaries.

BONAPARTE'S GULL
Black 'W' broken by pale grey back and confused by broad black trailing edge to wing. Underwing very pale.

KITTIWAKE
Black 'W' broken by pale grey back. 'Infilled' by pale, even white, inner primaries and secondaries. Bold black line over nape.

Ross's Gull *Rhodostethia rosea*

white trailing edge

wedge-shaped tail
difficult to see

**ADULT
WINTER**

black necklace

black "W"

wedge
tail tipped
black

white "infill"

pink wash

**FIRST
WINTER**

ADULT SUMMER

J F M A M J J A S O N D

Status: Small Arctic-dwelling gull that occasionally
wanders southwards to temperate latitudes in winter.
Identification: 29–31cm (12in). Adult in summer is grey
above, pink below, and marked by a black neck ring, quite
unmistakable. In winter, loses colour, closely resembles
winter Little Gull. Wedge-shaped tail often difficult to see
– but diagnostic. Underwing white. First winter shows
black 'W' across wing like Little Gull, but with white
secondary and primary 'in-fill'.
Voice: High *keu*, but vagrants usually silent.
Habitat: Breeds tundra river systems. Winters pack ice.
Similar Species: Little Gull, but seldom overlaps.

Ivory Gull *Pagophila eburnea*

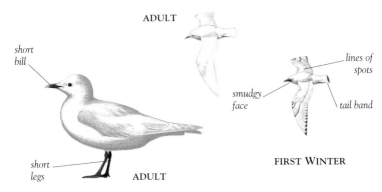

ADULT

short
bill

lines of
spots

smudgy
face

tail band

short
legs

ADULT

FIRST WINTER

Status: Small, dove-like gull that wanders southwards
from the pack ice in winter. Circumpolar. Vagrant to
Scotland, Norway and elsewhere.
Identification: 40–43cm (16in). Adult is only all-white
gull and with rounded head, short bill and short black legs
has a pigeon-like appearance. First winter has spotted
wings that create lines in flight, and darkly smudged face.
Long wings extend well beyond tail. Mostly found at
northern fishing harbours where very tame.
Voice: Harsh, tern-like cries.
Habitat: Breeds high Arctic islands. Winters pack ice.
Similar Species: None.

J F M A M J J A S O N D

Kittiwake *Rissa tridactyla*

JUVENILE

nape mark

'gentle head'

yellow bill

black 'W'

pale hind wing

black tips no mirrors

black legs

ADULT SUMMER

ADULT WINTER

J F M A M J J A S O N D

Status: Marine gull that is summer visitor to precipitous cliffs of northern Europe.
Identification: 38–43cm (15½–16½in). Totally maritime gull adult similar to Common Gull. Both have small head, short yellow bill and benign expression. Kittiwake has shorter legs and longer, narrower wings; black wingtips lack white 'mirrors'; and pale innerwing. Immatures show black inverted 'W' in flight.
Voice: Repeated *kitti-week*.
Habitat: Breeds colonially on cliffs. Winters at sea.
Similar Species: Common Gull as above. Immature Sabine's Gull shows less marked 'W' across wings.

Sabine's Gull *Larus sabini*

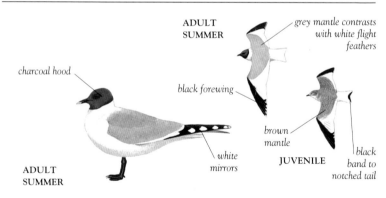

ADULT SUMMER

grey mantle contrasts with white flight feathers

charcoal hood

black forewing

white mirrors

brown mantle

JUVENILE

black band to notched tail

ADULT SUMMER

J F M A M J J A S O N D

Status: Regular autumn migrant to Biscay, storm-driven to Ireland and Channel.
Identification: 32–34cm (12½–13½in). Pelagic gull. At rest, adult pale grey above, with black wingtips marked by white mirrors. In summer, grey hood bordered by clear black collar. In winter, hood largely lost. In flight shows black forewing, white inner primaries; grey coverts and back. Juveniles have brownish mantle.
Voice: Raucous, higher-pitched than other gulls.
Habitat: Breeds tundra. Winters at sea.
Similar Species: Juvenile Kittiwake and Little Gull.

Gull-billed Tern *Gelochelidon nilotica*

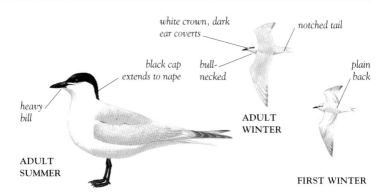

white crown, dark ear coverts

notched tail

black cap extends to nape

bull-necked

plain back

heavy bill

ADULT WINTER

ADULT SUMMER

FIRST WINTER

J F M A M J J A S O N D

Status: About same size and colour as Sandwich Tern. Feeds predominantly over marshes and adjacent dry land.
Identification: 35–39cm (14–15in). Pale grey above and white below make this one of palest European terns. Shiny black cap, lacking ragged crest, and thick bill with distinct gonys separate from Sandwich. In winter and juvenile, cap reduced to dark mark behind eye. In flight, wingtips how little black, and thick, bull-necked appearance very obvious. Black legs longer than Sandwich.
Voice: Harsh *ack-ack*.
Habitat: Marshes, lagoons, estuaries and rice fields.
Similar Species: Sandwich Tern lacks robust build.

Caspian Tern *Sterna caspia*

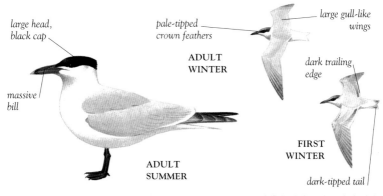

large head, black cap

pale-tipped crown feathers

large gull-like wings

ADULT WINTER

dark trailing edge

massive bill

FIRST WINTER

ADULT SUMMER

dark-tipped tail

Status: Huge tern, same size as Herring Gull; summer visitor Baltic, regular Atlantic and Mediterranean coasts.
Identification: 48–56cm (19–22in). Upperparts grey, with bold black crest terminating vertically. Underparts white. Bill blood-red and massive, with black band near tip when not breeding. Legs black and long for tern. In flight, recalls gull, with leisurely wingbeats.
Voice: Loud, harsh *kraa*.
Habitat: Breeds on low-lying islands off rocky coasts, but also on lagoons. In winter, frequents coasts, estuaries.
Similar Species: Royal is only other large tern with red bill, but bill is far less massive than Caspian's.

J F M A M J J A S O N D

Lesser Crested Tern   *Sterna bengalensis*

ADULT
WINTER

FIRST
WINTER

ragged crest

*darker grey than
Sandwich*

*thin yellow
bill*

ADULT SUMMER

J F M A M J J A S O N D

Status: Recent arrival to coastal waters that has bred in
Europe over past few years. Increasingly regular.
Identification: 38–43cm (15–17in). Similar in size and
appearance to Sandwich Tern, but with darker grey
upperparts and long yellow bill. Confusion more likely
with larger, paler Royal Tern which has heavier orange-
red bill and is no more than a rare vagrant.
Voice: Scratchy *kea-rik* similar to Sandwich Tern.
Habitat: Nests on sandy beaches, colonially, often with
Crested Tern. When not breeding, essentially coastal
along beaches and coastal lagoons but also well out to sea.
Similar Species: Royal Tern and Crested Tern.

Sandwich Tern   *Sterna sandvicensis*

ADULT–JULY
ONWARDS

*white
forehead*

*long black bill,
yellow tip*

ragged crest

pale grey

white

scaled back

*black
legs*

ADULT SUMMER

JUVENILE

J F M A M J J A S O N D

Status: Summer visitor to northern coasts, widespread
coasts on passage and winter visitor to Mediterranean.
Identification: 38–43cm (14–17in). Sandwich is much
paler than other terns (except Gull-billed and Roseate),
and has black legs and long, black bill with yellow tip that
can only be seen at close range. Black cap forms ragged
crest on hind crown. Confined to coastlines where dives
for food. Forms dense colonies.
Voice: Loud *keer-rik*, like rusty hinge on opening door.
Habitat: Essentially maritime. Breeds on low islands. On
passage and in winter along shorelines.
Similar Species: Compare Gull-billed Tern.

Common Tern   *Sterna hirundo*

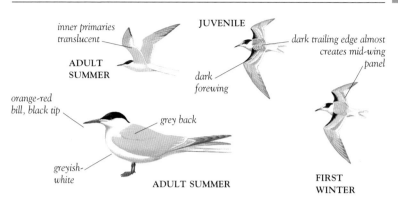

inner primaries translucent

ADULT SUMMER

JUVENILE

dark trailing edge almost creates mid-wing panel

dark forewing

orange-red bill, black tip

grey back

greyish-white

ADULT SUMMER

FIRST WINTER

J F M A M J J A S O N D

Status: Summer visitor to most temperate coasts as well as inland in concentrated colonies.
Identification: 30–36cm (11–14in). Pale grey above; washed pale grey below. Black cap; red legs. Bill usually orange-red with black tip but sometimes pure red or almost black. Juvenile has black leading edge to wing that forms bar on folded wing, and lacks white trailing edge to inner wing.
Voice: Harsh *kee-arr; kirri-kirri.*
Habitat: Sand and shingle bars; coasts and estuaries.
Similar Species: Beware separating Common Terns from Arctic or Roseate Terns by bill colour alone.

Arctic Tern   *Sterna paradisaea*

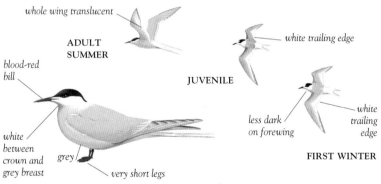

whole wing translucent

ADULT SUMMER

white trailing edge

JUVENILE

blood-red bill

white between crown and grey breast   *grey*

less dark on forewing

white trailing edge

FIRST WINTER

very short legs

Status: Summer visitor; very similar to Common Tern but breeds farther north along coasts and among tundra.
Identification: 30–39cm (11–15in). Like Common Tern but with shorter, blood-red bill (without black tip), longer tail and fully translucent wing when seen from below. Common Tern has translucent patch only on inner primaries. Greyer below with white cheeks. Juvenile has less black on leading edge of wing than juvenile Common Tern and prominent white trailing edge to secondaries.
Voice: Harsh *key-rr*, similar to Common Tern, but briefer.
Habitat: Shingle bars and beaches. Maritime in winter.
Similar Species: Common Tern as above. See page 176.

J F M A M J J A S O N D

Juvenile and First-Winter Sea Terns

In late summer and autumn mixed flocks of terns often gather along beaches near favoured feeding grounds and present excellent opportunities for comparison. Juveniles of the three regular European terns may, at first sight, seem dauntingly similar as all have black bills and white foreheads. But knowing what to look for actually makes them easier to identify than accompanying adults.

ROSEATE TERN: Black legs. Back heavily marked creating scaly pattern and folded wing shows black bar, though not as black as Common. In flight, black forewing fades through grey mid-wing to white trailing edge.

COMMON TERN: Red legs. Back gingery and folded wing shows bold black bar. In flight, black forewing and grey trailing edge enclose pale grey mid-wing panel.

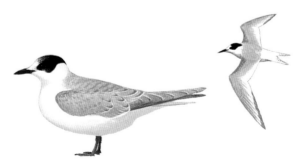

ARCTIC TERN: Red legs. Back grey with darker barring and folded wing shows only a hint of black bar. In flight, white trailing edge very obvious.

Roseate Tern *Sterna dougallii*

pale wings

dark forehead

ADULT SUMMER

almost spotted back

black bill

white not grey (pinkish spring)

paler grey than Common or Arctic

long tail streamers

ADULT SUMMER

JUVENILE

J F M A M J J A S O N D

Status: Rarest of breeding terns with a few isolated colonies, mostly on islands. Late-arriving summer visitor.
Identification: 32–40cm (12–15in). Best picked out from more abundant Common and Arctic Terns by paler colour – almost white above and below. Identification confirmed by black bill (some Common Terns have almost complete black bill and many Roseates have basal half of bill red by mid-summer) and long tail streamers (may become broken). In spring has pink flush on breast.
Voice: Similar to Common Tern: *kee-a, pee-pee-pee.*
Habitat: Breeds on low islets; winters coasts.
Similar Species: Common and Arctic Terns.

Little Tern *Sterna albifrons*

very narrow wings

white forehead

yellow bill, black tip

ADULT

black leading edge

JUVENILE

Status: Declining summer visitor to coasts and rivers that flies on sickle-like wings.
Identification: 23–26cm (9–10in). Tiny fast-flying tern. Long narrow wings, almost swift-like in shape, flicker in fast wingbeats. Essentially marine, feeding close inshore, diving for small fish. Legs and bill yellow, the latter with black tip. Black cap always incomplete; forehead white. Juvenile has black bill, black forewing and scaly upperparts.
Voice: Various chatterings; high-pitched, sharp *kittik.*
Habitat: Shingle beaches along shoreline and inland along large rivers. Winters along shorelines.
Similar Species: Small size separates from other 'sea' terns.

J F M A M J J A S O N D

Whiskered Tern   *Chlidonias hybridus*

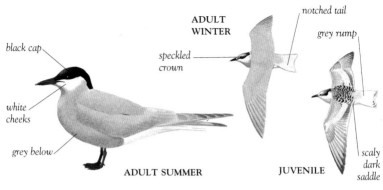

ADULT WINTER

notched tail

grey rump

speckled crown

black cap

white cheeks

grey below

ADULT SUMMER

JUVENILE

scaly dark saddle

J F M A M J J A S O N D

Status: Summer visitor to south and central Europe. Locally abundant.
Identification: 26–29cm (10–11in). In summer, upperparts grey, underparts darker grey, with distinct white cheek patch and black cap. Bill and feet dark red. Juvenile has dusky 'saddle' between grey wings, like White-winged Black Tern, but lacks pale rump of that species. Adult winter has vestigial cap, lacks white collar, and has black ear coverts that align with eye.
Voice: A rasping, but abrupt, *tchank*.
Habitat: Shallow, freshwater lakes and marshes.
Similar Species: Black and White-winged Black Terns.

Juvenile and First-Winter Marsh Terns

In summer plumage the three species of 'Marsh Terns' are not only beautiful, but also easy to separate. In winter plumage they need considerably more care, while juveniles are positively confusing, especially when resting. In flight a combination of dark or pale saddle, with a dark or pale rump, and dark or pale wings offers sufficient to identify each species. At rest such features disappear and careful examination of head pattern is required for accurate diagnosis.

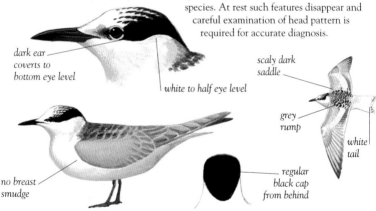

dark ear coverts to bottom eye level

white to half eye level

scaly dark saddle

grey rump

white tail

no breast smudge

regular black cap from behind

WHISKERED TERN

Largest of the three with longer bill. Juvenile Whiskered in flight shows scaly dark saddle contrasting with pale wings; not a black saddle contrasting with pale innerwing and dark primaries of White-winged. Rump pale grey and tail white; not white rump and grey tail of White-winged. Whiskered is a pale tern with a dark back; others are dark terns with pale features.

BLACK TERN

Dark grey wings and back lack contrasting dark/black mantle of others. Smudgy dark patch at sides of breast diagnostic. Head has 'waisted', water-drop-like pattern, but not as marked as White-winged. Ear coverts extend below eye level, and white behind ear coverts to top of eye.

WHITE-WINGED BLACK TERN

Pronounced black saddle contrasts with white (not grey) rump. Wing dark with pale innerwing. Head always appears whiter than Black by lacking dark breast smudge and having more white on crown. Head has marked 'waisted' water-drop-like pattern on nape, and dark ear coverts extending well below eye (almost a cheek 'water-drop') with white behind extending well above eye.

Black Tern *Chlidonias niger*

white forehead

ADULT SUMMER

grey wings

smudge at side of breast

smudge at side of breast

ADULT WINTER

black, dark grey wings

JUVENILE

ADULT SUMMER

J F M A M J J A S O N D

Status: Summer visitor to most of Europe and regular passage migrant elsewhere.
Identification: 23–26cm (9–10in). Summer adult all black with dark grey wings. Juvenile and winter grey above and white below, with black cap, white forehead, diagnostic black smudge at side of breast and black ear coverts that extend below line of eye. Tail notched. Black Terns take insects from surface of water in flight.
Voice: High-pitched *kik*.
Habitat: Freshwater lakes and pools. Marine in winter.
Similar Species: None in breeding plumage. See juvenile and winter White-winged Black and Whiskered Terns.

White-winged Black Tern *Chlidonias leucopterus*

no smudge at breast sides

ADULT SUMMER

dark saddle

black body and wing linings

no smudge at breast sides

pale rump

tiny bill

ADULT WINTER

white undertail

JUVENILE

ADULT SUMMER

J F M A M J J A S O N D

Status: Summer visitor and passage migrant to eastern Europe.
Identification: 22–24cm (9–9½in). Body black, contrasting with almost white wings and tail. Underwing coverts black. Winter adult similar to Black Tern, but has black patch behind eye, and only a hint of greyish cap and lacks smudge at side of breast. Juvenile similar to juvenile Black Tern, but has black 'saddle' and pale rump. Juvenile Whiskered Tern has grey rump with white tail.
Voice: Loud *keer*.
Habitat: Shallow lakes with emergent reeds.
Similar Species: Black and Whiskered Terns as above.

Common Guillemot *Uria aalge*

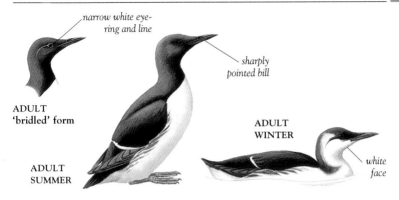

narrow white eye-ring and line

sharply pointed bill

ADULT 'bridled' form

ADULT WINTER

white face

ADULT SUMMER

J F M A M J J A S O N D

Status: Strictly maritime.
Identification: 40–44cm (16–17in). Usually found in flocks. Comes to land to breed, when forced to do so by storms, or when 'oiled'. Stands upright on land and forms dense colonies on cliff ledges. Upperparts blackish brown; underparts white. In winter, neck and sides of face white. Some have white eye-ring and line extending across face – known as bridled form.
Voice: Various moaning and growling notes.
Habitat: Cliffs in summer; winters offshore.
Similar Species: Brünnich's Guillemot, Razorbill.

Brünnich's Guillemot *Uria lomvia*

thick bill, white mark

cap extends below eye

WINTER

SUMMER

Status: Though there is some overlap, this species replaces Common Guillemot at higher latitudes. A rare vagrant farther south and then usually found dead on the tideline.
Identification: 40–44cm (16–17in). Closely resembles Guillemot, but virtually black above, with thicker and shorter bill. At all seasons, whitish line at base of bill best field mark, but in winter black cap extends below eye and there is no thin line across ear coverts.
Voice: Various growling notes.
Habitat: Breeds on fearsome cliffs of high Arctic. Winters on adjacent seas except where frozen.
Similar Species: Common Guillemot as above.

J F M A M J J A S O N D

Razorbill   *Alca torda*

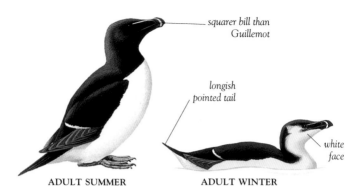

squarer bill than
Guillemot

longish
pointed tail

white
face

ADULT SUMMER   **ADULT WINTER**

J F M A M J J A S O N D

Status: Breeds in north and west, often on same cliffs as
Common Guillemot. Britain is world headquarters.
Identification: 39–43cm (15–16½in). Similar to
Guillemot; often forms mixed flocks. Generally blacker
above. Bill shape much deeper than Guillemot, with
distinctive vertical white line. In flight, at sea, pointed tail
particularly useful feature; gives bird elongated silhouette.
Like Guillemot, black neck lost in winter.
Voice: Various growls and grunts.
Habitat: Breeds in crevices on sea cliffs. Winters along
rocky shores and at sea.
Similar Species: Common Guillemot.

Black Guillemot   *Cepphus grylle*

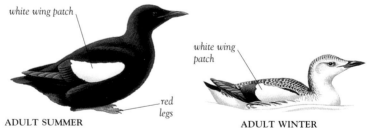

white wing patch

white wing
patch

red
legs

ADULT SUMMER   **ADULT WINTER**

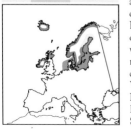

J F M A M J J A S O N D

Status: Resident around northern cliffs where it breeds
and all but unknown elsewhere. Less gregarious than
other auks.
Identification: 33–35cm (12½ – 13½in). Most often seen
on water below nesting cliffs. In summer, plumage all black
with bold white oval patch on wings. Feet and inside of
mouth bright red. In winter, mottled greyish all over, with
darker wings still marked by whitish ovals.
Voice: High-pitched, somewhat plaintive *peeeee*.
Habitat: Breeds among screes and rockfalls at foot of cliffs.
In winter, inhabits same areas of shallow seas.
Similar Species: None.

Little Auk   *Alle alle*

SUMMER

ADULT WINTER

tiny, stubby bill

white face

J F M A M J J A S O N D

Status: Starling-sized autumn and winter visitor in variable numbers.
Identification: 20–22cm (8–9in). Upperparts black, underparts white. Throat and breast black in summer, white in winter. Bill short and stubby. Flies fast on whirring wings. Tiny size and rapid flight best features at sea. Highly gregarious, though 'wrecks' may leave individuals miles inland.
Voice: Chattering at colonies; silent at sea.
Habitat: Breeds in vast colonies among Arctic mountain screes often some distance from sea. Winters at sea.
Similar Species: Other small auks may wander from Pacific to the Atlantic.

Puffin   *Fratercula arctica*

white face

multi-coloured bill

reduced bill

large head

less white face

ADULT SUMMER

ADULT WINTER

Status: Small, comical seabird; forms colonies on offshore islands and stacks in north and west.
Identification: 30cm (12in). Upperparts black; underparts white; face white. Outstanding feature is large parrot-like bill vertically striped in yellow and red. Size of bill reduced (horny plates at base shed) and colours paler in winter and juvenile plumages. At sea, short, rapidly whirring wings and large head with white face are best features.
Voice: Deep, purring *arr-arr*.
Habitat: Breeds among land slips on cliffs lacking terrestrial predators. Winters at sea.
Similar Species: Common Guillemot, Razorbill.

J F M A M J J A S O N D

Black-bellied Sandgrouse *Pterocles orientalis*

black-white-black
flight pattern

pointed tail

♂

black
belly

SUMMER ♂

SUMMER ♀

J F M A M J J A S O N D

Status: Pigeon-like bird of arid areas most often seen flighting to and from water in morning and evening.
Identification: 33–35cm (13–14in). In flight, weight-forward, bullet-shape on fast, pointed wings picks out as sandgrouse. Broad black band across belly, white wing linings and black flight feathers. Head and breast pale blue-grey separated by narrow black line from pinkish-buff lower breast and black belly. Tail pointed, but not extended. Gregarious, flies in small flocks.
Voice: Low bubbling.
Habitat: Stony, sparsely vegetated steppes and plains.
Similar Species: Pin-tailed Sandgrouse.

Pin-tailed Sandgrouse *Pterocles alchata*

♂

white
belly

extended
'pin-tail'

SUMMER ♀

white
belly

SUMMER ♂

J F M A M J J A S O N D

Status: Typical, bullet-shaped sandgrouse mostly seen in fast-flying flocks morning and evening.
Identification: 31–39cm (12–15in). Upperparts mottled brown and buff; head greenish with orange wash on face and black chin. Orange breast band bordered above and below by narrow black band. Underparts white. Long tail with extended 'pin-tail'.
Voice: Loud *guet-tar*.
Habitat: Dry lowland plains, dried out marshes and poor stony grasslands; scant vegetation.
Similar Species: See Black-bellied Sandgrouse, but Pin-tailed is only likely white-bellied sandgrouse in our area.

Rose-ringed Parakeet *Psittacula krameri*

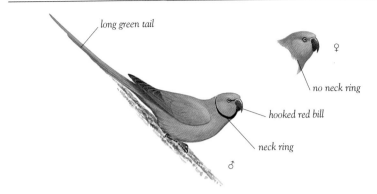

long green tail

♀

no neck ring

hooked red bill

neck ring

♂

J F M A M J J A S O N D

Status: Europe's only feral parrot; escaped from captivity in 1960s in England and has since spread to adjacent Continent. Often called Ring-necked Parakeet.
Identification: 37–43cm (14½–17in). Plumage mainly green with blackish outerwings. Extremely long, pointed tail. Large hooked red bill. Male has narrow neck ring of pink and black lacking in female. Gregarious and noisy especially at roosts.
Voice: Screaming *keeo-keeo*.
Habitat: In Europe in orchards, parks and large gardens. In native range in open deciduous woodland.
Similar Species: None.

Great Spotted Cuckoo *Clamator glandarius*

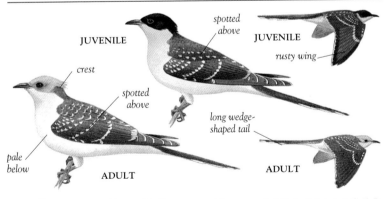

JUVENILE

spotted above

JUVENILE

rusty wing

crest

spotted above

long wedge-shaped tail

pale below

ADULT

ADULT

Status: Noisy, summer visitor to Mediterranean with a distinct south-west and south-east divide.
Identification: 38–41cm (15–16in). Larger than Common Cuckoo, but with similar long tail, sharply pointed wings and shallow wingbeats; obviously a cuckoo. Upperparts dark brown variously spotted white on wings and back. Head pale grey with erectile crest; tail dark brown, long and graduated, tipped white. Underparts warm buff.
Voice: Distinctive, raucous *kittera-kittera-kittera*.
Habitat: Orchards and groves, plains with copses, cork plantations, fields and thickets in dry country.
Similar Species: Common Cuckoo.

J F M A M J J A S O N D

Common Cuckoo *Cuculus canorus*

hepatic phase

ADULT ♀

JUVENILE

ADULT

small head
and bill

grey head
and neck

long
narrow wings

JUVENILE

barred
below

ADULT

long wedge-
shaped tail

Status: Widespread and common summer visitor virtually throughout Europe. Familiar song is characteristic sound of spring. The world's best known brood parasite.
Identification: 32–34cm (12½–13½in). Usually seen in flight when long pointed wings, long tail and small head and bill are reminiscent of a hawk or small falcon. When perched, often on overhead wire, appears ungainly and off-balance; seems to have difficulty folding wings. Upperparts and breast grey; underparts barred dark brown and white. Sexes similar. Hepatic female is rare colour phase with rich chestnut-brown upperparts heavily barred black; head and breast warm buff barred black; belly white heavily barred. Juvenile is heavily barred above and below with dark brown upperparts and white belly.
Voice: Familiar *cuck-oo* repeated; female has bubbling call.
Habitat: Occupies huge range of landforms from marshes and lowland woods, to open heaths and copses, and mountain moorland. Parasitizes wide range of small birds. Females are host specific, laying eggs that mimic the preferred host.
Similar Species: See Great Spotted Cuckoo.

J F M A M J J A S O N D

Rock Dove *Columba livia*

wingbars

white rump

pale grey

wingbars

J F M A M J J A S O N D

Status: Highly localized resident in remote wildernesses; feral birds widespread and numerous.
Identification: 31–35cm (12–14in). Genuine Rock Doves now confined to cliffs in extreme north and west and a few southern mountains. Elsewhere, they have interbred with domesticated Rock Doves escaped from captivity. Genuine wild bird pale grey with patch of metallic purple and green at sides of neck. Folded wing shows two black bars. Rump white; tail broadly tipped black.
Voice: Familiar *oo-roo-coo*, repeated.
Habitat: Sea cliffs, mountain gorges and cliffs; feral towns.
Similar Species: Stock Dove lacks white rump.

Stock Dove *Columba oenas*

no white rump

mid-grey

tiny wingbars

whole wing bordered black

Status: Widespread resident through western Europe; summer visitor to central and east. Nowhere common.
Identification: 31–35cm (12–14in). Grey above and paler grey below, with pale pink breast and less marked double wingbar than Rock Dove. In flight, shows grey wings with broad black borders. Tail broadly tipped black, lacks white rump. Though found in similar areas to Wood Pigeon, can be distinguished by lack of white on neck and wing.
Voice: A *coo-roo-oo* repeated monotonously.
Habitat: Forest or woodland edges with plentiful old trees.
Similar Species: Rock Dove, Wood Pigeon; beware feral Rock Dove lacking white rump.

Wood Pigeon *Columba palumbus*

white neck
slash

white bar
across wing

white
wing edge

J F M A M J J A S O N D

Status: Widespread, often abundant, resident in the west and summer visitor to the north and east.
Identification: 39–43cm (15½–17½in). Largest of the pigeons; marked by white neck slash and broad white bar across open wings. Grey above, pinkish below. In flight, outerwing is dark; tail grey with black terminal band. Juvenile lacks glossy patch and white bar on neck.
Voice: Endlessly repeated *coo-coo-coo-cu-coo*.
Habitat: Variety of woodlands from pure deciduous to pure conifer, with access to fields and crops.
Similar Species: No pigeons or doves are as large and show white bar across wing.

Collared Dove *Streptopelia decaocto*

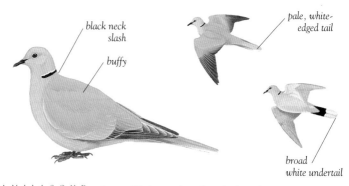

black neck
slash

buffy

pale, white-
edged tail

broad
white undertail

J F M A M J J A S O N D

Status: Widespread resident; highest densities in south-east; twentieth-century expansion north-westwards.
Identification: 29–32cm (11–12½in). Pale buffy above, pinkish below; neat black line (collar) on sides of neck. In flight, undertail has black base and broad white tip; uppertail buff with white margins and tip. Juvenile lacks black collar.
Voice: Plaintive *weer*; repeated *coo-coooo-coo*.
Habitat: Originally dry savannah type country, but westwards spread associated with villages and gardens.
Similar Species: Turtle Dove has brown upperparts; Laughing Dove is smaller and lacks collar.

Turtle Dove *Streptopelia turtur*

dark, white-edged tail

black and brown

bold black and white neck slash

narrow white tail tip

J F M A M J J A S O N D

Status: Small, fast-flying dove that is summer visitor to most of Europe, whose purring call is characteristic of late spring.
Identification: 26–29cm (10–11½in). Grey-brown on head and back; pinkish below. Wing coverts black; each feather broadly edged rust; creating turtle-shell appearance. Shows rufous back and wing coverts in flight. Black tail edged white; smudged black and white neck slash. Forms flocks in autumn.
Voice: Purring *roor-rr* repeated.
Habitat: Dry lowlands with copses, plantations, hedgerows and plentiful open land. Avoids human habitation.
Similar Species: Collared Dove.

Laughing Dove *Streptopelia senegalensis*

white tail margins

blue wing coverts

blue wing coverts

chestnut necklace

white undertail

J F M A M J J A S O N D

Status: Resident Bosphorus and south-east Turkey where frequently called Palm Dove. Abundant and widespread in many parts of Africa.
Identification: 25-27cm (10-10½in). Dainty, darkish dove with pale blue wing coverts and chestnut and black necklace. In flight shows broad white undertail and uppertail margins.
Voice: Laughing *poo, poo, pooo, pooo, poo.*
Habitat: Cities, towns, oases.
Similar Species: No similar-sized dark dove occurs in our area.

Barn Owl *Tyto alba*

bold facial disc

pale rounded wings

flat white face

white breast

dark breasted form

Status: The world's most widespread owl. Found through most of Europe, though nowhere common.
Identification: 33–36cm (12½–14in). Most often seen quartering fields at dusk. Western and southern forms identified by white underparts. Eastern forms have spotted buff underparts. Upperparts pale orange-buff with darkish spots. Flat-face with dark ring around white facial disc.
Voice: Variety of shrill shrieks, hisses and snoring notes.
Habitat: Extensive areas of rough grassland, with copses. Nests in barns and other artifacts.
Similar Species: All other owls are brown or grey mottled black, except Snowy Owl, which is white all over.

Snowy Owl *Nyctea scandiaca*

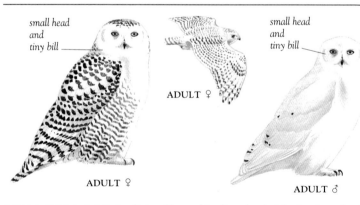

small head and tiny bill

ADULT ♀

small head and tiny bill

ADULT ♀

ADULT ♂

Status: Huge, white diurnal owl of the Arctic tundra that occasionally erupts southwards into boreal forests.
Identification: 53–66cm (21–26in). Smaller male white with few spots of black on wing coverts. Larger female white, liberally spotted black on upperparts with bars on breast and underparts. Rounded head, well-feathered bill and crouching attitude more reminiscent of seal than bird. In flight wings large and rounded.
Voice: Various barks and mews, but generally silent.
Habitat: Open tundra and bare mountain slopes, with well-drained ridges and a plentiful food supply of lemmings.
Similar Species: None.

Scops Owl *Otus scops*

GREY
ADULT

bold ears

RUFOUS ADULT

slimline
shape

tail
shorter
than Little Owl

wings appear
longer than
Little Owl

J F M A M J J A S O N D

Status: Tiny owl that is summer visitor to southern Europe and totally nocturnal; more often heard than seen.
Identification: 18–20cm (7–8in). Slim upright posture with noticeable 'horns' heavily streaked above and below, and prominent facial disc, sufficient to identify. Majority of birds are grey, but a proportion are more rufous.
Voice: Monotonously repeated *poo-poo-poo*, with each note separated by over a second of silence, is characteristic sound of Mediterranean summer.
Habitat: Orchards, groves, copses, fields, towns, villages.
Similar Species: Pygmy Owl is even smaller. Little Owl, much larger and more rounded in shape.

Pygmy Owl *Glaucidium passerinum*

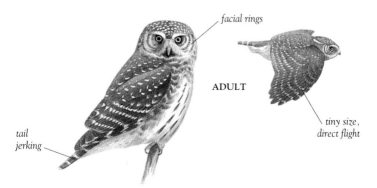

facial rings

ADULT

tail
jerking

tiny size,
direct flight

Status: Tiny owl, resident in conifer forests, and one of the most elusive of European birds.
Identification: 16–17cm (6½in). Chubby shape, smallish head, and longish barred and frequently cocked tail best features. Grey-brown, heavily barred above; white-streaked on belly, but barred on sides of breast, below. Has prominent short, white supercilia. Often sits at angle rather than upright; fidgets. Hunts at dawn and dusk.
Voice: Repeated double-note similar to call of Scops, but higher pitched and more closely spaced.
Habitat: Conifer forests, particularly of silver fir.
Similar Species: Only Eurasian Scops Owl.

J F M A M J J A S O N D

Tawny Owl *Strix aluco*

large rounded head

dark eyes

flat head

warm brown

broad rounded wings

J F M A M J J A S O N D

Status: Common and widespread owl and source of the most familiar owl hoots and shrieks. Totally nocturnal.
Identification: 36–40cm (14–15½in). Upperparts brown, mottled buff; underparts buffy, broadly streaked brown. Well-marked facial disc set off by large, dark eyes. In flight, wings long and rounded.
Voice: *Hoo…hoo-hoo* wavering at end; harsh *ke-wick*.
Habitat: From edges of conifer forests, through deciduous woods to farmland with copses and shelter belts. Also locally in city parks as well as churchyards and gardens.
Similar Species: Replaced northwards by Ural Owl. Long-eared Owl may be confused in flight.

Hawk Owl *Surnia ulula*

dark sides to face

short, pointed wings

pale scapulars

long tail

J F M A M J J A S O N D

Status: Owl of great northern conifer forests. Mainly active during day and frequently perches quite openly.
Identification: 33–41cm (13–16in). Black and grey owl with long tail and large, well-marked rounded head. Particularly fierce expression. Facial disc accentuated by broad black marks at either side and bold whitish supercilia. Yellow eyes. Densely barred breast, pale grey (spotted) scapulars and long tail avoid confusion with any other owl.
Voice: Rattling *ki-ki-ki*.
Habitat: Boreal forests from edge of taiga to steppes.
Similar Species: None, but check Ural and Great Grey Owls..

Ural Owl *Strix uralensis*

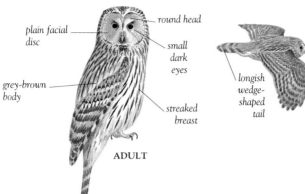

plain facial disc

round head

small dark eyes

grey-brown body

streaked breast

longish wedge-shaped tail

ADULT

J F M A M J J A S O N D

Status: Large owl of northern boreal forests that resembles a pale Tawny Owl, but is half as large again.
Identification: 60–62cm (24in). Grey-brown heavily streaked above; creamy and prominently streaked below. Clear-cut facial disc creamy with only dark markings around eyes. Crown clearly streaked. Long, clearly barred, wedge-shaped tail produces impression of large Accipiter in flight. Only similar owl is Great Grey which is larger.
Voice: A deep hooting *hoo-oo, hoo-hu-hoo-hoo* that begins softly and gains in volume.
Habitat: Conifer forests with other trees and glades.
Similar Species: See Great Grey Owl as above.

Great Grey Owl *Strix nebulosa*

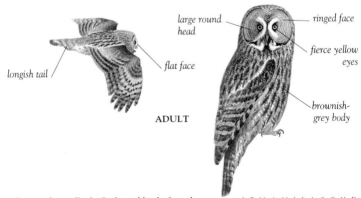

large round head

ringed face

fierce yellow eyes

longish tail

flat face

brownish-grey body

ADULT

Status: Large, almost Eagle Owl-sized bird of northern conifer forests with circumpolar distribution.
Identification: 65–70cm (25½–27½in). Upperparts grey, heavily barred and streaked with row of white spots on wing coverts and scapulars (a feature shared with Ural Owl). Large, rounded head with bold facial disc emphasized by rows of parallel barring around piercing yellow eyes. Frequently hunts during day unlike Ural Owl.
Voice: Deep and deliberate *whow-whow-whow-whow* repeated 8–12 times.
Habitat: Mature forests of pine and fir with open glades.
Similar Species: Ural Owl is greyer.

J F M A M J J A S O N D

Eagle Owl   *Bubo bubo*

huge rounded wings

bold ears

orange eyes

ADULT

Status: Huge, extremely powerful, nocturnal predator that has surprisingly survived in many parts of Europe despite persecution and a changing landscape.

Identification: 60–75cm (23½–29½in). Brown upperparts heavily barred and mottled black and buff. Underparts buffy, heavily streaked black, especially on breast. Large pale buffy facial disc with paler outer ring. Large orange-red eyes and large ear tufts. In flight, huge rounded wings are brown and buff and heavily barred; tail always appears short. Brown coloration like Long-eared Owl, and sheer size preclude confusion with any other European species.

Voice: Low-pitched *ooo-hu*; deep but far-carrying.

Habitat: Mostly mountains, precipitous hillsides and brown barren countryside with little or no human habitation or activity. Nests in cliff caves, on ground and in abandoned tree nests of other species. Surroundings mostly open with quantity of suitable large prey.

Similar Species: Great Grey Owl is only species anywhere near the size of Eagle Owl.

J F M A M J J A S O N D

Long-eared Owl   *Asio otus*

dark carpals

dark belly

orange-based primaries

orange eyes

ear tufts

finely streaked back

orange face

J F M A M J J A S O N D

Status: Strictly nocturnal owl, mostly of old conifer forests and belts, that stands very slim and upright.
Identification: 34–37cm (13–14in). Medium-sized owl with striking orange eyes, prominent facial disc and conspicuous ear tufts. Upperparts mottled buff and brown; underparts buffy, streaked brown. Scarce and secretive owl, lacking obviously distinctive voice. Forms communal roosts in winter. Pale orange patches on wings.
Voice: Low *oo-oo-oo*; juvenile has rusty hinge-like squeak.
Habitat: Boreal and other forests, small copses and plantations often conifers.
Similar Species: Tawny Owl is also nocturnal.

Short-eared Owl   *Asio flammeus*

gliding, hovering, harrier-like flight on long wings

dark carpals

creamy-based primaries

rounded head, yellow eyes

pale belly

blotchy back

white trailing edge

Status: Diurnal owl of marshes and moorland that breeds in north and is a winter visitor to most of Europe.
Identification: 36–39cm (14–15in). The owl most frequently seen hunting during daylight over marshes and open moors. Flat head and long rounded wings with dark carpal patches. Pale, almost white, below with dark wingtips and carpal patches. Quarters territory like harrier – hovers and glides with wings held in shallow 'V'.
Voice: High-pitched *kee-aw*; deep *boo-boo-boo*.
Habitat: Rough open country, rolling moorland of grass and heather, bogs, rough grazing, marshes and dunes.
Similar Species: None.

J F M A M J J A S O N D

Little Owl   *Athene noctua*

alert posture

bold supercilia, fierce expression

resting posture

rounded wings, bouncing flight

J F M A M J J A S O N D

Status: Small, buffy-brown owl, most often seen perched openly during daylight. Resident temperate Europe.
Identification: 21–23cm (8–9in). Brown upperparts boldly spotted whitish. Whitish underparts heavily streaked brown. Large, rounded head with black-edged facial disc, bold supercilia and staring yellow eyes create fierce expression. Sits openly, resembling round stone; when alert stands upright on long legs. Flies with distinctive bouncing flight, like a woodpecker.
Voice: Plaintive *keeoo*.
Habitat: Open countryside with copses and hedgerows.
Similar Species: Scops Owl is nocturnal.

Tengmalm's Owl   *Aegolius funereus*

heart-shaped head

bold facial disc

bold braces

bold braces

ADULT

J F M A M J J A S O N D

Status: Small, forest dwelling owl, about same size as Little Owl, but with much larger head and bold facial disc.
Identification: 24–27cm (9½–10½in). Upperparts dark grey-brown spotted with white on wings and scapulars; underparts white, streaked brown. Large pale facial disc with yellow eyes and distinct 'eye-bags'; black margins at sides. Tail short. Nests in tree holes.
Voice: A rapid *po-po-po-pop* repeated in quick succession after gap of less than second.
Habitat: Boreal and mixed forests; frequently uses Black Woodpecker holes.
Similar Species: See Hawk Owl and Little Owl.

European Nightjar *Caprimulgus europaeus*

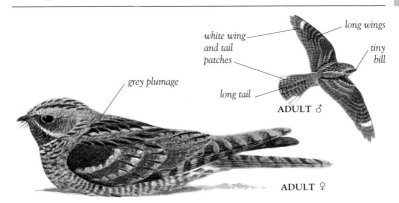

grey plumage

white wing and tail patches

long wings

tiny bill

long tail

ADULT ♂

ADULT ♀

J F M A M J J A S O N D

Status: Widespread, but scarce, summer visitor most often seen at dawn and dusk.
Identification: 25–28cm (10–11in). Heavily camouflaged in browns, buffs and greys. Male has conspicuous white patches on wings and tail, lacking in female. Best located by distinctive churring call. Long narrow wings and tail produce hawk-like silhouette as it flies silently, changing direction erratically and easily.
Voice: Distinctive churring similar to that made by vibrating tongue in mouth.
Habitat: Lowland heaths, felled forest clearings.
Similar Species: See Red-necked Nightjar.

Red-necked Nightjar *Caprimulgus ruficollis*

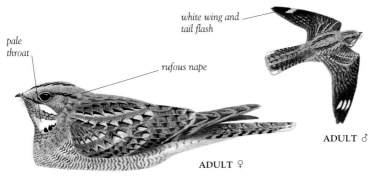

white wing and tail flash

pale throat

rufous nape

ADULT ♂

ADULT ♀

Status: Summer visitor to Iberia. Very similar to European Nightjar and most easily separated by different 'song'.
Identification: 30–32cm (12in). Mottled and barred in dark browns and buffs, and considerably more rufous than more widespread European Nightjar. Has large patch of white on sides of chin, particularly male, and broad rufous collar marks rear of neck. In flight, underparts rufous (difficult to see); both sexes show white in wing and tail.
Voice: Song quite distinct: repeated *cut-ok*, much slower than churring of European Nightjar, each syllable clear.
Habitat: Open, bare sandy areas, open woodlands.
Similar Species: European Nightjar as above.

J F M A M J J A S O N D

Common Swift   *Apus apus*

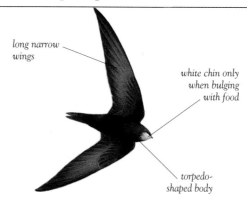

long narrow
wings

white chin only
when bulging
with food

torpedo-
shaped body

J F M A M J J A S O N D

Status: Common, often abundant, summer visitor throughout Europe mostly to towns and cities.
Identification: 16–17cm (6in). Superficially similar to swallows and martins but easily distinguished by longer and narrower sickle-shaped wings and all-black coloration. Most aerial of birds, coming to land (buildings and caves) only to lay and incubate eggs and feed young. Flickers wings and forms 'screaming' parties over colonies on summer evenings.
Voice: High-pitched screaming.
Habitat: Nests mainly in buildings in urban areas.
Similar Species: See Pallid Swift.

Pallid Swift   *Apus pallidus*

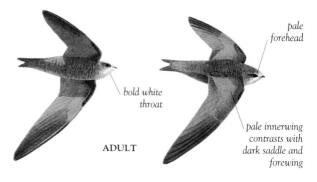

pale
forehead

bold white
throat

pale innerwing
contrasts with
dark saddle and
forewing

ADULT

J F M A M J J A S O N D

Status: Summer visitor to Mediterranean where often commonest swift along the coast.
Identification: 16–17cm (6½in). Long, sickle-shaped wings; slender, torpedo-shaped body; forked tail; and dark coloration all shared with Common Swift. Pallid has prominent white throat and is dark brown with pale innerwing contrasting with dark saddle and primaries. Structural differences include heavier body, broader wings and shorter forked tail.
Voice: High-pitched screaming.
Habitat: Coastal cliffs and large buildings.
Similar Species: Common Swift as above.

Alpine Swift *Apus melba*

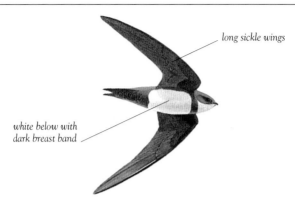

long sickle wings

white below with
dark breast band

J F M A M J J A S O N D

Status: Summer visitor Mediterranean and south European uplands; in lowlands uses human artifacts as nest sites.
Identification: 20–22cm (8–9in). Brownish plumage broken by white chin, and underparts separated by brown breast band. Only swift that shows this pattern. Size may not be apparent when flying high overhead, though slower wingbeats may help. Gregarious, forming dense feeding flocks and large colonies. Spends long periods away from colonies foraging over huge areas.
Voice: Loud chittering.
Habitat: Upland cliffs and crags, buildings, walls.
Similar Species: None.

White-rumped Swift *Apus caffer*

narrow white rump

long, deeply forked tail

long pointed wings

Status: First colonized Europe 30 years ago, now scarce summer visitor to south and central Spain.
Identification: 14cm (5½in). Smaller than other regular European swifts. Uniform sooty plumage broken by narrow 'horseshoe' white rump and paleness on chin. Deeply forked tail often obvious. Arrives late (May) and breeds in Red-rumped Swallow's nests. Vagrant Little Swift is smaller, with square white rump and square-cut tail.
Voice: Low twittering.
Habitat: Cliffs and caves in mountains, but also now in road culverts and concrete buildings.
Similar Species: Vagrant Little Swift has white rump.

J F M A M J J A S O N D

White-breasted Kingfisher *Halcyon smyrnensis*

massive red bill

chocolate head

white throat and breast

shining blue

white wing patch

J F M A M J J A S O N D

Status: A widespread Asiatic species that finds an outpost along the south-western shores of Turkey.
Identification: 26–28cm (10in). Large brown and blue kingfisher marked by large red bill and white breast. Head and nape is a rich chocolate-brown contrasting with white chin and breast, and blue back, tail and flight feathers. Wing coverts (shoulders) and belly are dark, rich brown. Huge red bill is obvious at all times.
Voice: Loud laughing calls.
Habitat: Watersides with perches including telegraph wires, trees and bushes. In Asia even in dry areas.
Similar Species: None.

Common Kingfisher *Alcedo atthis*

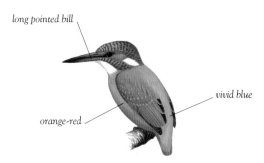

long pointed bill

vivid blue

orange-red

J F M A M J J A S O N D

Status: Exotic, jewel-like bird, most often seen as a flash of bright blue as it dashes over river or lake.
Identification: 15–16cm (5½–6in). Upperparts blue-green with vividly blue rump; underparts bright orange-red with white bib and nape mark. Catches fishes by diving head-first into water.
Voice: Metallic *chee* or *chee-kee* rapidly repeated.
Habitat: Confined to streams, rivers and lakes, though southern birds also use seashores with still, clear water. Northern birds may move to tideline in severe winters.
Similar Species: None, but White-breasted and Pied Kingfishers share behaviour characteristics.

Pied Kingfisher   *Ceryle rudis*

heavy black bill

black crest

hovers

double breast band

pied upperparts

♂

♂

J F M A M J J A S O N D

Status: Only black and white kingfisher in our area, resident in southern Turkey.
Identification: 24–26cm (9½–10in). Boldly black and white kingfisher that is both obvious where present and easily identified. Frequently seen in flight, when regularly hovers over water. Male has one broad and one narrow breast band. Black crown, white supercilium and black eye-stripe. Upperparts mottled black and white; underparts white. Large black bill. Female lacks second breast band.
Voice: Loud chattering.
Habitat: Rivers and ponds with adjacent trees and bushes.
Similar Species: None.

European Roller   *Coracias garrulus*

bulky head and body

chestnut back

blue head and body

black and blue wings

Status: Chunky, colourful summer visitor to southern and eastern Europe, most often seen perched on telegraph poles or wires, or in tumbling display flight.
Identification: 30–32cm (11–13in). Large head and entire underparts pale blue, back chestnut-brown, wings blue and black. In flight, blues shine in sunlight producing dramatic effect. Juvenile buffy brown with blue and black wings. No other European bird can be confused.
Voice: Harsh *kraak-ak*.
Habitat: Old oak and pine forests with clearings and dead or damaged trees for nest sites.
Similar Species: None

J F M A M J J A S O N D

Blue-cheeked Bee-eater *Merops superciliosus*

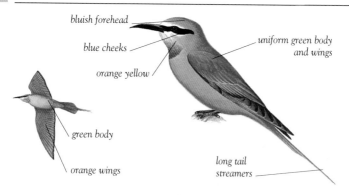

bluish forehead

blue cheeks

orange yellow

uniform green body and wings

green body

orange wings

long tail streamers

J F M A M J J A S O N D

Status: Summer visitor that just creeps across the Syrian border into Turkey, but which often overshoots to Europe. **Identification:** 28–31cm (11½in). Longer overall than European Bee-eater, but Blue-cheeked is smaller, slimmer. Similar in shape and behaviour, but overall green plumage broken only by distinctive head pattern of blue forehead and ear coverts (cheeks) and orange-yellow throat. Long tail streamers and uniform pale orange underwing. **Voice:** Liquid *preep* that, though similar to European Bee-eater, is clearly different to those who know that bird well. **Habitat:** Arid lowlands, often near water. **Similar Species:** Beware Little Green Bee-eater.

European Bee-eater *Merops apiaster*

chestnut back

yellow throat

buffy underwing

green-blue breast

tail streamers

J F M A M J J A S O N D

Status: Gregarious and noisy summer visitor to southern and eastern Europe. An aerial jumble of bright colours. **Identification:** 27–29cm (11in). Adult brown on head, nape and folded wings; with dark eye-stripe, yellow chin and blue underparts. Tail green with two extended central feathers forming 'pin-tail'. Flies fast and acrobatically on pointed wings with much gliding; underwing rich buff. Juveniles more green and blue, but brownish crown separates from rare Blue-cheeked Bee-eater. **Voice:** Very distinctive, rich, liquid *quip-quip*. **Habitat:** Dry, open areas, often near water, with sand banks. **Similar Species:** See Blue-cheeked Bee-eater above.

Hoopoe   *Upupa epops*

crest

black and
white wings

decurved bill

short legs

J F M A M J J A S O N D

Status: Distinctive summer visitor throughout temperate and Mediterranean Europe. Some winter southern Iberia.
Identification: 27–29cm (10½–11½in). Distinctive at rest and in flight. Sandy fawn above and below, marked by long erectile crest with black tip. Wings and tail black with broad white bars. Short legs and long black decurved bill. Spends much time on ground where may be surprisingly inconspicuous; also perches freely in trees.
Voice: Distinctive, far-carrying *poo-poo-poo*, repeated.
Habitat: Orchards, open woodland, agricultural land with dry-stone walls, old barns and disused buildings.
Similar Species: None.

Wryneck   *Jynx torquilla*

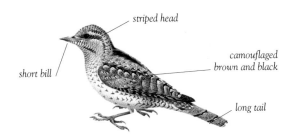

striped head

camouflaged
brown and black

short bill

long tail

Status: Highly elusive summer visitor that spends much of its time on the ground or hidden in bushes.
Identification: 15–16cm (5½–6in). Highly camouflaged relative of the woodpeckers. Does not behave like a woodpecker, although voice similar to Lesser Spotted. Upperparts brown, variously mottled, streaked and barred with black, buff and grey. Short bill, striped head pattern and long tail produce unusual appearance.
Voice: Far-carrying *kyee-kyee-kyee* repeated. Silent once eggs laid.
Habitat: Open woods, parks, clearings, orchards, groves.
Similar Species: None.

J F M A M J J A S O N D

Grey-headed Woodpecker *Picus canus*

grey forehead

♀

grey nape

red forehead

black moustache

no barring

♂

J F M A M J J A S O N D

Status: Like Green Woodpecker but smaller; more confined to uplands and areas with continental climate.
Identification: 25–26cm (10in). Upperparts green, underparts yellowish-grey, or grey. Head grey marked with red forehead in adult male and fine black moustache in adult male and female. Lacks barring on flanks and has smaller bill than Green Woodpecker.
Voice: Flute-like *ku-ku* repeated five to eight times. Drums.
Habitat: Usually at greater altitudes; in smaller areas of woodland; and often among stands of pure conifers.
Similar Species: Green Woodpecker, as above, has red crown in all plumages.

Green Woodpecker *Picus viridis*

yellow rump

red crown

black and red moustache

♀

red crown

black moustache

barred above and below

♂

JUVENILE

J F M A M J J A S O N D

Status: Large green and yellow woodpecker that is resident through most of Europe. Often forages on ground for ants.
Identification: 30–33cm (11½–13in). Bright red crown, moustachial stripe red, bordered black in male, pure black in female. Upperparts green, rump yellow, tail dark, barred and pointed. Dagger-like silver-grey bill; grey legs. Typical undulating flight. Juvenile has heavily streaked face and barred underparts.
Voice: Loud, laughing *keu-keu-keu-keu*. Rarely drums.
Habitat: Mature open deciduous and mixed forests, but also open country with copses, heathland, gardens.
Similar Species: See Grey-headed Woodpecker.

Great Spotted Woodpecker   *Dendrocopos major*

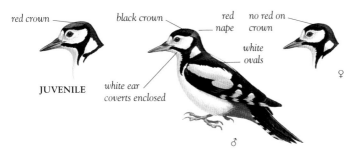

red crown

black crown

red nape

no red on crown

white ovals

JUVENILE

white ear coverts enclosed

♀

♂

Status: Widespread, often common, resident of woodlands throughout Europe. The standard 'pied' woodpecker.
Identification: 22–24cm (8–9in). Upperparts black broken by white cheeks, neck patch, and two bold white ovals on back. Adult male has red patch on hind crown (lacking in female). Juvenile has red crown. Both sexes frequently drum on dead wood producing loud, far-carrying hollow sound. Deeply undulating flight.
Voice: Sharp *chik*, repeated and terminating in chatter.
Habitat: Virtually any type of woodland.
Similar Species: Syrian and Middle Spotted Woodpeckers See Woodpecker Backs page 207.

J F M A M J J A S O N D

Syrian Woodpecker   *Dendrocopos syriacus*

lacks cheek stripe

open-ended ear coverts

white faced

lacks cheek stripe

white ovals

♀

♂

Status: Very similar to Great Spotted Woodpecker. Resident south-eastern Europe around villages.
Identification: 22–23cm (9in). Like Great Spotted black and white, with red undertail coverts; also male has red spot on nape; and female no red on crown. Major distinction is lack of black bar joining moustachial streak to crown creating 'open-ended' ear coverts and a 'white-faced' appearance.
Voice: Loud *schik*; drumming.
Habitat: Villages and gardens.
Similar Species: Great Spotted and Middle Spotted Woodpeckers. See Woodpecker Backs page 207

J F M A M J J A S O N D

Middle Spotted Woodpecker   *Dendrocopos medius*

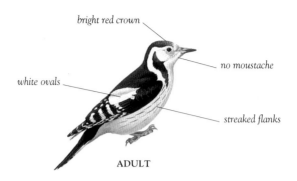

bright red crown

no moustache

white ovals

streaked flanks

ADULT

J F M A M J J A S O N D

Status: Smaller version of Great Spotted Woodpecker, resident through most of temperate Europe.
Identification: 20–22cm (8–8½in). One of three 'pied' woodpeckers with bold white ovals on back. Similar to Great Spotted and Syrian Woodpeckers, but noticeably smaller with fulvous wash on breast that is finely streaked on flanks. In all plumages bright red crown separates from other species, except juvenile Great Spotted and Syrian.
Voice: Repeated *qua-qua* four to six times; drumming.
Habitat: Mature deciduous woods, with hornbeam and oak.
Similar Species: Great Spotted and Syrian Woodpeckers as above. See Woodpecker Backs page 207.

White-backed Woodpecker   *Dendrocopos leucotos*

red crown

ladder-backed wings

moustachial streak

♀

white rump

streaked flanks

♂

J F M A M J J A S O N D

Status: Shade larger than Great Spotted Woodpecker, but resident of hill and montane forests.
Identification: 24–26cm (9½–10in). Like Great Spotted Woodpecker, but larger, longer-necked and longer-billed. 'Ladder-back' pattern across wings rather than white ovals. White rump extending up lower back. Underparts heavily streaked picks out from all other 'pied' woodpeckers. Males have red crowns.
Voice: Quick *juk-juk*; drumming.
Habitat: Mature forests with dead and decaying wood.
Similar Species: Smaller Middle Spotted Woodpecker. See Woodpecker Backs page 207.

Lesser Spotted Woodpecker *Dendrocopos minor*

♀ *buffy crown*

red crown

ladder back

streaked underparts

♂

J F M A M J J A S O N D

Status: Tiny, sparrow-sized woodpecker that spends most of its time among woodland canopy, easily overlooked.
Identification: 14–15cm (5¹/₂–6¹/₂in). Agile climber, often on thin twigs near tops of trees. Male has red crown, female buffy white. Upperparts black, boldly barred white across back; white cheeks. Both sexes drum, producing faster, higher pitched sound than other woodpeckers.
Voice: High-pitched *kee-kee-kee-kee* repeated.
Habitat: Open broad-leaved woods. Avoids conifers.
Similar Species: Small size and canopy foraging preclude confusion with any other European woodpecker. See Woodpecker Backs below.

Woodpecker Backs

White-backed Woodpecker	Great Spotted Woodpecker	Syrian Woodpecker	Middle Spotted Woodpecker	Three-toed Woodpecker	Lesser Spotted Woodpecker

Back patterns of the 'pied' woodpeckers are not only an important clue to their identity, but often the only view obtained as the birds climb tree trunks. A cursory glance is sufficient to divide the six species into 'ladder-backs' and 'white-wing ovals'. The 'ladder-backs' offer more clues from the rear. Two have white backs – White-backed is large and white is confined to the rump. Three-toed is smaller with white extending from rump to nape (a 'proper' white-back). Lesser Spotted has a pure, uninterrupted 'ladder-back' and is much smaller. The 'white-wing ovals' – Great Spotted, Syrian and Middle Spotted must then be separated by further views of crown and face. These are the species that cause most problems and frustrations, but a clear order of decreasingly complex face pattern runs: Great Spotted, Syrian, Middle Spotted, or GSM.

Three-toed Woodpecker *Picoides tridactylus*

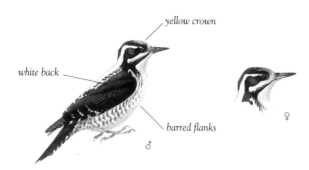

yellow crown

white back

barred flanks

♂

♀

Status: Strictly a coniferous woodland woodpecker of Continental mountains and northern boreal forests.
Identification: 21–22cm (8½in). Distinct from other 'pied' woodpeckers in lacking bold pattern of white in wings. Very 'black' woodpecker, with black head marked with white lines, heavily barred underparts, largely black wings and white rump and back. Adults have yellow on crown.
Voice: Quiet *tuk-tuk*; drumming.
Habitat: In north favours damp, marshy woodland. In south prefers high-level forests.
Similar Species: White-backed woodpecker as above. See Woodpecker Backs page 207.

Black Woodpecker *Dryocopus martius*

red forehead

black forehead

large tail

♂

♀

J F M A M J J A S O N D

Status: Largest European woodpecker, resident through forests and woods of temperate and northern Europe.
Identification: 45–47cm (18in). Virtually size of crow, which it frequently resembles in flight. Completely black, except crown, which is red in male and red at rear crown in female. Despite size, difficult to see. Far-carrying calls often best signs of presence. Habitat requirements help concentrate search for this sought-after bird.
Voice: Yelping *kee-aa, kee-aa, kee-aa*; also *kwick-kwick*; and loud drumming.
Habitat: Conifer forests, with stands of deciduous trees.
Similar Species: May resemble Crow, Rook or Jackdaw.

Calandra Lark *Melanocorypha calandra*

massive bill

large dark
underwing

black neck
patch

white
trailing
edge

short tail

J F M A M J J A S O N D

Status: Large, chunky lark, resident of grasslands and steppes from the Mediterranean eastwards.
Identification: 18–20cm (7–8in). Large, thick-set lark with stout bill, short tail and broad, rounded wings. Upperparts streaked dull brown; underparts white with streaking and two bold black crescents on breast. Most often seen flying when almost 'no-necked, bull-headed' appearance and big, rounded wings most obvious characters. Look for white trailing edge on wings.
Voice: Nasal *kreet*; elaborate song in circling flight.
Habitat: Open grasslands and steppes, but also on crops.
Similar Species: Bimaculated Lark lacks white wing edge.

Bimaculated Lark *Melanocorypha bimaculata*

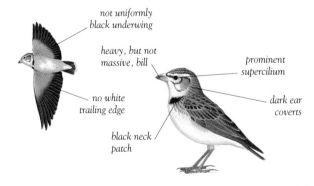

not uniformly
black underwing

heavy, but not
massive, bill

prominent
supercilium

no white
trailing edge

dark ear
coverts

black neck
patch

Status: Large, chunky lark very similar to Calandra that is summer visitor to stony plains of Turkey.
Identification: 16–17cm (6½in). Slightly smaller than Calandra Lark; shares robust build, heavy bill and black neck patches. Best distinguished in flight when lack of white trailing edge to wing is diagnostic. Underwing not uniformly black. More prominent supercilium and dark margined ear coverts create less bland face than Calandra.
Voice: Mellow *prrp*; song similar to Calandra.
Habitat: Stony uplands, dry stony heaths and semi-desert.
Similar Species: Calandra Lark as above. Beware – in parts of Turkey the two species can occur together.

J F M A M J J A S O N D

Short-toed Lark   *Calandrella brachydactyla*

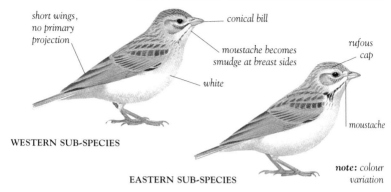

short wings, no primary projection

conical bill

moustache becomes smudge at breast sides

rufous cap

white

moustache

WESTERN SUB-SPECIES

EASTERN SUB-SPECIES

note: *colour variation*

J F M A M J J A S O N D

Status: Torpedo-shaped lark that flies low and strong in small parties. Summer visitor to Mediterranean.
Identification: 13–15cm (5–6in). Best feature, apart from shape in flight, is black moustache that widens to a smudge on side of neck. Pale, stubby bill, sandy or greyish upperparts and darkish bar across closed wing best field marks, but thickset shape, size and white underparts characteristic, even in flight.
Voice: Hard *chi-chirrp*.
Habitat: Dry grassland steppe, dried out sandy and muddy areas.
Similar Species: See Lesser Short-toed Lark.

Lesser Short-toed Lark   *Calandrella rufescens*

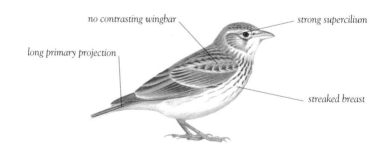

no contrasting wingbar

strong supercilium

long primary projection

streaked breast

J F M A M J J A S O N D

Status: Scarce resident in south-eastern and south-western corners of our area that frequents dry areas.
Identification: 13.5–14.5cm (5½in). Very similar to Short-toed Lark and to be distinguished with care. Small, round-headed and short-billed lark that lacks black neck patches of Short-toed, as well as black bar on wing coverts. Streaking on breast and sides of throat diagnostic, but beware 'false streaking' when head turned or feathers ruffled. Strong pale supercilia meet over bill.
Voice: Rolled *prrt*.
Habitat: Poor, bare stony ground, gravels and dry clays.
Similar Species: Short-toed Lark as above.

Crested Lark   *Galerida cristata*

large bill

spiked crest

lightly
streaked breast

rufous outertail

J F M A M J J A S O N D

Status: Widespread resident through temperate Europe. Resembles Sky Lark, but marked by boldly spiked crest.
Identification: 16.5–17.5cm (6½–7in). Upperparts brown and buff; underparts pale with extensive streaking on breast. Tail short with rufous outer feathers. Bill long and decurved. Rufous underwing often difficult to see. Only really confusable with Thekla Lark from which it must be distinguished with greatest care.
Voice: Liquid *wee-wee-ooo*.
Habitat: Grassy, lowland plains, open fields, margins of saltpans and marshes.
Similar Species: Thekla Lark overlaps only in Iberia.

Thekla Lark   *Galerida theklae*

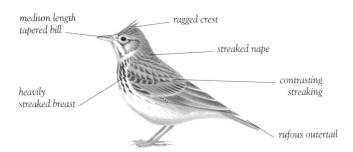

medium length
tapered bill

ragged crest

streaked nape

contrasting
streaking

heavily
streaked breast

rufous outertail

J F M A M J J A S O N D

Status: Resident Iberia and south-western France. Often at altitude but to sea level if appropriate landform found.
Identification: 15.5–16.5cm (6in). Generally more upland bird than very similar Crested with less 'spiked' crest, smaller, straighter bill, and more heavily streaked breast with streaking extending across 'collar' to nape. If visible, underwing grey, not rufous, at least in European form.
Voice: Similar to Crested Lark, but a flute-like whistled *tu-twee-ooo* with a rise and fall in the final note.
Habitat: Dry and bare areas among rocks and boulders or thick scrub; oleandar scrub in dry stream beds.
Similar Species: Crested Lark as above.

Wood Lark *Lullula arborea*

supercilia
meet at nape

white corners
to tail

black and
white mark at
bend of wing

no flank
streaking

short tail

J F M A M J J A S O N D

Status: Small, stockily build lark of tree heaths and open woodland. Locally common resident or summer visitor.
Identification: 14.5–16cm (6–6½in). Favours areas of short grass with scattered trees and shrubs. Similar to Sky Lark but tail obviously shorter and only hint of crest; prominent pale supercilia meet at nape to create capped appearance. Small black and white patch at bend of wing. Upperparts streaked brown and buff. Distinctive song uttered from tree-top or in flight.
Voice: Fluty *too-loo-eet* distinctive and far-carrying.
Habitat: Open areas with scant vegetation, scattered trees.
Similar Species: See Tree Pipit, which is slimmer.

Sky Lark *Alauda arvensis*

faint
supercilium

small flat crest

whitish
trailing edge

streaked breast
and flanks

white outertail

J F M A M J J A S O N D

Status: Common and widespread resident in west, summer visitor in east. Huge numbers move westwards to winter.
Identification: 17–18cm (6½–7in). Heavily-streaked, ground-dwelling bird of wide variety of habitats. Most often seen in towering song flight during spring and early summer. Bulky shape distinguishes from pipits; flat crest and long, white-edged tail separate from Wood Lark.
Voice: Liquid *chirrup*; fine persistent warbling song uttered in towering flight.
Habitat: Heaths, commons, grassland and plough; also hillsides and open taiga, moorland, marshes.
Similar Species: See Wood Lark.

Shore Lark   *Eremophila alpestris*

white
outertail

black and yellow
face pattern

WINTER

♂ **SUMMER**

J F M A M J J A S O N D

Status: Resident Balkan mountains and summer visitor
Scandinavian mountains, tundra; winter visitor to shores.
Identification: 16–17cm (6–6½in). Difficult to locate
until it flies. Buffy- brown above and white below. Shows
white outertail feathers; distinctive black and yellow face
pattern and two tiny black' horns' on top of head. Face
pattern subdued in winter but still unmistakable. Usually
in small flocks, often in areas occupied by Snow Buntings.
In summer, head pattern more clear-cut and colourful.
Voice: Shrill *tseep* or *tseep-tseep* like wagtail or pipit.
Habitat: Mountain plateaux. Winters shingle beaches.
Similar Species: None.

Dupont's Lark   *Chersophilus duponti*

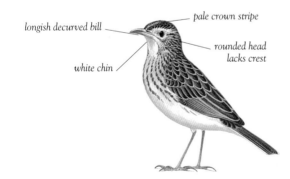

pale crown stripe

longish decurved bill

rounded head
lacks crest

white chin

Status: Highly secretive and crepuscular lark that runs
rather than flies when disturbed. Resident Spain.
Identification: 17–18cm (7in). More difficult to locate
than to identify. Streaked upperparts, with rounded crest-
less head, which shows pale crown stripe. Buffy breast with
fine lines of dark streaking and white belly. Longish
decurved bill. Slimmer, more upright than Crested Lark.
Voice: Greenfinch-like nasal calls as well as twittering song.
Habitat: Dry, flat, open areas with clumps of vegetation.
In winter, mixes with other larks on cereal fields.
Similar Species: Length of bill and lack of crest preclude
confusion with adult Crested and Thekla Larks.

J F M A M J J A S O N D

Sand Martin   *Riparia riparia*

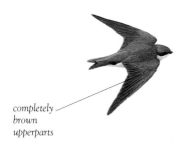

completely brown upperparts

breast band

J F M A M J J A S O N D

Status: Summer visitor throughout Europe, though locally restricted by lack of suitable nesting habitat.
Identification: 11–12cm (4½–5in). Swallow-like with shallow, forked tail and sharply angled wings. Erratic flight with less frequent glides than similar species. Upperparts sandy brown; underparts white. Distinctive brown breast band. Always gregarious. In winter and on passage, roosts among dense reeds, often in company with Barn Swallows.
Voice: Thin *chirruping* twitter.
Habitat: Nests sandy cliffs and banks.
Similar Species: Larger Crag Martin.

Crag Martin   *Ptyonoprogne rupestris*

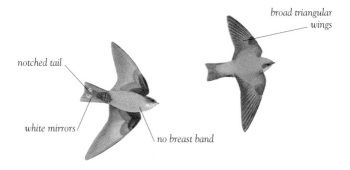

broad triangular wings

notched tail

white mirrors

no breast band

J F M A M J J A S O N D

Status: Chunky 'swallow' that is resident or summer visitor to hills and mountains of Mediterranean.
Identification: 14.5–15cm (5½in). Predominantly alpine bird, but descending to sea level in winter. Brown above and buff below, lacking breast band of Sand Martin, only other 'swallow' of similar colour. Square-cut tail shows row of pale spots when spread. Much thicker set, with heavier body, than other 'swallows'; wings broader and more triangular, glides more frequently.
Voice: Thin *chirruping*.
Habitat: Mountain and hill crags and gorges.
Similar Species: Sand Martin is lighter in build.

Barn Swallow *Hirundo rustica*

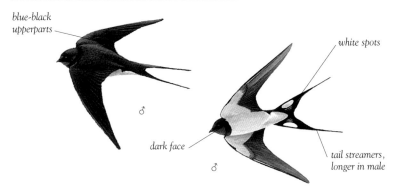

blue-black upperparts

♂

white spots

dark face

♂

tail streamers, longer in male

J F M A M J J A S O N D

Status: Common and widespread summer visitor virtually throughout our region. Familiar in towns and villages.
Identification: 16–22cm (6½–8½in). Long angled wings and deeply-forked tail streamers in adult; streamers longer in male than female. Spread tail shows row of white spots. Upperparts dark metallic blue; face and throat red, bordered below by narrow, dark breast band. From below is only hirundine with dark head.
Voice: High-pitched *vit-vit-vit* of alarm; song a twittering trill.
Habitat: Nests in buildings and caves.
Similar Species: See Red-rumped Swallow.

Red-rumped Swallow *Hirundo daurica*

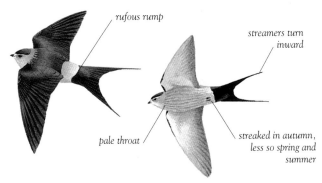

rufous rump

streamers turn inward

pale throat

streaked in autumn, less so spring and summer

J F M A M J J A S O N D

Status: Summer visitor that has successfully expanded range northwards.
Identification: 17–18cm (6½–7in). Body more robust and torpedo-like than Barn Swallow's, a shape accentuated by tail streamers that turn distinctly inwards. Upperparts black; entire underparts, narrow collar and broad rump rusty-pink.
Voice: Soft *chirrup*.
Habitat: Mountain and sea caves and cliffs, but increasingly bridges and road culverts, as well as unfinished buildings.
Similar Species: Barn Swallow as above.

House Martin *Delichon urbica*

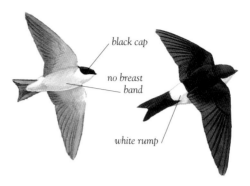

black cap

no breast band

white rump

J F M A M J J A S O N D

Status: Common summer visitor that nests under eaves of buildings forming colonies, often overlapping nests.
Identification: 12–13cm (4½–5in). Compact, black and white, swallow-like bird. Requires nearby source of soft mud to construct nearly spherical nest. Blue-black on crown and back; black wings and tail; prominent white rump and pure white underparts. Gregarious but does not join communal roosts of Barn Swallows and Sand Martins in reedbeds.
Voice: Harsh *chirrup*, quite unlike other hirundines.
Habitat: Mountain and sea caves; now mostly in towns.
Similar Species: See Barn Swallow.

Swallow and Martin Nests

Few birds leave such easily identifiable signs of their presence as the hirundines – the swallows and martins. In their absence, even after the birds themselves have left, proof of breeding can be obtained by locating and correctly identifying their nests. All are constructed of reinforced mud droplets, but unmistakable shape is characteristic.

Barn Swallow: Simple, shallow cap, usually resting on ledge inside building or cave. Trailing grasses or feathers.

Red-rumped Swallow: Flask-shaped structure with narrow entrance tunnel widening to form nest chamber. Fixed to horizontal undersurfaces of culvert, drainage pipe or unfinished building.

House Martin: Neatly gourd-shaped nest with narrow half-oval entrance. Usually fixed to building, most often in angle of wall and overhanging roof. Colonial.

Crag Martin: Deep, open cup fixed to cliff wall and protected by overhang, or inside shallow cave or cave entrance.

Richard's Pipit   *Anthus novaeseelandiae*

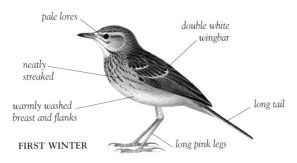

pale lores

double white wingbar

neatly streaked

warmly washed breast and flanks

long tail

long pink legs

FIRST WINTER

J F M A M J J A S O N D

Status: Scarce, but regular, mainly autumn visitor, from Siberia to Europe, mainly Britain.
Identification: 18cm (7in). Largest European pipit, only Tawny Pipit comparable in size. Olive-brown, heavily streaked upperparts. White underparts neatly streaked on breast and washed orange-buff on breast and flanks. Strong yellowish bill. Size and particularly upright stance separate from all European pipits save Tawny, which has less streaked back, even in first winter plumage.
Voice: Loud distinctive sparrow-like *shreep*.
Habitat: Damp grasslands.
Similar Species: See Tawny Pipit and above.

Tawny Pipit   *Anthus campestris*

dark spots form line across wing

unstreaked

finely streaked

ADULT

JUVENILE MOULTING TO FIRST WINTER

J F M A M J J A S O N D

Status: Summer visitor to south and east Europe.
Identification: 16–17cm (6–6½in). Substantially larger than other pipits, generally paler with less streaking, particularly on underparts. Adults sandy above, with streaking confined to margins of flight feathers. Underparts pale buff. Line of dark spots forms prominent bar across closed wing. Juveniles darker and more streaked on back and upper breast, but always paler and greyer than any northern pipit.
Voice: Wagtail-like *tseep*.
Habitat: Low, dry, flat landscapes, sparse grasslands.
Similar Species: See equally large Richard's Pipit.

Water Pipit   *Anthus spinoletta*

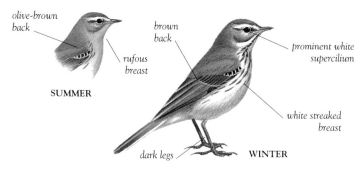

olive-brown
back

*rufous
breast*

SUMMER

brown
back

*prominent white
supercilium*

*white streaked
breast*

dark legs   **WINTER**

J F M A M J J A S O N D

Status: High altitude breeder that is widespread winter
visitor to southern and western Europe.
Identification: 15–16.5cm (6–6½in). The combination of
unstreaked back, bold supercilium and white outertail
make for straightforward separation from other pipits at all
times. Finely streaked white breast in winter; unstreaked
creamy buff in spring. Recently separated from Rock Pipit
as distinct species.
Voice: Clear *weest*.
Habitat: Open stony mountain plateaux with scant
vegetation. Winters freshwater margins.
Similar Species: Other pipits.

Rock Pipit   *Anthus petrosus*

*dull
upperparts*

*grey
outer-tail*

dark legs

petrosus

*pale supercilium
more prominent*

*darker than
Meadow
Pipit*

*fewer
streaks on
whiter belly*

dark legs

littoralis **SPRING**

J F M A M J J A S O N D

Status: Summer visitor to Scandinavian shores, resident
British shores winter visitor.
Identification: 15–16.5cm (6–6½in). Distinct subspecies.
British Rock Pipit *A.p.petrosus* is streaked black on olive
above, black on buff below; short supercilium; grey
outertail. Scandinavian Rock Pipit, *A.p.littoralis*, streaked
brownish above with prominent supercilium. White belly;
fine streaking on pinkish breast; grey outertail. Darker and
more uniformly than Meadow Pipit at all seasons.
Voice: Clear *weest*.
Habitat: Mostly along rocky shorelines.
Similar Species: Meadow and Red-throated Pipit.

Red-throated Pipit   *Anthus cervinus*

boldly streaked

rusty throat

boldly streaked

white bib

boldly streaked

ADULT SUMMER   **ADULT WINTER**

J F M A M J J A S O N D

Status: Summer visitor to northern Scandinavia, passage migrant through eastern Europe.
Identification: 14–15cm (5¾in). Upperparts very heavily streaked to rump; underparts white, heavily streaked black. Overall effect is to produce more heavily streaked and more 'contrasted' bird than Meadow Pipit. In spring and summer, unstreaked throat pale pink; in winter, throat still obvious as white bib.
Voice: Thin *tseez*.
Habitat: Breeds open shrubby tundra and Arctic meadows. On passage on stony ground with poor vegetation.
Similar Species: Meadow Pipit as above.

Meadow Pipit   *Anthus pratensis*

streaking less contrasting

white outer-tail

streaked breast

pale legs

darker/greyer type

J F M A M J J A S O N D

Status: Common and widespread breeder and winter visitor. Resident north-western Europe.
Identification: 14–15cm (5½–6in). Olive-brown or grey-brown above with broad dark streaking; streaked buffy breast and white belly, streaked flanks. Legs pinkish-brown; white outertail feathers. Often gregarious outside breeding season.
Voice: High-pitched *tissip* or *eest*; accelerating *trill* in parachuting display flight.
Habitat: Mountains, moors, heaths, marshes, estuaries.
Similar Species: Rock Pipit along shorelines; see also Tree and Red-throated Pipits.

Tree Pipit *Anthus trivialis*

clean markings

white outertail

'clean' streaking
on yellowish
breast

white belly

pale legs

J F M A M J J A S O N D

Status: Summer visitor to open woodlands.
Identification: 14–16cm (5½–6½in). Buffy upperparts
lightly streaked brown; underparts pale yellowish with
clear lines of black streaking that extends flanks. A clean-
cut, neatly marked bird compared with Meadow Pipit.
Well-marked creamy supercilium is a further feature.
Voice distinct, frequently uttered in flight, starting and
terminating on perch.
Voice: Loud descending *trill* with drawn-out *see-see-see*
ending. Also harsh *tees*.
Habitat: Woodlands and overgrown heaths with perches.
Similar Species: Meadow Pipit less cleanly marked.

Pied Wagtail *Motacilla alba*

sooty back

JUVENILE PIED

grey back

WHITE ♀ SUMMER

black of chin
never meets
black of crown in
White Wagtail

PIED ♀ SUMMER

white chin

black chin

WHITE ♂ WINTER

white chin

PIED ♂ WINTER **PIED ♂ SUMMER**

black chin

WHITE ♂ SUMMER

J F M A M J J A S O N D

Status: Widespread resident, but summer visitor north and
east Europe.
Identification: 17–18cm (6½–7in). Subspecies in Britain is
M.a.yarrellii. Male mainly black above with white face and
outertail. Black bib terminates in broad black breast band;
remaining underparts white. Juvenile and first winter have
grey backs. Continental subspecies *M.a.alba*, White
Wagtail, has pale grey back.
Voice: Harsh *chis-ick*; disjointed *twitter*.
Habitat: Open areas, with or without water.
Similar Species: Citrine and Grey Wagtails, especially
first winter, almost lacking yellow on underparts.

Grey Wagtail   *Motacilla cinerea*

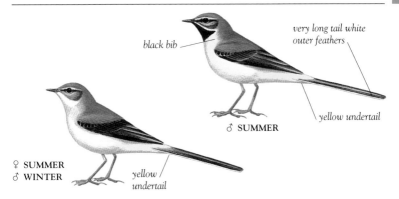

black bib

very long tail white outer feathers

♂ SUMMER

yellow undertail

♀ SUMMER
♂ WINTER

yellow undertail

J F M A M J J A S O N D

Status: Closely associated with water.
Identification: 18–20cm (7–8in). Large, clean-looking wagtail with longer tail than other species that is constantly wagged. Upperparts grey with white supercilium, yellow-green rump, and long, white-edged, black tail. Underparts white with yellow undertail coverts and variable yellow on breast. In summer, male has black bib.
Voice: Metallic *tzitzi*.
Habitat: Fast-flowing streams with boulders and an overhang of trees; also slower streams with weirs
Similar Species: Compare Yellow Wagtail (green back) and Citrine Wagtail (grey back).

Citrine Wagtail   *Motacilla citreola*

grey back

yellow face

bold double wingbar

grey back

bold double wingbar

grey back

bold double wingbar

ADULT ♂

ADULT ♀

JUVENILE

Status: Summer visitor to Russia and Ukraine; scarce passage migrant through Balkans; vagrant Europe.
Identification: 16–17cm (6–6½in). Like Yellow Wagtail, but larger in body and shorter in tail. Head and underparts yellow; back pale grey. Summer male has black half-collar at base of nape. Juvenile white below and pale grey above, with black and white wings. In all plumages, grey back and bold white double wingbar are best features.
Voice: Metallic *tsreep*.
Habitat: Marshy tundra with thickets and bushes.
Similar Species: Yellow Wagtail as above; Pied Wagtail lacks bold white double wing bar.

J F M A M J J A S O N D

Yellow Wagtail *Motacilla flava*

flava

cinereocapilla

iberiae

thunbergi

feldegg

green back

yellow underparts

♂

JUVENILE

yellow-green back

flavissima

♀

leucocephala

lutea

beema

pygmaea

simillima

Status: Widespread summer visitor to damp marshes and meadows. Several subspecies can be recognized in the field, mainly by the head pattern of summer males.

Identification: 16–17cm (6½–7in). Slim, elegant summer visitor distinguished by yellow underparts, green back and typical wagtail bounce of long, white-edged, black tail. Spends much time walking, often around domestic stock. Eleven subspecies, recognized mainly by head colour of breeding males, each of which occupies separate range, have occurred in our area. Hybrids are frequent where ranges meet and individuals can show characters of other subspecies and are not sure guide to wandering or vagrancy. Ten heads illustrated, plus one fully illustrated subspecies

J F M A M J J A S O N D

M.f.flavissima. Several subspecies may occur together on migration, especially in eastern Mediterranean. M.f.*flavissima* Britain; M.f.*lutea* Lower Volga; M.f.*flava* north-central Europe; M.f.*beema* Volga-Ural to Siberia; M.f.*leucocephala* Mongolia; M.f.*cinereocapilla* Italy; M.f.*iberiae* Spain and Portugal; M.f.*pygmaea* Egypt; M.f.*feldegg* Greece and Turkey; M.f.*thunbergi* Scandinavia; M.f.*simillima* eastern Siberia. In all subspecies particular attention must be paid to supercilium, colour of ear coverts, colour of throat and colour of crown. The difference, for example, between *thunbergi* and *feldegg* is the former's white throat. Between *cinereocapilla* and *iberiae* the latter's bold supercilium.

Voice: A loud *see-ip.*

Habitat: Damp grasslands, marshes and floods.

Similar Species: See Citrine Wagtail.

Yellow-vented Bulbul *Pycnonotus xanthopygos*

crest

eye-ring

black head

short rounded wings

long tail

J F M A M J J A S O N D

Status: The only representative of this Old World tropical family to penetrate our area, in Turkey.
Identification: 19cm (7½in). Bulbuls are well-proportioned birds marked by longish tails and a crested appearance, often with contrasting head and undertail coloration. This species has upperparts and tail greyish-brown shading darker to black over crested head. Underparts buffy with yellow vent. Clear pale eye-ring. Several other bulbuls also show yellow vents, but are not found in our area.
Voice: Clear, loud flute-like whistles.
Habitat: Wide variety of landscapes with trees and shrubs.
Similar Species: None in our area.

Waxwing *Bombycilla garrulus*

crest

black bib

yellow on wings and tail

Status: Chubby, northern forest bird that erupts south and west irregularly.
Identification: 17–18.5cm (7in). Decidedly Starling-like shape and size, but pinkish brown in colour. Swept-back crest, black lores and chin patch broken by white moustachial streak produce 'cross' expression. Black wings marked by tiny wax-like spots of red and yellow; black banded tail tipped yellow. Highly gregarious in winter.
Voice: Tinkling *trill*.
Habitat: Conifer forests; during eruptions roams hedgerows and gardens in flocks.
Similar Species: Starling, in flight.

J F M A M J J A S O N D

Dipper *Cinclus cinclus*

JUVENILE

scaly

short cocked tail

ADULT

white breast

J F M A M J J A S O N D

Status: Resident of fast-running streams throughout temperate Europe.
Identification: 17–18.5cm (7in). Portly, short-tailed, blackish bird marked by bold white gorget; reminiscent of large, white-breasted Wren. Spends much time searching for food among tumbling, rock-strewn waters where wades, swims and dives with complete mastery. Usually solitary, often perching openly on rocks. Territory can be 2km or more long but only as wide as a river or stream.
Voice: Clear *zit-zit*.
Habitat: Permanent, fast-running streams.
Similar Species: None.

Wren *Troglodytes troglodytes*

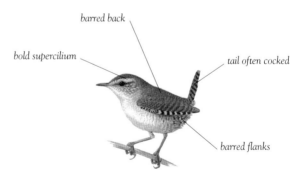

barred back

bold supercilium

tail often cocked

barred flanks

J F M A M J J A S O N D

Status: One of most widespread and numerous birds of Europe. Tame in gardens.
Identification: 9–10cm (3½–4in). Easily recognized by small size and cocked tail. Chestnut above, with clear pale supercilium and barred back and wings. Underparts buffy; some barring on flanks. Spends much time hunting through dense ground cover, where presence betrayed only by characteristic calls and loud wheezing song. Tame in gardens.
Voice: Repeated *tic-tic*; loud rippling warble ending in wheezy *churr*.
Habitat: Vast range, from sea cliffs to city gardens.
Similar Species: This is the only Old World wren.

Hedge Accentor *Prunella modularis*

thin bill

grey face

streaked flanks

ADULT

J F M A M J J A S O N D

Status: Widespread and tame; also called Dunnock.
Identification: 14–15cm (5½–6in). Spends most of time crouched low on ground searching for food. Seldom moves far from cover, usually perches openly only when singing. Flicks wings continuously. Flies low and briefly in undulating flight. Grey foreparts and thin bill separate from House Sparrow. Back and wings brown, liberally streaked with black; brown streaking on flanks. Juvenile less grey on head, entire underparts streaked.
Voice: Jangling *staccato* warble.
Habitat: Hedgerows, gardens, heaths, woodland.
Similar Species: See Alpine Accentor.

Alpine Accentor *Prunella collaris*

double white wingbar

chestnut wing patch

spotted gorget

chestnut streaked flanks

Status: Resident all mountains of south and central Europe.
Identification: 17–19cm (6½–7½in). Chunky and considerably larger than more widespread Hedge Accentor. Greyish on crown with some slight streaking; back and wings brown with bold black streaking and prominent line of white spots on wing coverts. Chin spotted black and white to form gorget; remaining underparts grey with bold chestnut streaks on flanks.
Voice: Liquid *chirrup*.
Habitat: Mountain screes and rocks, usually above tree line.
Similar Species: Distinct Snow Finch inhabits similar areas.

J F M A M J J A S O N D

Radde's Accentor *Prunella ocularis*

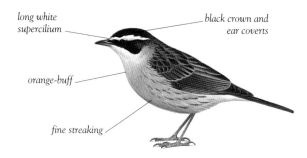

long white
supercilium

black crown and
ear coverts

orange-buff

fine streaking

J F M A M J J A S O N D

Status: Resident high mountains of central Turkey.
Identification: 14–15cm (5½in). Typical Hedge
Accentor-like bird, which spends much of its time
shuffling horizontally over bare ground among bushes
and scrub, flicking its wings. Head black marked by long,
bold white supercilium and greyish throat. Rest of
upperparts mottled chestnut and black. Breast
orange-buff, whitish on belly and undertail, lightly
streaked chestnut on flanks.
Voice: Jingling song like Hedge Accentor.
Habitat: High rocky mountain pastures and gullies.
Similar Species: Alpine Accentor occurs in same areas.

Rufous Scrub-robin *Cercotrichas galactotes*

bold supercilium and
eye-stripe

tail cocked

outer tips
black and white

J F M A M J J A S O N D

Status: Scarce summer visitor to south-west and south-
east Europe.
Identification: 14–16cm (5½–6in). Distinctly marked by
rufous plumage and long fan-shaped tail. Upperparts rich
rufous with bold supercilium and prominent white double
wingbar, tail long, graduated, tipped black and white, and
often cocked and fanned. Underparts white.
Voice: Harsh *tek-tek*.
Habitat: Scrub-covered river courses, cactus belts,
thickets.
Similar Species: Nightingales are darker rufous and lack
all other characteristics of this species.

Thrush Nightingale *Luscinia luscinia*

less rufous

mottled breast

ADULT

J F M A M J J A S O N D

Status: Summer visitor that replaces Nightingale in eastern Europe. Sometimes called Sprosser.
Identification: 16–17cm (6¼–6¾in). Though the two species of nightingale overlap in range, this species prefers marshy and flooded forests, rather than dry woodland and bush country favoured by Nightingale. Thrush Nightingale darker, less rufous brown with mottling of brown on breast. Tail less rusty.
Voice: Song similar, but louder than Nightingale. Lacks crescendo.
Habitat: Flooded woodland, waterside thickets.
Similar Species: Nightingale as above.

Nightingale *Luscinia megarhynchos*

warm brown

rufous tail

ADULT

rufous tail

scaled

JUVENILE

Status: Temperate and Mediterranean Europe in summer.
Identification: 16–17cm (6¼–6¾in). Almost always hidden deep in vegetation; males occasionally perch openly to sing. Tail spread in song display. When disturbed, dives into nearest cover. Adult rufous-brown above merging with creamy-white underparts. Juvenile marked with scale-like crescents, as juvenile Robin. Rust-red tail characteristic.
Voice: Fabulous songster more often heard than seen. Song a virtuoso performance of liquid trills ending in crescendo; commonly heard after dark, also during the day.
Habitat: Woods, heaths, thickets.
Similar Species: See Thrush Nightingale.

J F M A M J J A S O N D

Bluethroat *Luscinia svecica*

white spotted *cyanecula*

FIRST WINTER

bold supercilium

moustache

blue breast

rusty tail patches

red spotted *svecica*

♂ SUMMER

♂ SUMMER

♀

J F M A M J J A S O N D

Status: Secretive, summer visitor to Continental Europe.
Identification: 13–15cm (5–6in). Adult male has distinctive cobalt-blue throat and breast with dark blue and red breast bands. Spot in centre of breast is red in *L.s.svecica* and white in *L.s.cyanecula*. Adult female has white throat and breast marked by dark brown breast band extending as moustache to base of bill. First-winter males have just a hint of blue and red above breast band; females lack both colours on breast.
Voice: Penetrating *tic-tic*; thin *wheet*.
Habitat: Damp thickets, often near water.
Similar Species: None.

Red-flanked Bluetail *Tarsiger cyanurus*

blue upperparts

♀

short supercilium

white chin

orange flanks

blue tail often flicked

orange flanks

blue tail

♂

J F M A M J J A S O N D

Status: A distinctive chat that breeds in eastern Finland, but is otherwise a rare vagrant throughout Europe.
Identification: 13.5–14.5cm (5½in). A secretive, ground-dwelling Robin-like chat. Summer male is unmistakable with blue upperparts and tail and orange-washed flanks. Female and juvenile have white throat, buffy breast band, orange flanks, blue tail. Useful features are pale supercilium and eye-ring; tail frequently flicked.
Voice: Hard *tik-tik* reminiscent of Robin.
Habitat: Woodlands with understorey, often near water.
Similar Species: None.

White-throated Robin *Irania gutturalis*

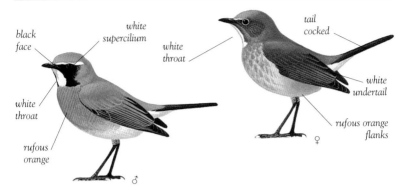

black face

white supercilium

white throat

white throat

rufous orange

♂

tail cocked

white throat

white undertail

rufous orange flanks

♀

J F M A M J J A S O N D

Status: Large Robin-like chat with rufous-orange breast. Summer visitor to much of Turkey. Nowhere common.
Identification: 16–17cm (6½in). Spends much time on ground among dense vegetation frequently cocking longish tail. Male grey above with black face bordered by white supercilium and white throat. Most of underparts rich rufous-orange; belly and undertail coverts white. Female buffy-grey. White undertail a prominent field mark.
Voice: Calls and short song reminiscent of Nightingale.
Habitat: Upland ravines, gullies with thick undergrowth.
Similar Species: Adult male none. Female and juvenile see Bluethroat, Robin, Redstart.

Black Redstart *Phoenicurus ochruros*

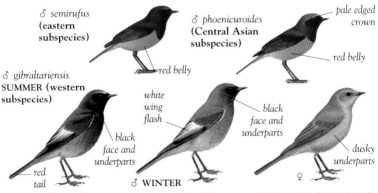

♂ *semirufus* (eastern subspecies)

♂ *phoenicuroides* (Central Asian subspecies)

pale edged crown

red belly

♂ *gibraltariensis* SUMMER (western subspecies)

white wing flash

red belly

black face and underparts

red tail

black face and underparts

dusky underparts

♂ WINTER

♀

Status: Widespread summer; winters in southern Europe.
Identification: 14–15cm (5½–6in). Perches openly with rusty tail shimmering. Pounces to ground in search of food. Summer male has black head, back, breast and belly; bold white flash in wing. In winter, black areas become dark, leaden-grey; black remains on throat; underparts dirty white. Female brown, darker above, paler below; juvenile as female but lightly barred; both have rust-red tails.
Voice: Song is a brief warble. Call a short *sip* or *tissic*.
Habitat: Cities, towns, cliffs, burnt-over woodland.
Similar Species: Female and juvenile are duskier versions of Common Redstart.

J F M A M J J A S O N D

Whinchat   *Saxicola rubetra*

supercilium

white wing patches

bold white supercilium

white tail patches

pale orange

♀

♂

J F M A M J J A S O N D

Status: Widespread summer visitor and passage migrant, most often seen perching openly atop a bush.
Identification: 12–13cm (4³⁄₄–5in). Summer male has brown upperparts, heavily streaked black; white flash in closed wing. Prominent, creamy white supercilium; dark ear coverts. Underparts pale creamy-orange. In flight, shows white patch on innerwing and white patches either side of tail. Female a more subdued version of male.
Voice: Metallic *tic-tic*; brief warble.
Habitat: Heaths, downland, scrub.
Similar Species: Stonechat lacks supercilium, though vagrant eastern subspecies show bold one.

Stonechat   *Saxicola torquata*

no supercilium

grey-brown head

white rump

black head, white half collar

♀

♂

J F M A M J J A S O N D

Status: Common resident in west; summer visitor to east.
Identification: 12–13cm (4³⁄₄–5in). Perches prominently on tops of bushes and pounces to ground. Flies low, showing greyish white rump and white patches on wings. In summer, male has black head bordered by prominent white half collar. Back and wings dark brown, streaked black; tail dark brown. Breast orange-red. In winter, male paler with less reddish breast. Female with dark, not black, head.
Voice: Metallic *chak-chak*; jingling warble.
Habitat: Heaths, scrubby hillsides, hedgerows.
Similar Species: See Whinchat.

Robin *Erithacus rubecula*

red face and breast

scaled above and below

ADULT

JUVENILE

J F M A M J J A S O N D

Status: Widespread and numerous resident; Scandinavian birds are migrants.
Identification: 13–15cm (5–6in). Upright, plump little bird; perches openly and hops on the ground. Adult warm olive-brown with red face, chin and breast. Sides of breast pale grey; belly white. Juvenile brown head, wings and tail with brown barring on buffy back and breast; impossible to distinguish from adult after moult (June–August).
Voice: Thin *tic-tic*; leisurely warble.
Habitat: Gardens, woods and hedgerows.
Similar Species: See Redstart, Stonechat and Red-breasted Flycatcher.

Common Redstart *Phoenicurus phoenicurus*

white forehead

grey back

black face

♂ WINTER

buff brown

♂

red tail

buffy

red tail

♂ SUMMER

♀

Status: Widespread summer visitor throughout Europe.
Identification: 13.5–14.5cm (5¼–5¾in). Summer male has dove-grey crown and back; wings brown. White supercilia meet on forehead; rest of face black. Underparts orange-red; tail orange-red with darker centre. Female also has orange-red tail but is buffy brown above, buffy below. Juvenile similar to female but speckled. Perches on lower branches of trees and makes pouncing sallies to ground. Orange-red tail frequently shimmered.
Voice: Brief warble; quiet *hooet*.
Habitat: Woodland margins, orchards and heaths.
Similar Species: Black Redstart always darker.

J F M A M J J A S O N D

Cyprus Pied Wheatear   *Oenanthe cypriaca*

darker crown

white crown margins

grey crown

black back

black face joined to black wings

warm underparts

warm underparts

♀

♂

J F M A M J J A S O N D

Status: Summer visitor only to Cyprus, formerly regarded as a well-marked subspecies of Pied Wheatear.
Identification: 13–14cm (5½in). Slightly smaller than Pied Wheatear; sexes almost identical. Summer male black face joined to black wings and back. Crown variably grey, white supercilium. Underparts warm buff. Rump white, narrow black tail band forms prominent 'T' shape. Female darker crown, off-black upperparts and warmer breast.
Voice: A cricket-like buzzing.
Habitat: Stony hillsides with trees and bushes.
Similar Species: Pied and Finsch's Wheatears also have black of face and wings joined.

Pied Wheatear   *Oenanthe pleschanka*

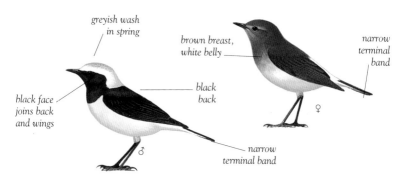

greyish wash in spring

brown breast, white belly

narrow terminal band

black face joins back and wings

black back

narrow terminal band

♂

♀

J F M A M J J A S O N D

Status: Summer visitor to Crimea and southern Ukraine.
Identification: 15cm (5½in). Male bold black and white with black face joined to black wings and back. Crown washed grey and underparts lightly washed buffy, but both become whiter during breeding season. In fresh (autumn) plumage crown almost brown, underparts buffy pink and black face and wings speckled brown. Female dark brown, paler brown head and breast. Tail has narrow terminal band to accentuate 'T' pattern.
Voice: Harsh *zack-zack*. Song a fluty warble with mimicry.
Habitat: Dry rocky hillsides with little vegetation.
Similar Species: See Cyprus Pied and Finsch's Wheatears.

Black-eared Wheatear *Oenanthe hispanica*

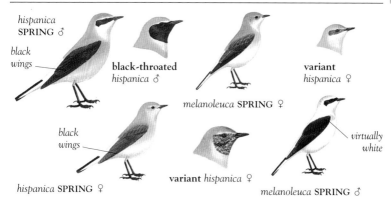

hispanica
SPRING ♂

black
wings

black-throated
hispanica ♂

variant
hispanica ♀

melanoleuca SPRING ♀

black
wings

hispanica SPRING ♀

variant *hispanica* ♀

melanoleuca SPRING ♂

virtually
white

J F M A M J J A S O N D

Status: Summer visitor throughout Mediterranean.
Identification: 14–15cm (5½–6in). Males of western
subspecies, *O.h.hispanica*, have black wings contrasting
with sandy back and crown, and white belly. Two distinct
forms show either black mask (white-throated), or black
mask, chin and throat (black-throated). Males of eastern
subspecies, *O.h.melanoleuca* are paler, often white rather
than sandy. More white outertail than Northern Wheatear.
Voice: Harsh *zerrk*.
Habitat: Open and rocky areas.
Similar Species: Eastern subspecies, with care from
Finsch's and Red-tailed Wheatears.

Finsch's Wheatear *Oenanthe finschii*

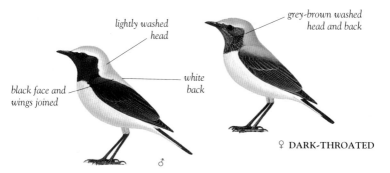

lightly washed
head

grey-brown washed
head and back

black face and
wings joined

white
back

♀ DARK-THROATED

♂

Status: Summer visitor to and resident in south and
eastern Turkey. Winters Cyprus.
Identification: 15cm (5½in). Male a 'pied' wheatear with
black of face and wings joined as Pied and Cyprus
Wheatears; but back white not black. Female has grey-
brown head and back. Autumn male has plain face with
grey crown and back like male Northern Wheatear, but
lacks dark ear coverts. Low flight often erratic.
Voice: Sharp *sak* of alarm. Song clear, scratchy warble.
Habitat: Dry, rocky plains, hillsides and ravines.
Similar Species: Pale black-throated form of Black-eared
Wheatear has white back, but face and wings not joined.

J F M A M J J A S O N D

Black Wheatear   *Oenanthe leucura*

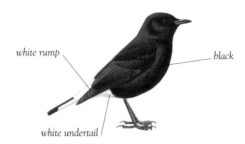

white rump

black

white undertail

Status: Resident of rocky hillsides Iberia.
Identification: 17–19cm (6½–7½in). Large, chunky wheatear, significantly larger than Northern Wheatear. Whole plumage black, except white undertail coverts and rump, and black and white tail. Inhabits open rocky country, often among mountains where it is difficult to find until it flies, when white rump and tail flash conspicuously.
Voice: Harsh *chak*.
Habitat: Dry rocky hillsides, gullies, screes.
Similar Species: Beware vagrant White-crowned Black Wheatear.

Red-tailed Wheatear   *Oenanthe xanthoprymna*

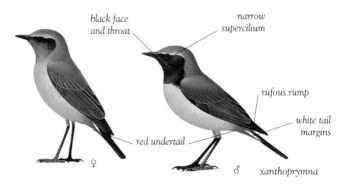

*black face
and throat*

*narrow
supercilium*

rufous rump

*white tail
margins*

red undertail

♀

♂   *xanthoprymna*

Status: Small, slim wheatear, breeds in eastern Turkey.
Identification: 14.5–15cm (5½in). Male Turkish birds (*O.x.xanthoprymna*) have black face and throat, bordered above by narrow supercilium, separated from black wings. The rump is rufous, the sides of the tail white in a normal wheatear T-shape. The upperparts are buffy-grey. Females sometimes lack black face, but share the tail pattern. Eastern birds from Iran (*O.x.chrysopygia*) lack black face and have sides of tail rufous not white.
Voice: Warbling song and a distinctive *thrr-thrr*.
Habitat: Dry, rocky hillsides and scrub.
Similar Species: Smaller than Red-rumped Wheatear.

Identification of Wheatears in Flight

The name 'wheatear' is derived from the countryman's name that refers to the white rump; the most obvious of the species' shared plumage characteristics. The extent of white in rump and tail varies between species and is often a crucial element in identification. Most have an inverted 'T' of black set against a white background. But some have short shanks and others long ones. Some have thick crosses, others very thin ones. These features also apply to females and first-winter birds. Tail, rump and back patterns, combined with the joining (or not) of black face to black wings, are a major means of clinching identification.

NORTHERN WHEATEAR:
Regular black 'T' with extensive white rump terminating in grey of back.

BLACK-EARED WHEATEAR:
Very narrow terminal band and long-shanked 'T', a pattern shared with Pied Wheatear which has black (not sandy or white) back.

PIED WHEATEAR: Narrow terminal band and long shanked 'T' like Black-eared. Black back separates from that species as well as Finsch's.

ISABELLINE WHEATEAR:
Broad terminal band, but very short shanked 'T' creates unique tail pattern.

FINSCH'S WHEATEAR:
Regular black 'T' like Northern Wheatear. White rump extends over back to crown; a pattern shared with pale eastern subspecies of Black-eared Wheatear.

CYPRUS PIED WHEATEAR:
Broad terminal band and short-shanked 'T' are one of major distinctions from Pied Wheatear, especially in worn, white summer plumage.

RED-TAILED WHEATEAR:
Very broad terminal band extends to rufous rump leaving only small white patches either side at base of tail.

Isabelline Wheatear   *Oenanthe isabellina*

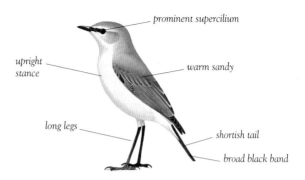

prominent supercilium

upright stance

warm sandy

long legs

shortish tail

broad black band

J F M A M J J A S O N D

Status: Summer visitor to much of Turkey, where expanding range. Migrant through Cyprus and elsewhere in eastern Mediterranean.
Identification: 16–17cm (6⅕in). Closely resembles female and first-winter Northern Wheatear, but larger with bigger, more rounded head and larger bill. Stands very upright on long legs creating a short-tailed impression. Frequently runs. Warm sandy above, creamy below. Tail shows longer black terminal band than Northern.
Voice: Loud *wheet*. Loud warbling song includes mimicry.
Habitat: Dry stony plains with scant vegetation.
Similar Species: Northern Wheatear as above.

Northern Wheatear   *Oenanthe oenanthe*

hint of mask

white rump and outertail

pale supercilium dark ear coverts

grey crown and back

black wings

black mask

♀

♂

AUTUMN

J F M A M J J A S O N D

Status: Widespread summer visitor to open country.
Identification: 14–15.5cm (5½–6in). Typical upright posture with sudden darting movements; frequently 'bobs'. In flight, white rump and tail pattern distinctive. Adult male has grey crown and back with black 'mask'. Wings black; underparts creamy-buff. Adult female grey-brown above with only hint of face mask. Juvenile sandy crown and back, pale margins to dark wing feathers; hint of mask. Greenland subspecies *O.o.leucorhoa* larger and longer wings.
Voice: Hard *chak-chak*; brief warble.
Habitat: Heaths, moors, beaches and downs.
Similar Species: Other female wheatears. See page 235.

Rock Thrush   *Monticola saxatilis*

short orange tail

warm wash

blue head

blue-white rump

orange

♀

♂

J F M A M J J A S O N D

Status: Scarce summer visitor to southern Europe.
Identification: 18–20cm (7–8in). Male has pale blue head and neck with darker back; pale blue-white rump and rufous tail; breast and underparts warm rufous forming breast band against blue neck. Female buffy, heavily marked with pale crescents above and dark crescents below, creating scaly appearance. Female Blue Rock Thrush similar, but much darker. Both sexes stand upright and have shortish tails.
Voice: Harsh *chak*; loud warbling.
Habitat: Rocky screes and walls in dry uplands.
Similar Species: Female Blue Rock Thrush as above.

Blue Rock Thrush   *Monticola solitarius*

short dark tail

barred dark

black wings

dark blue

♀

♂

J F M A M J J A S O N D

Status: Widespread Mediterranean scrub and mountains.
Identification: 20–21cm (8in). Considerably more abundant than Rock Thrush. Male dark blue with darker upperparts and almost black wings. Pointed head and bill, triangular-shaped wings and short tail create starling-shape both when perched and in the air. Has habit of perching motionless atop large rocks for considerable periods. Female similar in shape, but very dark brown marked by pale crescents. At distance, both sexes appear virtually black.
Voice: Fluted, Blackbird-like warble.
Habitat: Large rocks from near sea level to altitude.
Similar Species: Common Starling; female Rock Thrush.

Ring Ouzel *Turdus torquatus*

silvery wing panel

silvery wings

white crescent

♂

♀

Status: Summer visitor to hills and mountains that winters in south-west and south-east.
Identification: 23–25cm (9–10in). Behaviour much as Blackbird but much less confiding. Flies swift and low showing silvery wings. On passage, often skulks in dense cover. In summer, male black with brownish wash; distinctive white crescent across breast. Silvery wing edges form pale panel on folded wing. In winter, male browner with scaly markings.
Voice: Angry, harsh *chook-chook*; loud *peu-u peu-u*.
Habitat: Upland moors and rocky screes.
Similar Species: Blackbird lacks white crescent, silver wings.

Blackbird *Turdus merula*

yellow eye-ring

yellow bill

♂

♀

dark breast with faint spots

Status: Familiar, widespread and common resident, or summer visitor, throughout Europe.
Identification: 24–27cm (9½–11in). All black male has yellow bill and eye-ring. Female browner, with subdued speckling on breast varying considerably from rufous-brown to greyish brown. First-winter males retain brown wing feathers; distinguishes from older, black-winged birds; also lack yellow on bill.
Voice: Loud chatter of alarm; fluty warbled song.
Habitat: Gardens to woods, moorland to fields; highly adaptable.
Similar Species: Ring Ouzel.

Song Thrush *Turdus philomelos*

plain face

warm brown
back

buff with
speckles

Status: Widespread resident or summer visitor; winter
visitor Iberia and Mediterranean.
Identification: 23cm (9in). Neat, medium-sized thrush.
Brown above; white neatly spotted with black below;
creamy-yellow wash on breast. Plain face lacks
distinguishing features. Flight fast, strong and direct unlike
Mistle Thrush.
Voice: Variety of phrases, each repeated three or four
times.
Habitat: Woods, gardens, fields and hedges.
Similar Species: Mistle Thrush larger and greyer; Redwing
with distinctive face pattern.

J F M A M J J A S O N D

Redwing *Turdus iliacus*

rufous underwing
shared with Song
Thrush

bold supercilium

whitish with
speckles

rufous flanks

Status: Summer Fennoscandia; winter visitor south, west.
Identification: 20–22cm (8–9in). Smallest regular thrush
marked by bold supercilium and rufous flanks. Brown above,
with brown ear coverts separating and accentuating bold
supercilium and double moustachial streak; face markings
give distinctly 'cross' look. Whitish underparts spotted in
clear streaks, with bold rust-red flanks. Flight fast and
direct like Song Thrush; (unlike undulating flight of
Mistle Thrush). Often in large flocks in winter.
Voice: Quiet *seeip* in flight.
Habitat: Birch forests; fields, often in large flocks, in winter.
Similar Species: Song Thrush slightly larger.

J F M A M J J A S O N D

Fieldfare *Turdus pilaris*

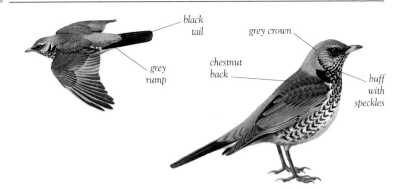

black tail

grey rump

grey crown

chestnut back

buff with speckles

J F M A M J J A S O N D

Status: Resident or summer visitor to north, central and eastern Europe; widespread winter visitor elsewhere.
Identification: 24–27cm (9½–10½in). Large, typical thrush with densely speckled breast washed buffy yellow. Head, nape and rump dove-grey – latter useful field mark in flight. Wings and back chestnut-brown; tail black. Pattern of head and face markings produce 'cross' expression. Generally gregarious, forming substantial winter flocks.
Voice: Harsh *chak-chak* in flight.
Habitat: Scrubby hillsides; winters fields and hedgerows.
Similar Species: Other 'spotted' thrushes lack grey head and rump.

Mistle Thrush *Turdus viscivorus*

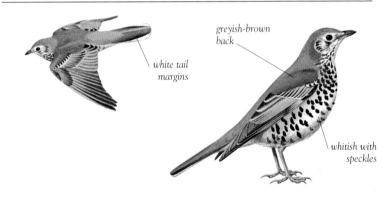

greyish-brown back

white tail margins

whitish with speckles

J F M A M J J A S O N D

Status: Largest of the thrushes; resident, but only summer visitor Fennoscandia.
Identification: 26–28cm (10–11in). Distinctly greyer and paler appearance than Song Thrush. Upperparts buffy grey-brown with pale margins to flight feathers. Underparts white, heavily spotted black. In undulating flight, shows grey-brown rump and white corners to tail. Generally less gregarious than other thrushes.
Voice: Loud *tuk-tuk*; song like Blackbird, but faster.
Habitat: Open woods, gardens, groves.
Similar Species: Song Thrush is smaller and browner. See Fieldfare.

Fan-tailed Warbler   *Cisticola juncidis*

thin decurved bill

boldly streaked

short rounded tail

J F M A M J J A S O N D

Status: Resident Mediterranean, extending northwards along Atlantic coasts. Also called Zitting Cisticola.
Identification: 9–11cm (3½–4½in). Tiny warbler with character unique among European birds. Heavily streaked above with rounded head, longish, decurved bill and short, cocked tail. In flight, rounded wings and short tail particularly obvious and bird 'bounces' in sky as if suspended on piece of elastic, uttering repetitive call.
Voice: Repeated *zip-zip-zip-zip*, etc.
Habitat: Damp fields, marshes, cereals.
Similar Species: Many streaked 'marshy' warblers have similar plumage, all lack features described.

Graceful Prinia   *Prinia gracilis*

short decurved bill

distinctly streaked

long cocked tail, feathers tipped black and white

buffy flanks

long pinkish legs

Status: Tiny warbler-like bird found in scrubland only in southern Turkey. The only prinia in our area.
Identification: 10cm (4in). A very small, dull-brown bird marked by a long rounded tail often held cocked above back. Upperparts brown-buff finely streaked black. Underparts whitish, with buffy flanks. A hint of pale supercilium. Long, graduated tail has feathers tipped black and white, easily seen when fanned. Legs bright pinkish-red and long for size. Bill short and decurved.
Voice: A rolling trill and a repeated *tebbit-tebbit*.
Habitat: Arid scrub, neglected thorn hedges, water margins.
Similar Species: Fan-tailed Warbler lacks long tail.

J F M A M J J A S O N D

Cetti's Warbler *Cettia cetti*

pale supercilium

chestnut-brown

*prominent
rounded tail often
spread*

J F M A M J J A S O N D

Status: Resident west and south Europe, expanding
northwards.
Identification: 13.5–14.5cm (5–5¹/₂in). Always secretive
and elusive, but presence revealed by uniquely explosive
call. Usually sighted as dark brown bird flitting from one
bush to another. Clearer views reveal rich chestnut-brown
upperparts with clear, pale supercilium and strongly
rounded tail. Underparts whitish.
Voice: Explosive *chetti-chetti-chetti*.
Habitat: Dense bushy undergrowth adjacent water.
Similar Species: Darker than any similar-sized bird,
including Nightingale.

Grasshopper Warbler *Locustella naevia*

faint supercilium

lightly streaked back

rounded tail

J F M A M J J A S O N D

Status: Localized summer visitor to marshes and damp
thickets mostly located by song.
Identification: 12–13cm (4¹/₂–5in). One of 'streaked-back'
marshy warblers; upperparts brown streaked black; short
and inconspicuous pale supercilium. Underparts buff with
faint breast streaking. Most frequently observed at dawn or
dusk when produces continuous reeling call.
Voice: Ventriloquial reeling – like rewinding fishing reel.
Habitat: Marshes, thickets, young conifer plantations.
Similar Species: Sedge Warbler has bolder streaking and
bolder supercilium; Savi's Warbler song similar, but lower
pitched, reeling.

River Warbler   *Locustella fluviatilis*

unstreaked back

short primary projection

streaked breast

barred undertail

J F M A M J J A S O N D

Status: Scarce summer visitor to eastern Europe.
Identification: 13.5–14cm (5$\frac{1}{2}$in). Slightly larger than Grasshopper Warbler, though similar in shape and behaviour. Upperparts unstreaked dull-brown; underparts streaked grey-brown on sides of neck and breast, barred undertail. Best identified by song.
Voice: Two notes (one high, one low) run together to create a rhythmic chuffing. Quite different from Grasshopper and Savi's more uniform reeling.
Habitat: Waterside thickets, damp hedges.
Similar Species: Other 'plain backed' marshy warblers lack breast streaking.

Savi's Warbler   *Locustella luscinioides*

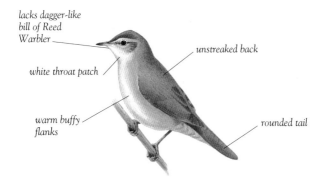

lacks dagger-like bill of Reed Warbler

unstreaked back

white throat patch

warm buffy flanks

rounded tail

Status: Widespread summer visitor to reedbeds.
Identification: 13–14cm (5–5$\frac{1}{2}$in). Often perches on reed tops. Reeling song similar to Grasshopper Warbler, but lower pitched and usually with briefer phrases. Upperparts uniform buff-brown; underparts buff. Faint supercilium; distinctly rounded tail. Very similar to Reed Warbler, though lacking sloping forehead and long bill.
Voice: Reeling.
Habitat: Reedfen, swamps, marshes.
Similar Species: Reed and Marsh Warblers are similarly unstreaked above, dagger-like bills. Check River Warbler.

J F M A M J J A S O N D

Moustached Warbler *Acrocephalus melanopogon*

dark cap

bold supercilium ends
squarely

clear eyestripe

contrasting
streaking

J F M A M J J A S O N D

Status: Resident Mediterranean; summer visitor in east.
Identification: 12–13cm (5in). Similar to Sedge Warbler
with streaked upperparts and bold supercilium. Upperparts
more contrasting in warm buff and black; underparts paler,
often white. Crown much darker than Sedge, giving
capped appearance; supercilium white, broadening behind
eye and terminating squarely.
Voice: Song similar to Reed Warbler but breaks into
Nightingale-like *tu-tu-tu* repeated.
Habitat: Reedbeds among extensive marshes.
Similar Species: Sedge Warbler can show same features,
especially juvenile; but never as prominently.

Aquatic Warbler *Acrocephalus paludicola*

bold crown stripes

bold striped pattern

J F M A M J J A S O N D

Status: Rare, localized summer visitor mostly to Poland;
endangered. Vagrant westwards autumn.
Identification: 12–13cm (4½–5in). Upperparts sandy
coloured with clear black streaks, forming more
contrasting pattern than Sedge or any other similar
warbler. Creamy central crown stripe contrasts with dark
lateral stripes and long creamy supercilia to produce
striped effect.
Voice: Simple, short phrases repeated softly.
Habitat: Low sedge marshes.
Similar Species: No warblers so contrastingly streaked.

Sedge Warbler *Acrocephalus schoenobaenus*

dark crown

streaking more contrasting than adult

streaked back

JUVENILE

bold creamy supercilium

rounded tail

ADULT

J F M A M J J A S O N D

Status: Common and widespread summer visitor to variety of wetlands, except Iberia and southern France.
Identification: 12–13cm (4½–5in). Upperparts heavily streaked black on brown; streaked crown often quite dark, giving capped appearance. Broad, creamy supercilium extends almost to nape; contrasts with narrow black eye-stripe. Underparts buffy, especially on flanks. Often well hidden, but also perches openly. Has brief song flight.
Voice: Harsh grating notes mixed with melodic phrases.
Habitat: Reedbeds, ditches and dykes, bushy margins.
Similar Species: See Moustached, Aquatic and Grasshopper Warblers.

Paddyfield Warbler *Acrocephalus agricola*

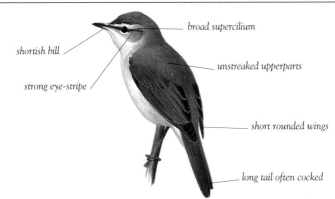

shortish bill

strong eye-stripe

broad supercilium

unstreaked upperparts

short rounded wings

long tail often cocked

Status: Scarce and localized summer visitor to Black Sea region that is extremely rare elsewhere.
Identification: 12–13cm (5in). Only unstreaked *Acrocephalus* warbler that with prominent supercilium. Reed Warbler marked by longer tail; shorter bill; and shorter wings with small primary projection. Cream-coloured supercilium widens behind the eye and contrasts with clear dark eye-stripe. Raising crest produces large-headed appearance; tail often cocked.
Voice: A hard *chik-chik*.
Habitat: Frequents reeds and other aquatic vegetation.
Similar Species: All unstreaked *Acrocephalus* warblers.

J F M A M J J A S O N D

Blyth's Reed Warbler *Acrocephalus dumetorum*

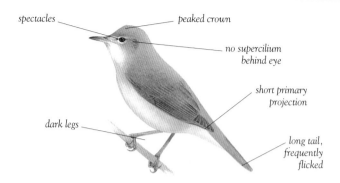

spectacles

peaked crown

no supercilium behind eye

short primary projection

dark legs

long tail, frequently flicked

J F M A M J J A S O N D

Status: Scarce in summer south-east Finland; migrates east.
Identification: 12–13cm (5in). Forms species triangle with Reed and Marsh Warblers. Upperparts olive-brown, generally greyer than Marsh Warbler; pale supercilium terminates just behind eye; lacks pale tips to tertials. Look for bunched primaries on folded wing; tail appears longish in comparison and is regularly flicked. Bill and legs dark. Resembles Marsh Warbler, but more peaked crown.
Voice: Varied, musical phrases, repeated.
Habitat: Bushy wetland margins.
Similar Species: See above; identified with great care.

Marsh Warbler *Acrocephalus palustris*

steep forehead

thin supercilium

shorter bill than Reed

uniform underparts

pale legs

pale tips to tertials

longer wings than Reed

J F M A M J J A S O N D

Status: Summer visitor central and eastern Europe westwards to southern England.
Identification: 12–13cm (4½–5in). Uniform olive-brown upperparts and buff and white underparts. Very similar to Reed Warbler, but generally more olive above and whiter below, with flatter crown and slightly longer wings. Best identified by song.
Voice: Remarkable mimic with Greenfinch-like notes.
Habitat: Thickets, willows and rushes near water, rather than pure reedbeds.
Similar Species: Reed Warbler as above; see Blyth's Reed Warbler.

Reed Warbler   *Acrocephalus scirpaceus*

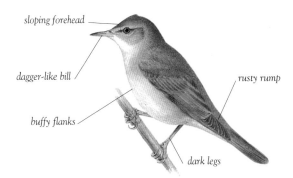

sloping forehead

dagger-like bill

buffy flanks

rusty rump

dark legs

J F M A M J J A S O N D

Status: Common, widespread summer visitor to reedbeds.
Identification: 12–13cm (4½–5in). Tends to skulk in deep cover but will perch on reed-tops, especially while singing. Upperparts warm brown, with distinct rufous wash on rump unlike Marsh or Blyth's Reed Warbler. Underparts white with buffy flanks. Sloping forehead reaches peak at top of crown, accentuating length of dagger-like bill. Dark legs.
Voice: Harsh, grating *jag-jag, chirrug-chirrug*.
Habitat: Extensive reedbeds and reedy margins.
Similar Species: See Marsh, Savi's and Blyth's Reed Warblers.

Great Reed Warbler   *Acrocephalus arundinaceus*

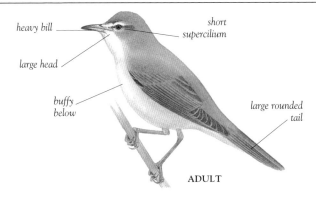

heavy bill

short supercilium

large head

buffy below

large rounded tail

ADULT

Status: Widespread summer visitor, except Fennoscandia.
Identification: 18–20cm (7–8in). Similar to Reed Warbler, but much larger and bulkier bird, with loud song quite unmistakable. Upperparts brown, marked by short supercilium and dark eye-stripe that extends from bill to behind eye. Underparts creamy-buff. Large bill and head, large rounded tail and short rounded wings. In flight, resembles thrush rather than warbler. .
Voice: Loud, strident discordant notes.
Habitat: Reedbeds, margins of freshwaters.
Similar Species: Much larger than Reed and other plain-backed warblers.

J F M A M J J A S O N D

Booted Warbler *Hippolais caligata*

marked supercilium

rounded crown

greyish-brown 'tea' coloured

short primary projection

medium length bill

long tail flicked upwards

J F M A M J J A S O N D

Status: Vagrant westwards from Russia; may breed Finland.
Identification: 11.5–12cm (4½in). Smallest *Hippolais* warbler, much more like *Phylloscopus* with shortish bill, rounded head with distinct supercilium and square tail. Short wings, long tail and broad-based bill useful marks. Brownish-grey above; whitish below. Frequently flicks tail upwards.
Voice: Sharp *chick*.
Habitat: Variable wet or dry scrub, orchards.
Similar Species: Dull *Phylloscopus* warblers; see Chiffchaff.

Upcher's Warbler *Hippolais languida*

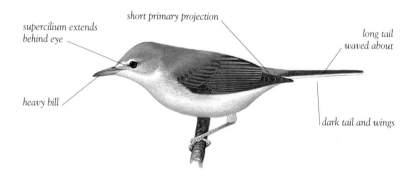

supercilium extends behind eye

short primary projection

long tail waved about

heavy bill

dark tail and wings

J F M A M J J A S O N D

Status: Scarce summer visitor to southern Turkey.
Identification: 13–15cm (5½in). Featureless, medium-sized warbler easily confused with other 'washed out' greyish *Hippolais* warblers, especially Olivaceous and Olive-tree. Upcher's greyish (like Olive-tree) rather than olive or brown. Sloping forehead and dagger-like bill resemble other *Hippolais*, but bill is heavier than Olivaceous and neither as long or as heavy as Olive-tree. Grey upperparts contrast with dark tail and wings.
Voice: Metallic *chuk*. Chattering song.
Habitat: Dry semi-desert scrub with thickets.
Similar Species: Olivaceous and Olive-tree.

Principles of Warbler Identification

Warblers are mostly small, ever active, slim rather than chunky, have thin well-proportioned bills and are mainly summer visitors. Some are well marked (many of the genus *Sylvia* for example), others are plain, featureless and confusing. As with all birds, identification involves knowing what to look for and having the patience to watch and the strength of character to resist 'seeing' what cannot be seen; that is avoiding the phenomenon of 'self-hoodwinking'.

SIZE
Warblers (unlike waders) offer size comparison with the vegetation among which they are found. Nevertheless, separating them into small (like a Goldcrest), medium (like a Garden Warbler) or large (like a Great Reed Warbler) is about as far as one can go in the field.

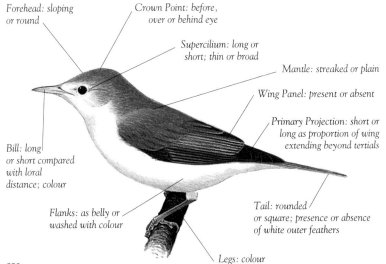

Forehead: sloping or round

Crown Point: before, over or behind eye

Supercilium: long or short; thin or broad

Mantle: streaked or plain

Wing Panel: present or absent

Primary Projection: short or long as proportion of wing extending beyond tertials

Bill: long or short compared with loral distance; colour

Flanks: as belly or washed with colour

Tail: rounded or square; presence or absence of white outer feathers

Legs: colour

WING LENGTH
Wing length and shape are often critical in distinguishing very similar species such as the short, rounded-winged Blyth's Reed from the long-winged Marsh Warbler. Length of wing is indicated by primary projection, the length of primaries visible beyond the tertials expressed as a percentage of total length of the folded wing. Savi's, River, Olivaceous and Melodious have short wings.

WING FEATURES
Most obvious of all wing markings are the pale wingbars shown by several of the rarer *Phylloscopus* warblers. However, the presence of a pale mid-wing panel in Olive-tree, Icterine and Olivaceous Warbler is of vital importance.

BILL AND HEAD
The length and shape of a warbler's bill is a significant feature, but is influenced by the shape of the head. A sharply sloping forehead accentuates bill length, a rounded head shape makes the bill appear less dagger-like.

LEGS
Leg colour may clinch an identification, but should never be used to make one. Both Icterine and Olive-tree Warblers have blue legs, but this should not eliminate Melodious or Olivaceous Warblers respectively.

Blyth's Reed Warbler: Olive-brown warbler very similar to Marsh Warbler. Sloping forehead accentuates bill length, though not to extent of Reed Warbler. Supercilium extends just beyond eye; pale eye-ring. Uniform, not dark centred, feathers to short wings (short primary projection). Flicks tail. Wetland margins.

Marsh Warbler: Warm olive-brown warbler, more olive than Reed but warmer than Blyth's Reed, though nearer the latter. Forehead less sloping and bill less dagger-like than Reed. Long primary projection and pale tips to dark-centred tertials. Thickets rather than reeds.

Olivaceous Warbler: Chunky, largish warbler with uniform olivish upperparts and large, yellowish, dagger-like bill. Crown peaks behind eye, which shows pale ring. Short primary projection. Overall corpulent appearance and lack of facial markings are good features.

Upcher's Warbler: Larger than Olivaceous, smaller than Olive-tree Warbler. Brownish-grey with rounded head and dagger-like bill. Thin supercilium in front of eye. Long primary projection and long tail that is frequently cocked and waved. Pale wing panel and pale edges to tail.

Olive-tree Warbler: Largest of warblers. Brownish-grey with prominent pale wing panel. Clear narrow supercilium; sloping forehead with huge dagger-like yellow bill. Long primary projection, but relatively shortish tail. Strong legs.

Confusing Featureless Warblers

Many of the Warblers of the genera *Hippolais*, *Acrocephalus* and *Locustella* are plainly coloured above and below and confusing. At first sight, they appear dauntingly similar and virtually devoid of the field characteristics and marks that are used to identify other warblers. Some *Acrocephalus* and *Locustella* warblers have streaked backs and heads, but those dealt with here are, like the *Hippolais*, plain-backed. The only 'plain' *Sylvia* warbler is also shown.

Savi's Warbler: Warm, buffy warbler confined to reedbeds. Bill relatively short; rounded head shows comparatively bold supercilium. White patch on throat (bib) particularly obvious when singing. Short wings.

River Warbler: Warm olive-brown warbler more likely to be mistaken for a Marsh than a Reed Warbler. Rounded head, rather than sloping forehead, makes bill appear shorter. Breast streaking, prominently barred undertail coverts and short primary projection are good features.

River Warbler: Warm brown and buff warbler marked by sloping forehead that accentuates length of dagger-like bill. Long wings (primary projection) and clear rusty rump. Mostly confined to reeds.

Booted Warbler: Small olive-brown warbler, more like *Phylloscopus*, than other *Hippolais*. Small bill less dagger-like; prominent supercilium. Pale legs and noticeable white outertail feathers.

Warbler Heads and Bills

Acrocephalus and Locustella

River Warbler: Olive-brown flat crown, but relatively short dark brown, pink-based bill. Short, thin supercilium and noticeable pale eye-ring.

Savi's Warbler: Warm buffy-brown, with rounded crown and shortish dark brown bill, with pale brown base. Supercilium broad, especially in front of eye.

Blyth's Reed Warbler: Olive-brown, with flat forehead and crown peak behind eye. Dagger-like bill with pale horn-coloured lower mandible. Supercilium broad in front of eye, absent behind.

Marsh Warbler: Olive-brown, with less sloping forehead than confusing species and apparently shorter bill as a result. Yellow lower mandible, grey upper. Short, broad supercilium in front of eye.

Reed Warbler: Warm brown with sloping forehead and dagger-like bill, with yellowish lower mandible. Inconspicuous supercilium in front of eye.

Paddyfield Warbler: Warm buffy-brown with rounded head, shortish bill and very clear broad supercilium. The only *Acrocephalus* to show such a feature.

Warbler Heads and Bills

Hippolais Warblers

Booted Warbler: Rounded head with shortish bill. Upper mandible brown, lower pale yellow. Marked by long buffy supercilium that broadens and turns upwards behind eye. Dark eye-stripe, mottled ear coverts.

Olivaceous Warbler: Sloping forehead, though not viciously so, accentuates length of bill which, though dagger-like, is not as long as others in the genus. Upper mandible brown, lower straw. Crown peak behind eye.

Upcher's Warbler: Rounded head does not accentuate what is serious dagger-like bill. Upper mandible greyish, lower yellowish. Narrow supercilium.

Olive-tree Warbler: Sloping forehead accentuates length of pronounced dagger-like bill. Upper mandible greyish, lower yellow, creates impression of huge yellow bill. Narrow supercilium.

Icterine Warbler: More olive and yellow on head than other *Hippolais* except Melodious. Sloping forehead accentuates length of long bill. Upper mandible horn, lower yellow. Plain face with supercilium behind eye.

Melodious Warbler: Similar olive and yellow head to Icterine Warbler, but head more rounded and bill appears less striking as a result. Yellow supercilium prominent.

Vagrant *Phylloscopus* Leaf Warblers

Greenish Warbler: Shows single narrow wingbar, prominent supercilium and clear dark eye-stripe. Dark (not pale) legs and length of supercilium separate from larger Arctic Warbler.

Arctic Warbler: Similar to, but larger than Greenish Warbler. Single narrow wingbar and clear-cut dark eye-stripe separated by long narrow supercilium that extends to nape and terminates in upswept flourish. Legs pale flesh.

Pallas's Warbler: Shows every feature found on any European *Phylloscopus*. Pale crown-stripe, bold supercilium, dark eye-stripe, broad double wingbar, yellow rump patch and white-tipped tertials. Tiny, crest-like bird.

Yellow-browed Warbler: Similar to, and almost as small as, Pallas's Warbler and showing many of that species' full hand of field characters. Lacks only pale crown-stripe and yellow rump. Supercilium thinner and distinctly elongated and upswept.

Radde's Warbler: Large, robust, *Phylloscopus* marked by olive-brown plumage and broad supercilium with distinct upswept terminal flourish. Bill short and stubby; legs pale and strong. Orange undertail coverts diagnostic, but difficult to see.

Dusky Warbler: Similar to Radde's Warbler, but brown rather than olive-brown. Less pronounced supercilium and thinner more pointed bill give head quite different, more Chiffchaff-like feel. Distinctly ground-dwelling.

Paddyfield Warbler: Warm, brown warbler with uniform upperparts like Reed Warbler, but marked by bold creamy supercilium and upright stance. Short wings particularly noticeable as is raised crown.

Garden Warbler: Olive-grey warbler virtually devoid of field marks and the confusion species, particularly among *Hippolais* warblers. Short, stubby bill identifies.

Icterine Warbler: Though yellow and olive in fresh spring plumage, first winter birds are frequently 'washed-out' and lacking in colour. With the sloping forehead and dagger-like bill of this species, such autumn individuals are easily confused with other, greyer *Hippolais* such as Olivaceous and Upcher's Warblers. Note mid-wing panel.

Melodious Warbler: Though comparatively featureless, like other *Hippolais* warblers, Melodious is always distinctly yellow below and olive-green above like summer-plumaged Icterine Warbler. Lacks blue legs, pale mid-wing panel and sloping forehead of that bird.

Great Reed Warbler: Largest of all the featureless warblers. Brown above and buffy below marked by clear, short supercilium and large dagger-like bill. Only the grey Olive-tree Warbler approaches it in size.

Where Warblers are Found

HABITAT
Although all warblers have particular habitat requirements they are also the most mobile of all birds, many making journeys of several thousand miles each spring and autumn. Inevitably, such journeys cause them to land in strange places in completely the wrong habitat. In summer, however, they are distinctly creatures of habit and a woodland warbler just will not breed in a reedbed, or *vice versa*.

REEDBEDS
A considerable variety of warblers inhabit reedbeds, though relatively few are totally confined to them, even during the breeding season. Reed, Great Reed and Savi's are all reedbed specialists, though only Savi's is restricted to really extensive reed stands. The others may make do with small reed patches or water margins.

WETLAND MARGINS
Most *Acrocephalus* and *Locustella* warblers are tied to wetland habitats to a greater or lesser degree. River, Blyth's Reed, and Paddyfield Warblers are usually found among wetland scrub, though all may also be in a mixture of scant reeds and bushes. Marsh Warblers also breed in such areas, but may also be found in scrub some distance from water associated with meadowsweet.

HEATH AND SCRUB
Though it is the warblers of the genus *Sylvia* that are most typical of the thorny, dwarf Mediterranean *maquis*, scrub with shrubs does hold a number of plain confusing warblers of other genera. Indeed, all members of the *Hippolais* occur in thickets and tangles, even though they may construct their nests elsewhere.

WOODS
Woods are the natural home of the genus *Phylloscopus*, though other genera exploit their margins and clearings. Garden Warbler is the most woodland orientated of the confusingly plain warblers, but Icterine and Melodious also utilize similar woodland margins.

ORCHARDS AND GROVES
The open-ground quality of fruit orchards and olive groves is ideally suited to several warblers, particularly of the genus *Hippolais*. Olive-tree is generally associated with groves, as are Upcher's and Booted Warblers.

RANGE AND DISTRIBUTION
In the same way and for the same reasons that warblers appear on migration in quite unsuitable habitats, they can and do appear well away from their natural range. Indeed, such vagrants are the very stuff of birding as a field sport. Nevertheless, during the breeding season they are confined geographically and a knowledge of a species' distribution is a significant aid to its identification. Northern warblers include Blyth's Reed, Garden and Icterine, though Garden Warbler is found throughout Europe and Icterine is decidedly eastern. Blyth's Reed Warbler is the only purely northern European warbler. Southern warblers include many of the scrub and grove species such as Olivaceous, Olive-tree, Upcher's and Booted. But three of these are decidedly eastern as well. Eastern warblers form a decidedly large group and include River, Marsh, Olive-tree, Upcher's, Booted and Icterine.

Olivaceous Warbler *Hippolais pallida*

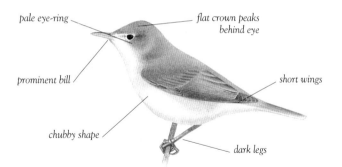

pale eye-ring

flat crown peaks behind eye

prominent bill

short wings

chubby shape

dark legs

Status: Summer visitor to Spain, Balkans and Turkey.
Identification: 12–14cm (4½–5½in). Washed-out, olive warbler with general lack of distinguishing features. Typical *Hippolais* warbler, with robust structure. Lack of yellow in plumage; large size; short rounded wings; general stockiness are best features. Bill long, accentuated by flat forehead; eastern subspecies, *H.p.elaeica*, has shorter bill than western, *H.p.opaca*.
Voice: Repeated babbling; hard *tec-tec*.
Habitat: Thickets and groves with taller trees.
Similar Species: See Booted, Olive-tree and Upcher's Warblers, all of which are washed-out olive-grey.

J F M A M J J A S O N D

Olive-tree Warbler *Hippolais olivetorum*

supercilium extends just behind eye

narrow wingbar

huge yellow bill

pale mid-wing panel

long primary projection

bluish legs

Status: Scarce summer visitor to woods and groves of south-east Europe.
Identification: 15–16cm (6in). Largest of the robust *Hippolais* warblers. Grey above, paler grey below; with huge yellow dagger of a bill accentuated by sloping forehead and crown peaked over eye. Pale grey supercilium terminates behind eye. Secondaries pale edged, forming pale panel on closed wing like first-winter Upcher's; long primary projection.
Voice: Slow, scratchy song; hard *tuc*.
Habitat: Deciduous woods, thickets, olive groves.
Similar Species: See Olivaceous and Upcher's Warblers.

J F M A M J J A S O N D

Icterine Warbler *Hippolais icterina*

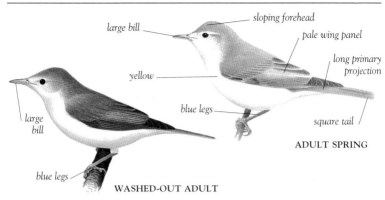

large bill — sloping forehead

large bill — pale wing panel

yellow — long primary projection

blue legs — blue legs

large bill — square tail

ADULT SPRING

WASHED-OUT ADULT

J F M A M J J A S O N D

Status: Summer visitor to central and eastern Europe.
Identification: 13–14cm (5–5½in). Largish, rather nondescript warbler with long bill and sloping forehead. Olive above, pale yellow below. Short yellow supercilium, bluish legs, square tail. Summer adults have pale panel in wing formed by margins of inner flight feathers. Long wings with exposed primaries, about a third of overall folded length.
Voice: Song resembles Marsh Warbler with mixed harsh and melodic notes; hard *tec* and *churr*.
Habitat: Scrubby woods, thickets.
Similar Species: Melodious Warbler.

Melodious Warbler *Hippolais polyglotta*

rounded head

large bill — no mid-wing panel

short, rounded wings

ADULT

greyish legs

J F M A M J J A S O N D

Status: Summer visitor to western Europe as far as Italy. Replaced eastwards by Icterine Warbler.
Identification: 12–13cm (4½–5in). Similar to Icterine Warbler, brownish-green above, creamy-yellow below, bill shorter, head more rounded and tail shorter, giving species distinctly plumper appearance. Wings short and rounded, exposed primaries forming only quarter of length of folded wing. Legs usually grey, though occasionally bluish.
Voice: Extended, melodic song with few harsh notes.
Habitat: Orchards, copses, thickets.
Similar Species: Icterine Warbler also yellowish; young *Phylloscopus* warblers may be as yellow.

Marmora's Warbler   *Sylvia sarda*

dark grey head

very long tail

dark grey

ADULT ♂

J F M A M J J A S O N D

Status: Resident west Mediterranean islands.
Identification: 12cm (4½in). Long tail and similar habits to Dartford Warbler. Adult male dark grey above with short rounded wings; underparts grey, paler on belly. Female grey above, but much paler below with warm pinkish wash. Both sexes have large head with 'crested' appearance and bulging chin; characteristic red eye-ring.
Voice: Pleasant twitter ending in trill; hard *tuc*.
Habitat: Low Mediterranean scrub.
Similar Species: Grey underparts distinguish from Dartford Warbler, but beware juveniles. Juvenile Marmora's much paler below.

Dartford Warbler   *Sylvia undata*

grey crown   very long tail

often cocked

vinous
brown

♂

pinker
than ♂

♀

Status: Resident of heaths and scrub western Europe to Italy.
Identification: 12–13cm (4½–5in). Tiny, elusive warbler most easily seen while singing in early spring. Upperparts grey-brown, greyer on head; underparts dark vinous brown with sparse white flecking on throat. Outstanding feature is long tail, often cocked when perching. Juveniles browner above and buffy below. Flies on rounded , whirring wings with long tail bouncing.
Voice: Scratchy warbling song; harsh *chur* or *tic*.
Habitat: Heaths with gorse; Mediterranean scrub.
Similar Species: Marmora's has similar long-tailed shape.

J F M A M J J A S O N D

Spectacled Warbler   *Sylvia conspicillata*

dark lores

white throat

brownish head

bunched secondaries
from orange-buff
patch

white primary margins

ADULT ♂

ADULT ♀

J F M A M J J A S O N D

Status: Summer visitor to western Mediterranean scrub; resident Cyprus.
Identification: 11.5–12.5cm (4½in). Small version of Common Whitethroat. Male has grey head; conspicuous white throat, which is often puffed out; pinkish breast; white belly. Brown wings prominently edged rufous; tail with white outer feathers. Female browner on head and back, less pink below, but has same rusty wings. Male differs from Whitethroat in size; significantly darker lores, producing 'masked' effect.
Habitat: Open expanses of low scrub.
Similar Species: Common Whitethroat as above.

Subalpine Warbler   *Sylvia cantillans*

buff-brown, not
rufous wings

white
throat

FIRST WINTER ♀

prominent
moustache

rich orange-red
breast

ADULT ♂

J F M A M J J A S O N D

Status: Locally common summer visitor Mediterranean scrub.
Identification: 11.5–12.5cm (4½–5in). Grey above, deep orange-red below with bold white moustachial streak. Wings short and rounded. In some plumages, wings rather rufous, but never rusty like Common Whitethroat or Spectacled Warbler. Bold white outertail feathers. Female much paler below, but with distinct moustache.
Voice: Sweet, but scratchy, jingle; hard *tuc-tuc-tuc*.
Habitat: Low scrubby gullies and thickets.
Similar Species: See Common Whitethroat and Spectacled Warbler.

Ménétries's Warbler *Sylvia mystacea*

eye-ring

grey nape

tail wagging

white moustache

salmon washed

♂

pale grey

tail wagging

black alula

♀

J F M A M J J A S O N D

Status: Summer visitor to south-eastern Turkey.
Identification: 12–13cm (5in). Male has black cap and grey back. Eye-ring yellow not red. Underparts salmon-pink with white moustache similar to darker Subalpine Warbler. Black tail has white outer feathers and is waved continually up and down and from side to side. Female similar to female Sardinian and Subalpine, but tail waving a sure field mark. Also paler both above and below.
Voice: Buzzing and chattering that are less harsh than Sardinian Warbler. Song less grating, many sweet notes.
Habitat: Riverside scrub, gardens and cultivation edges.
Similar Species: Sardinian and Subalpine Warblers.

Sardinian Warbler *Sylvia melanocephala*

red eye-ring

black cap

slate-grey

white throat

ADULT ♂

long tail even cocked

browner above

white outertail

white throat

ADULT ♀

white outertail

J F M A M J J A S O N D

Status: Common resident of Mediterranean scrub.
Identification: 12.5–14cm (5–5½in). Male has bold black cap that extends below prominent red-ringed eye. Upperparts slate-grey, tail broadly edged and tipped white. Underparts white with grey flanks. Female similar, but browner. Skulking behaviour, most often seen in flight between dense ground vegetation.
Voice: Harsh chattering and rattles.
Habitat: Scrubland, open woods, gardens, parks.
Similar Species: All black-headed 'scrub' warblers of genus *Sylvia*. Presume Sardinian until proved otherwise.

Rüppell's Warbler *Sylvia rueppellii*

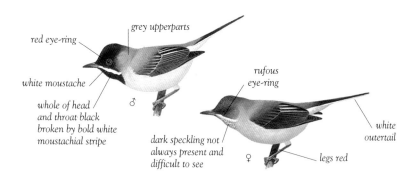

red eye-ring

grey upperparts

white moustache

whole of head
and throat black
broken by bold white
moustachial stripe

♂

rufous
eye-ring

dark speckling not
always present and
difficult to see

♀

white
outertail

legs red

J F M A M J J A S O N D

Status: Eastern Mediterranean scrub warbler.
Identification: 13.5–14.5cm (5½in). Male has entire head,
throat and upper breast black broken by bold white
moustachial stripe. Seemingly unmistakable, but beware
poorly seen male Cyprus Warbler. Female is grey above
with warm edges to flight feathers and wing coverts.
Rufous eye-ring and reddish legs distinguish.
Voice: Song similar to Sardinian, but with short repeated
phrases. Alarm a repeated harsh chacking.
Habitat: Scrub-covered hillsides.
Similar Species: Male to Sardinian Warbler, female to
Lesser Whitethroat.

Cyprus Warbler *Sylvia melanothorax*

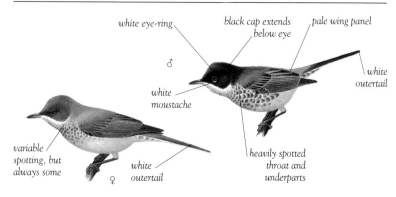

white eye-ring

black cap extends
below eye

pale wing panel

♂

white
moustache

white
outertail

heavily spotted
throat and
underparts

variable
spotting, but
always some

white
outertail

♀

J F M A M J J A S O N D

Status: Typical Mediterranean scrub warbler, but breeds
only in Cyprus; winters Israel.
Identification: 13cm (5in). Similar to Sardinian Warbler,
but male has bold black spotting and streaking on
underparts and broad white moustachial streak. Female
similar, but less spotted and streaked. Both sexes show pale
wing panel which, together with white moustache may
cause confusion with Rüppell's Warbler.
Voice: Song and calls similar to Sardinian Warbler with
harsh rattles and soft warbling broken by harsher notes.
Habitat: Low thorny scrub on rocky hillsides.
Similar Species: Rüppell's and Sardinian Warblers.

Orphean Warbler *Sylvia hortensis*

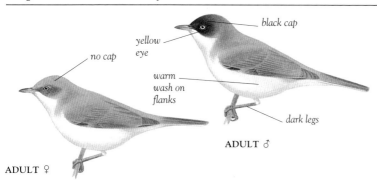

black cap

yellow eye

no cap

warm wash on flanks

dark legs

ADULT ♂

ADULT ♀

J F M A M J J A S O N D

Status: Scarce summer visitor to Mediterranean basin.
Identification: 14.5–16cm (5½–6½in). Like a large Sardinian Warbler with a bold yellow eye. Male has dull black cap that extends below prominent pale yellow eye and merges into sooty-grey upperparts; tail with white outer feathers. Throat white, remaining underparts buffy-pink. Female similar, but crown greyish, virtually matching upperparts.
Voice: Delicate warble with phrases repeated like Song Thrush; harsh *tac-tac*.
Habitat: Tall stands of vegetation and scrub.
Similar Species: Blackcap; Sardinian Warbler.

Barred Warbler *Sylvia nisoria*

stout bill

yellow eye

stout bill

dark eye, pale ring

barred below

white outertail

ADULT SUMMER

FIRST WINTER

barred undertail

white outertail

Status: Large, chunky warbler, summer visitor eastern Europe; migrates south-eastwards.
Identification: 14–16cm (5½–6½in). Easily identified in breeding plumages, but may pose problem in first winter. Adult grey above marked by two prominent pale wingbars. Tail has white outer feathers and is frequently cocked; prominently yellow eye. White underparts barred with grey crescents. First winter lacks barring except on flanks; lacks yellow eye, but has double wingbar and white-edged tail.
Voice: Variable warbling with harsh phrases.
Habitat: Woodland clearings, undergrowth, scrub, hedges.
Similar Species: Garden Warbler in autumn.

J F M A M J J A S O N D

Lesser Whitethroat   *Sylvia curruca*

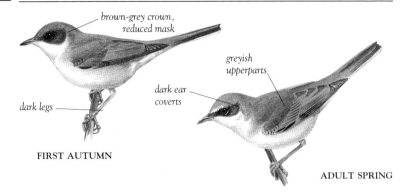

brown-grey crown,
reduced mask

greyish
upperparts

dark ear
coverts

dark legs

FIRST AUTUMN

ADULT SPRING

J F M A M J J A S O N D

Status: Widespread summer visitor, absent south and west; migrates south-easterly.
Identification: 13–14cm (5–5½in). Generally a skulking bird of bushy scrub, tall hedgerows and young conifers. Basically grey above, white below. Adult has prominent, dark ear coverts, giving masked appearance. Legs dark; white outertail feathers.
Voice: Rattle, similar to Yellowhammer, lacking final flourish; hard *tac-tac*.
Habitat: Tall thickets, heaths, scrubby woodland.
Similar Species: Common Whitethroat is rusty-winged; check other female *Sylvia* warblers.

Common Whitethroat   *Sylvia communis*

grey
crown

prominent rusty
wings

white
throat

brownish
crown

♂

buffy
legs

♀

J F M A M J J A S O N D

Status: Widespread and common summer visitor.
Identification: 13–15cm (5–6in). Marked by white throat; particularly obvious in singing male. Upperparts greyish brown. Broad rusty margins to wing feathers single most important feature. Head grey in male, buffy brown in female and juvenile. Breast pinkish, belly white, legs pale. Has short, dancing song flight.
Voice: Brief, scratchy warble; hard *tac-tac*.
Habitat: Brambles, thickets, hedgerows.
Similar Species: Spectacled Warbler smaller, but with similar pattern if grey head, white throat and (very) rusty wings.

Garden Warbler *Sylvia borin*

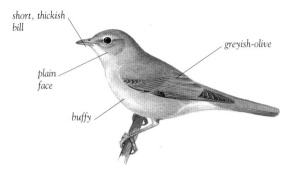

short, thickish bill

plain face

buffy

greyish-olive

J F M A M J J A S O N D

Status: Widespread summer visitor to hedges and thickets.
Identification: 13–15cm (5–6in). Virtually devoid of field
marks. Chunky, thick-set warbler with upperparts greyish
olive, underparts buffy white. Short, stubby bill and pale
eye-ring best features. Mostly skulks, even when singing.
Voice: Fine, quick warbling, like chattering Blackcap, but
lacking clear melodic notes of that bird.
Habitat: Woods, thickets, hedgerows.
Similar Species: Nondescript qualities cause confusion
with 'greyish' *Hippolais* warblers. But short, stubby bill
separates at all times. Beware juvenile Barred Warbler.

Blackcap *Sylvia atricapilla*

black cap

grey back

rust cap

♂

♀

J F M A M J J A S O N D

Status: Widespread and common summer visitor; winters
south and west.
Identification: 13–15cm (5–6in). Largish grey warbler
marked by black cap in male, rusty-brown cap in female,
that extends to eye. Female washed brown-grey above and
buff-grey on flanks. Juvenile has rusty-brown cap as female.
Voice: Extended, melodic song; more varied than Garden
Warbler, often compared to Nightingale.
Habitat: Woodland, thickets with trees, groves.
Similar Species: Red-capped female, none; black-capped
male, check Orphean Warbler.

Green Warbler   *Phylloscopus nitidus*

prominent supercilium

olive-green

single narrow wingbar

yellowish wash

white outertail tips

dark legs

Status: Summer visitor to mountains of northern and eastern Turkey.
Identification: 11cm (4½in). Typical *Phylloscopus* marked by single narrow wingbar and by more green and yellow in plumage than similar birds. Never as green and yellow as Wood Warbler. Upperparts olive-green, underparts washed yellow, often confined to throat. Yellowish supercilium never upturns behind eye like many Greenish.
Voice: Clear *chee-wee*. Willow Warbler-like string of notes.
Habitat: Montane forests, cliff thickets, streamside gullies.
Similar Species: Particularly Greenish Warbler and Yellow-browed Warbler of subspecies *humei*.

Greenish Warbler   *Phylloscopus trochiloides*

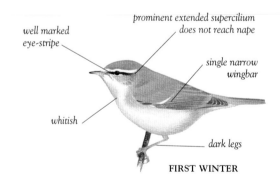

well marked eye-stripe

prominent extended supercilium does not reach nape

single narrow wingbar

whitish

dark legs

FIRST WINTER

Status: Summer visitor to Baltic; scarce westwards.
Identification: 10–11cm (4–4½in). Similar to Chiffchaff but pale wingbar formed by tips of greater coverts distinguish in summer and first winter. At other times, wingbar may be faint, or even absent, making for confusion with Chiffchaff, which has similar dark legs. Supercilium creamy and bold, more so than Chiffchaff.
Voice: Brief high-pitched *weedle-weedle-weedle*.
Habitat: Deciduous woods.
Similar Species: Arctic Warbler has larger bill, sloping forehead, brownish legs and is larger and heavier built. Supercilium reaches nape.

Arctic Warbler   *Phylloscopus borealis*

prominent eye-stripe

supercilium extends to nape

single narrow wingbar

pale legs

FIRST WINTER

J F M A M J J A S O N D

Status: Scarce summer visitor extreme north-east.
Identification: 12cm (4½). Like Willow Warbler, distinguished by single narrow, white wingbar, sometimes a second. Bill larger than other *Phylloscopus* warblers accentuated by sloping forehead. Supercilium long and extends well beyond eye, with upturn towards nape; accentuated by long dark eye-stripe.
Voice: Melodic trill followed by harsh note.
Habitat: Damp birch forest.
Similar Species: Greenish Warbler has shorter bill and supercilium, but great care required.

Pallas's Warbler   *Phylloscopus proregulus*

pale crown-stripe plus dark lateral crown-stripes

bold double wingbar

yellow rump

dark eye-stripe

FIRST WINTER

J F M A M J J A S O N D

Status: Autumn vagrant westwards from Asia mainly to Britain and Ireland.
Identification: 8.5–9.5cm (3¼–3½in). Relative of Chiffchaff that frequently hovers and behaves like Firecrest. Shows every major character by which *Phylloscopus* warblers identified. Bold supercilium; distinct eye-stripe; pale crown-stripe; bold double wingbar; prominent yellow rump. Upperparts olive-green.
Voice: Quiet *swee*; louder *chee-weet*.
Habitat: Bushes and scrub.
Similar Species: Firecrest, especially juvenile, and Yellow-browed Warbler.

Radde's Warbler   *Phylloscopus schwarzi*

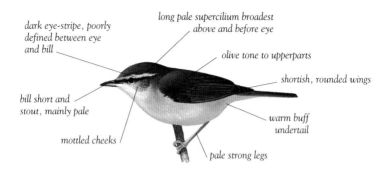

long pale supercilium broadest
above and before eye

dark eye-stripe, poorly
defined between eye
and bill

olive tone to upperparts

shortish, rounded wings

bill short and
stout, mainly pale

warm buff
undertail

mottled cheeks

pale strong legs

J F M A M J J A S O N D

Status: Rare autumn vagrant from eastern Asia.
Identification: 12–13cm (5in). Chunky build; short thick
bill; and long, bold, buffy-yellow supercilium, upswept
toward nape, distinguish from other *Phylloscopus* warblers.
Dark eye-stripe, dark band above supercilium, mottled
cheeks, buffy undertail coverts, pale margins to wing
feathers and strong palish yellow legs are additional
features. First winter dark olive; adult browner, easily to
confused with Dusky Warbler.
Voice: A soft *tuk-tuk* or louder *tak-tak*.
Habitat: Breeds taiga; winters scrub.
Similar Species: See Dusky Warbler and above.

Dusky Warbler   *Phylloscopus fuscatus*

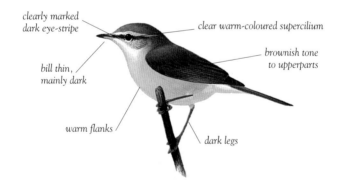

clearly marked
dark eye-stripe

clear warm-coloured supercilium

brownish tone
to upperparts

bill thin,
mainly dark

warm flanks

dark legs

J F M A M J J A S O N D

Status: Rare autumn vagrant from eastern Asia.
Identification: 11.5–12cm (4¾in). Like a brown
Chiffchaff, but with shorter wings and more prominent
rusty-buff supercilium contrasting with bold eye-stripe.
Thin dark bill and legs aid separation from more robust
adult Radde's Warbler. Habit of feeding on ground with
drooping wings and raised tail reminiscent of accentor.
Voice: Hard *tak-tak* similar to alarmed Radde's.
Habitat: Breeds deciduous woods and scrub, often along
streams.Winter and migrants in dense thickets.
Similar Species: See Chiffchaff and Radde's Warbler.

Bonelli's Warbler   *Phylloscopus bonelli*

greyish head
and back

yellow wing panel

yellow
rump

white
below

dark legs

J F M A M J J A S O N D

Status: Summer visitor to Mediterranean and west.
Identification: 11–12cm (4½in). Similar to Chiffchaff, but head, neck and foreparts washed-out grey, virtually devoid of field marks. Wings and tail with noticeable yellow margins to feathers; and bold yellow rump, obvious in flight. Underparts white; legs brown. Contrast of dull foreparts and yellowish hindparts best feature. By end breeding season adults have lost much yellow and may resemble similar aged Chiffchaff.
Voice: Rattled trill.
Habitat: Variety of woodlands.
Similar Species: Adult autumn Chiffchaff.

Wood Warbler   *Phylloscopus sibilatrix*

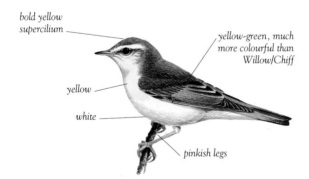

bold yellow
supercilium

yellow-green, much
more colourful than
Willow/Chiff

yellow

white

pinkish legs

Status: Summer visitor to deciduous woods; migrates south-east.
Identification: 12–13cm (4½–5in). Larger than Willow Warbler; greener above, with more yellow on wing and breast, contrasting with pure white belly. Pronounced yellowish supercilium with dark eye-stripe. Legs pale. Song flight on fluttering wings below tree canopy distinctive.
Voice: Plaintive *peu-peu* accelerates into buzzing trill in song flight.
Habitat: Dense deciduous woods with scant ground cover.
Similar Species: Juvenile Willow Warbler yellow, but never so bold as Wood Warbler.

J F M A M J J A S O N D

Yellow-browed Warbler *Phylloscopus inornatus*

bold yellow supercilium extends to nape

bold double wingbar

strong dark eye-stripe

mottled ear coverts

Status: Tiny Siberian waif that wanders westwards across Europe every autumn.
Identification: 9.5–10.5cm (3–4in). Smaller than Chiffchaff and marked by extended supercilium and bold double wingbar. Upperparts olive with broad, pale yellow supercilium extending to nape, and darkish stripe through eye. Wing has two whitish wingbars, rear one being extremely bold. Underparts white.
Voice: Characteristic hard *swee.*
Habitat: Any available cover.
Similar Species: Pallas's Warbler has coronal stripe and yellow rump.

J F M A M J J A S O N D

Willow Warbler *Phylloscopus trochilus*

marked supercilium

pale legs

ADULT SPRING

yellow breast

AUTUMN

J F M A M J J A S O N D

Status: Common, widespread summer visitor to wide variety of open wooded habitats.
Identification: 10.5–11.5cm (4–4½in). Very similar to Chiffchaff – olive-green above; washed yellow below. Clear supercilium extends well beyond eye; clear dark eye-stripe. Always cleaner-cut than Chiffchaff with pale (not dark) legs.
Voice: Sweet, descending trill; weak, two-part *hu-weet.*
Habitat: Heaths with birch and willow; woodland clearings and margins.
Similar Species: Chiffchaff as above; yellow autumn birds could be confused with larger Melodious Warbler.

Chiffchaff *Phylloscopus collybita*

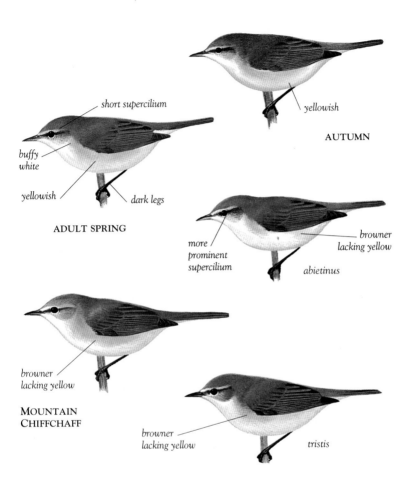

short supercilium

yellowish

AUTUMN

buffy
white

yellowish

dark legs

ADULT SPRING

more
prominent
supercilium

browner
lacking yellow

abietinus

browner
lacking yellow

**MOUNTAIN
CHIFFCHAFF**

browner
lacking yellow

tristis

Status: Named after characteristic call uttered over most of range. Summer visitor to north and east; winter visitor and resident in south and west.

Identification: 10.5–11.5cm (4–4½in). Slightly smaller than Willow Warbler with shorter, less well-marked supercilium. Upperparts browner; underparts more buffy, creating less 'clean' appearance. Dark legs. Young birds much more yellow and olive-green like Willow Warbler. Coloration varies geographically. Northern subspecies *abietinus* and eastern subspecies *tristis* much browner above and buffy-brown below; *tristis* has buffy-brown supercilium. Both resemble Mountain Chiffchaff *P.sindianus* and Dusky Warbler *P.fuscatus* which are separate species. Occurrences of vagrant *abietinus* and *tristis* may cause serious confusion with these species. All show a more marked supercilium than *collybita* of western Europe.

Voice: Distinctive *chiff-chaff-chiff-chaff* repeated. Iberian birds *tit-tit-tit-tit-tit-tit-tswee-tswee-tit-it-it*. Eastern *tristis* have tinkling warble. Also a single syllable *hweet*, separable from *hu-weet* of Willow Warbler.

Habitat: Variety of woodlands.

Similar Species: Willow and Dusky Warblers as above; beware Mountain Chiffchaff.

Goldcrest *Regulus regulus*

golden crest

plain head

plain face, no supercilium,
no eye-stripe

olive-green

JUVENILE

♀

moustache

♂

J F M A M J J A S O N D

Status: Smallest European bird, common widespread resident and winter visitor.
Identification: 8.5–9cm (3½in). Tiny rotund, with shortish tail. Crown has distinctive golden-orange blaze bordered by black. Face plain with large, dark eye and fine moustachial streak. Back olive-green; wings black with broad white margins and clear, single (sometimes double) wingbar. Underparts buffy white. Ever-active; flicks.
Voice: High-pitched *zi-zi-zi-zi*.
Habitat: Woods, particularly conifers; also gardens, hedges.
Similar Species: Firecrest has bold face pattern.

Firecrest *Regulus ignicapillus*

bold supercilium

yellow crest

bold white supercilium
bold eye-stripe

yellow-green

JUVENILE

♀

♂

J F M A M J J A S O N D

Status: Widespread resident south and west; summer visitor north and east.
Identification: 8.5–9cm (3½in). Similar to Goldcrest with similar high-pitched call and active, non-stop search for food among conifers. Greener on back with distinctive face pattern of bold white supercilium and prominent black eye-stripe. Easily identified if seen clearly. Different call and song; both stronger than Goldcrest.
Voice: High *zit-zit-zit*; similar song often ends abruptly.
Habitat: Conifers, low woodland.
Similar Species: Goldcrest has featureless face: see also vagrant Pallas's and Yellow-browed Warblers.

Spotted Flycatcher *Muscicapa striata*

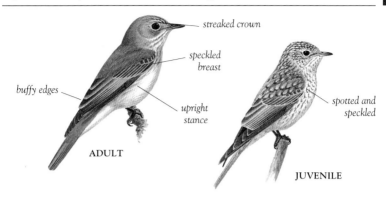

streaked crown

speckled breast

buffy edges

upright stance

ADULT

spotted and speckled

JUVENILE

J F M A M J J A S O N D

Status: Common and widespread summer visitor.
Identification: 13.5–14.5cm (5½–6in). Frequently seen perched upright on fence or twig, flying out to catch passing insect and returning to original perch. Agile flight on large wings. Upperparts greyish brown; narrow, pale edges to inner flight feathers and wing coverts. Crown streaked brown and buff. Underparts white; buff-brown streaking on breast. First winter birds differ in having broader buff margins to wing feathers.
Voice: Weak *tzee*.
Habitat: Gardens, hedges, open woods.
Similar Species: See Red-breasted Flycatcher.

Red-breasted Flycatcher *Ficedula parva*

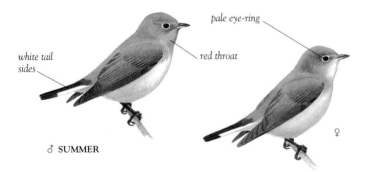

pale eye-ring

white tail sides

red throat

♂ **SUMMER**

♀

Status: Summer visitor to north and east.
Identification: 11–12cm (4½in). Summer male grey on head, grey-brown on back, wings and rump, but with distinctive black tail marked with bold white ovals at sides. Tail cocking shows this feature to advantage. Throat and upper breast rusty-red, remaining underparts white. Pale eye-ring prominent feature. Female and first-winter birds lack red throat, but have same black and white tail pattern.
Voice: Sharp *zeet*; trilled song.
Habitat: Deciduous woods, often damp or flooded.
Similar Species: Check female and first-winter Pied Flycatcher and relatives.

J F M A·M J J A S O N D

Semi-collared Flycatcher *Ficedula semitorquata*

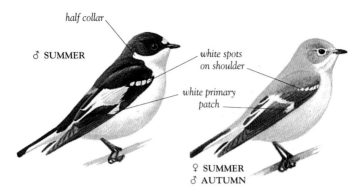

half collar

♂ SUMMER

white spots on shoulder

white primary patch

♀ SUMMER
♂ AUTUMN

J F M A M J J A S O N D

Status: Summer visitor south-east Europe.
Identification: 12–13cm (5in). Formerly considered conspecific with Collared Flycatcher. Male black and white with white half collar. Female as female Collared with small white patch in primaries. Both sexes show row of white spots on shoulder (median coverts) that is surest means of separation from both Collared and Pied Flycatchers.
Voice: Like Collared, but faster.
Habitat: Deciduous woods, often on hillsides.
Similar Species: As above.

Collared Flycatcher *Ficedula albicollis*

♀ FIRST WINTER &
♂ AUTUMN

collar

♂ SUMMER

large primary patch

white patch in primaries

J F M A M J J A S O N D

Status: Summer visitor eastwards from eastern France.
Identification: 12–13cm (5in). Very similar to Pied Flycatcher, particularly female and first winter. Male black above and white below marked by white collar, white rump and extensive white in wing. Female and first winter very close to equivalent plumages of Pied Flycatcher, but with more white in secondaries and small white rectangular patch on outer primaries.
Voice: Repetitive *see-see-see see-oo*.
Habitat: Tall deciduous woods.
Similar Species: Semi-collared and Pied Flycatchers, especially female and first winter.

Pied Flycatcher *Ficedula hypoleuca*

white forehead

white in wing

white in wing

cocked tail   ♂

♀ & AUTUMN ♂

J F M A M J J A S O N D

Status: Widespread and locally common summer visitor to north and temperate Europe.
Identification: 12–13cm (5in). Stout little bird with tiny bill. Perches openly watching for passing insects. Summer male black above with white forehead and bold area of white in wing; underparts white. Female, winter male and first-winter birds similar, but brown above with smaller white area in wing. Takes readily to nest boxes.
Voice: Repeated *zee-chi* ending in flourish; hard *tic*.
Habitat: Deciduous woods, often among hills.
Similar Species: Collared and Semi-collared Flycatchers, particularly female and first winter.

Long-tailed Tit *Aegithalos caudatus*

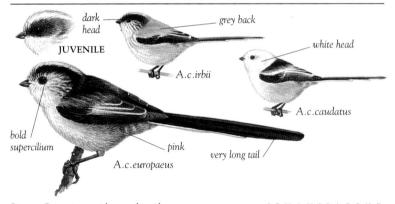

dark head

grey back

white head

JUVENILE

A.c.irbii

A.c.caudatus

bold supercilium

pink

very long tail

A.c.europaeus

Status: Gregarious, widespread resident.
Identification: 13.5–14.5cm (5½–5½in). Small, active bird with tail longer than body. Western subspecies *A.c.europaeus* has crown white with bold black stripe over eye extending to black back; tiny black bill. Wings black and white; tail black with white outer feathers; pink undertail coverts. Juveniles lack pink and have sooty black heads. Northern subspecies *A.c.caudatus* has all-white head. Spanish birds *A.c.irbii* have grey backs.
Voice: Continuous, high-pitched *zee-zee-zee*.
Habitat: Hedges, open woods, heaths and hedges.
Similar Species: None.

J F M A M J J A S O N D

Bearded Tit *Panurus biarmicus*

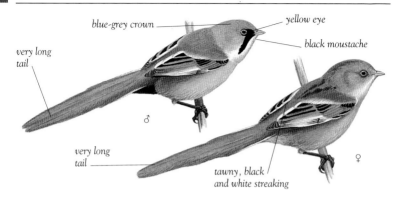

blue-grey crown

yellow eye

black moustache

very long tail

very long tail

tawny, black and white streaking

♂

♀

J F M A M J J A S O N D

Status: Highly localized resident of reedbeds that is gregarious at all seasons..
Identification: 16–17cm (6½–6½in). Small, buff-brown bird with long tail. Most often seen flying low on short whirring wings, long tail streaming out behind. Also perches on reed-tops. Male rich orange-brown above, with bold black and white margins to wings. Head blue-grey marked by droopy black moustache; both lacking in female.
Voice: *Pting-pting* repeated.
Habitat: Extensive reedbeds.
Similar Species: See Penduline Tit.

Penduline Tit *Remiz pendulinus*

black mask

pale chestnut back

chestnut back

ADULT ♂

JUVENILE

J F M A M J J A S O N D

Status: Patchily distributed resident of watersides; eastern birds are summer visitors.
Identification: 10.5–11cm (4½in). Male boldly marked, with chestnut back, and black mask through eye. Female paler above and has greyish head with only rudimentary mask. Juvenile 'washed out' version of female with pale chestnut back. Best located by call. Mostly found among overgrown wetland tangles and along dykes; builds penduline white nest overhanging water.
Voice: Plaintive *tseee*.
Habitat: Waterside trees and bushes.
Similar Species: See Bearded Tit.

Marsh Tit *Parus palustris*

glossy cap

small bib

uniform wing

J F M A M J J A S O N D

Status: Widespread resident, though absent from Mediterranean coasts.
Identification: 11–12cm (4½–5in). Typical tit with round head, short bill, black cap and uniform buff-brown upperparts. Great care needed to distinguish from very similar Willow Tit; Marsh Tit cap shiny (not dull), bib small (not large and diffuse); lacks pale panel in wing. Marsh Tit is neat and elegant; Willow Tit is scruffy.
Voice: Repeated *pitchoo-pitchoo-pitchoo*.
Habitat: Deciduous woods.
Similar Species: Willow Tit as above. See also larger Sombre and Siberian Tits.

Willow Tit *Parus montanus*

dull, sooty cap

pale wing panel

large bib

greyish back

montanus

borealis

white below

Status: Widespread resident, absent south except mountains.
Identification: 11–12cm (4½–5in). Very like Marsh Tit and found in similar habitats, especially damp alder and birch woods. Somewhat ill-kept appearance. Distinguished from Marsh Tit by dull black cap, larger white cheeks, larger and more diffuse black bib and (especially in winter) pale wing panel. Northern subspecies *P.m.borealis* has greyish back and more extensive white in folded wing.
Voice: Buzzing *erz-erz-erz*; high-pitched *zi-zi-zi*.
Habitat: Damp woods and scrub.
Similar Species: See Marsh, Sombre and Siberian Tits.

J F M A M J J A S O N D

Sombre Tit *Parus lugubris*

brown washed
upperparts

heavy bill

large bib

buffy flanks

J F M A M J J A S O N D

Status: Resident hillside woods and bushy scrub south-east Europe.
Identification: 14cm (5½in). Dull brown-black cap separated from substantial black bib by white cheeks. Upperparts dull brownish, underparts white with pale buffy flanks. Pattern similar to Willow Tit, but much larger with heavier bill and brown wash over cap.
Voice: Varied chattering, also *charr*.
Habitat: Montane hedges, scrubby woods and conifers; also archeological sites and ruins.
Similar Species: Siberian Tit does not overlap range of Sombre Tit.

Siberian Tit *Parus cinctus*

brownish wash

scruffy bib

rufous flanks

J F M A M J J A S O N D

Status: Resident birch and conifer woods of boreal zone of Fennoscandia.
Identification: 13–15.5cm (5–6in). Large, decidedly scruffy tit, even more so than similar, but smaller, Willow Tit. Black cap washed rusty; upperparts dull black washed with rust on back. Untidy chin patch more extensive than Willow Tit's; underparts white, rusty-brown along flanks.
Voice: Nasal *eeez* repeated four or five times.
Habitat: Virtually confined to conifer forests with birch and other scrub.
Similar Species: Willow Tit as above, but range also overlaps Marsh Tit.

Crested Tit *Parus cristatus*

black line surrounds face

crest streaked

J F M A M J J A S O N D

Status: Resident pinewoods throughout most of Europe; unknown away from breeding grounds.
Identification: 11–12cm (4½ –5in). Typically active, often associating with other tits. Grey-brown upperparts with prominent black and white streaked crest. Face white with clearly marked black eye-stripe, black bib and black line extending to enclose ear coverts. Underparts buffy.
Voice: Trilled *chirr-chirr-rr*.
Habitat: Pines with broken stumps and associated scattered birches.
Similar Species: No other European tit shows even the semblance of a crest.

Coal Tit *Parus ater*

white nape patch

grey back

bold double wingbar

Status: Widespread and common resident.
Identification: 10.5–11.5cm (4½in). Smallest tit, most often found among conifers. Grey above, with double white wingbar; underparts white. Crown and substantial bib glossy black; white patch on nape distinguishes from other tits.
Voice: High-pitched *zee-zee-zee*; also *weecho-weecho* repeated.
Habitat: Mostly associated with conifers, but even isolated belts or trees act as base for wider foraging to gardens .
Similar Species: Call like Goldcrest's; song like Great Tit's but usually distinctive.

J F M A M J J A S O N D

Blue Tit *Parus caeruleus*

greenish crown

blue crown

blue wings

supercilium and eye-stripe

JUVENILE

ADULT

J F M A M J J A S O N D

Status: Most common resident tit over most of Europe, especially in the west.

Identification: 11–12cm (4½–5in). Comes readily to bird tables and feeders; will occupy nest boxes and use bird baths. Wings pale blue with single white wingbar; back greenish. Underparts yellow with neat dividing line on centre of breast. White cheeks enclosed by dark line from eye to chin. Lacks black cap of most other European tits.

Voice: Harsh *churr*; also *tseee-tseee-tseee*.

Habitat: Woods, gardens, orchards, hedges, marshes.

Similar Species: See larger and darker Great Tit.

Azure Tit *Parus cyanus*

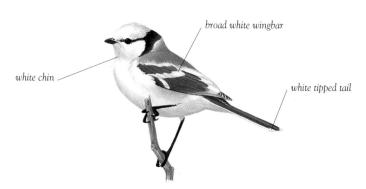

broad white wingbar

white chin

white tipped tail

J F M A M J J A S O N D

Status: Resident close relative of Blue Tit that just enters our area in western Russia.

Identification: 13cm (5¼in). Similar to 'washed out' Blue Tit but colours reduced to blue and white. Lacks dark bib. Has broad white wing patch, obvious both at rest and in flight. Even pale or albinistic forms of Blue Tit do not show these characters. Slightly larger than Blue Tit with white tail corners.

Voice: A *tsirr*, like Long-tailed Tit.

Habitat: Deciduous and mixed woodland, mostly around rivers and ponds. In winter, often in reedbeds.

Similar Species: Blue Tit as above.

Great Tit   *Parus major*

black crown

greyish crown

yellowish cheeks

JUVENILE

white cheeks

bold belly stripe

ADULT

J F M A M J J A S O N D

Status: Common and widespread resident; summer visitor northern Scandinavia.
Identification: 13.5–14.5cm (5½in). Most clearly marked of all the tits, with shiny black cap and bib joined by bold black line enclosing white cheeks; black stripe down yellow breast and belly (wider in male than female). Back green, wings and tail pale blue; latter with white outer feathers.
Voice: Wide variety of calls (57 described), including *teecha-teecha*.
Habitat: Woods, gardens, orchards, hedges.
Similar Species: Smaller Blue Tit.

European Nuthatch   *Sitta europaea*

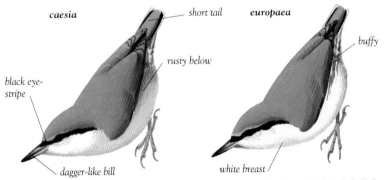

caesia

short tail

europaea

buffy

rusty below

black eye-stripe

dagger-like bill

white breast

J F M A M J J A S O N D

Status: Widespread resident of woodlands.
Identification: 13.5–14.5cm (5½in). Agile tree-climber, similar to woodpeckers but does not undulate in flight. Upperparts pale blue with bold black eye-stripe. Scandinavian birds *S.e.europaea* have white throat and breast with buff undertail. Southern birds *S.e.caesia* have whole underparts warm buff. Tail short and square. Produces sounds when hacking at food wedged in tree crevice.
Voice: High-pitched *chwit-chwit*; loud *kee-kee-kee*.
Habitat: Woodlands into gardens and orchards.
Similar Species: See other nuthatches.

Krüper's Nuthatch *Sitta krueperi*

black cap

short, uptilted bill

bold supercilium
and eye-stripe

rufous-orange chest patch

J F M A M J J A S O N D

Status: Small nuthatch found from Turkey to the Caspian.
Identification: 12cm (4¹/₄in). Pale blue-grey above, marked by black crown and prominent eye-stripe, separated by clear white supercilium. Diagnostic breast patch is warm rufous-orange. Juvenile duller lacking black on crown and eye-stripe, small rufous-orange breast patch.
Voice: A fast repetitive whistle on two notes. Call is harsh, Jay-like, running into a repetitive *keek-keek-keek*.
Habitat: Mountain forests of conifers, often spruce.
Similar Species: Smaller than other nuthatches found in same range with black cap and rufous-orange chest patch.

Corsican Nuthatch *Sitta whiteheadi*

♀

white supercilium,
black eye-stripe

black cap

♂

J F M A M J J A S O N D

Status: Endemic pines of Corsica.
Identification: 12cm (4¹/₄in). Smaller than European Nuthatch. Pale blue-grey above with black cap and bold black eye-stripe separated by clear-cut white supercilium. Underparts white with pinkish wash on flanks. White tips to outertail feathers; steel-grey bill smaller than Nuthatch. Best located by distribution calls; not difficult to identify once found.
Voice: Nasal *char*; rippling *po-po-po*.
Habitat: Forests of Corsican pine usually in mountains.
Similar Species: Only nuthatch on Corsica, but clearly related to Krüper's Nuthatch of Turkey.

Western Rock Nuthatch *Sitta neumayer*

white breast

unmarked tail

pinkish-orange

J F M A M J J A S O N D

Status: Resident hills south-east Europe and Turkey.
Identification: 13.5–14.5cm (5½in). About same size as
European Nuthatch, but inhabits rocky crags, usually at
some altitude. Like Nuthatch, pale blue-grey above with
prominent black eye-stripe; tail lacks white at tips found in
other nuthatches. Throat and breast white, underparts
washed pinkish-orange not orange-red. Constructs gourd-
shaped nest of mud.
Voice: Shrill piping on descending scale.
Habitat: Rock crags, canyons, ruins at altitude.
Similar Species: European Nuthatch as above; also
Eastern Rock Nuthatch.

Eastern Rock Nuthatch *Sitta trephronota*

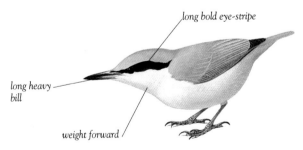

long bold eye-stripe

long heavy
bill

weight forward

Status: Resident central eastern Turkey, mostly at altitude.
Identification: 15–16cm (6–6½in). Large nuthatch, about
same size as Redwing. Similar to Rock Nuthatch, but
longer and heavier bill together with larger head and
longer neck create more weight-forward appearance. Black
eye-stripe both longer and wider than Rock Nuthatch.
Behaviour similar, but frequents trees as well as rocks.
Voice: *Peep-peep-peep* more deliberate and clear than Rock
Nuthatch. Also a repeated *kew-kew* and a Greenfinch-like
whee-whee.
Habitat: Cliffs, gorges and rocky screes in mountain areas.
Similar Species: Western Rock Nuthatch as above.

J F M A M J J A S O N D

Wallcreeper *Tichodroma muraria*

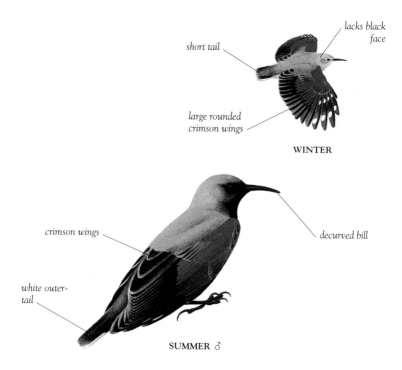

lacks black face

short tail

large rounded crimson wings

WINTER

crimson wings

decurved bill

white outer-tail

SUMMER ♂

Status: A well-marked, but highly elusive bird of mountain crags, most often associated with the sheer cliffs and buttresses that line deep gorges. Resident among the highest mountains, but descends to lower altitudes in winter and may undertake quite lengthy migrations and occur as a vagrant hundreds of miles off-course.

J F M A M J J A S O N D

Identification: 16–17cm (6½in). Whole of body, including rump and undertail is pale steel-grey. In breeding season face, chin and upper breast washed black, absent in winter and non-breeding birds. Upperwing coverts bright crimson, contrasting with black flight feathers and black tail; the latter with white tips, especially prominent at the corners. In flight large rounded, paddle-like wings are highly 'waisted', like a ping-pong bat; white-spotted primaries showing 'fingering', like a bird of prey. Seen from below crimson confined to lesser coverts and difficult to see. Bill long and decurved. Climbs easily and frequently flicks wings to expose crimson patches (fortunately). Unless they fly overhead, against the sky, Wallcreepers are very difficult to locate, even in known breeding areas. They do, however, have regular winter haunts, including churches and quarries, and may then become more localized. Cliff scanning for long periods is generally unproductive. In both summer and winter haunts keeping an alert watch on the sky is more likely to succeed.

Voice: A series of weak, high-pitched *zee-zee-zee* notes that, while more melodic, are similar to Eurasian Treecreeper. Often drowned by noise of rushing water.

Habitat: In summer frequents mountain gorges and clefts. In winter resorts to churches and quarries at lower altitudes. Vagrants may occur on sea cliffs.

Similar Species: Though there are no other wallcreepers, the rock nuthatches occupy similar habitats and behave in the same way. They do, however, lack the bat-like wings of the Wallcreeper.

Eurasian Treecreeper   *Certhia familiaris*

long decurved
bill

bold white
supercilium

streaked
upperparts

white flanks

pointed tail

J F M A M J J A S O N D

Status: Widespread resident of mainly upland conifer forests.
Identification: 12–13cm (4½–5½in). Small tree-climber. Well camouflaged and easily overlooked; streaked brown and buff above with rusty rump. White supercilium; double wingbar; tail feathers have protruding shafts. Underparts white. Joins mixed tit flocks in winter.
Voice: Goldcrest-like *tsee-tsee*.
Habitat: Conifer forests often at altitude; also deciduous woods in Britain where Short-toed Treecreeper is only a vagrant.
Similar Species: See Short-toed Treecreeper.

Short-toed Treecreeper   *Certhia brachydactyla*

supercilium not
prominent

tawny flanks

Status: Resident lowlands of south and central Europe. Absent Britain and Scandinavia.
Identification: 12–13cm (4½–5½in). Very similar to Eurasian Treecreeper and identified only with great care. Short-toed less rufous and more greyish-brown, with finer, less distinct and decidedly buffy (not white) supercilium. Below, flanks washed with buff-brown, but difficult to see in the field.
Voice: Similar to Eurasian Treecreeper, but Chaffinch-like *chiuk* distinctive.
Habitat: Deciduous forests, parks, gardens.
Similar Species: Eurasian Treecreeper as above.

J F M A M J J A S O N D

Golden Oriole *Oriolus oriolus*

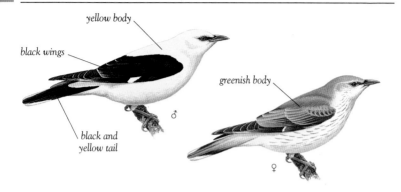

yellow body

black wings

black and
yellow tail

♂

greenish body

♀

J F M A M J J A S O N D

Status: Widespread summer visitor to Continental
Europe. Absent most of Fennoscandia and only recent
colonist Britain.
Identification: 23–25cm (9–10in). Boldly coloured but
self-effacing bird; more often heard than seen. Male bright
yellow with black wings and black centre to tail. Females
and younger males greenish and black, with varying
amounts of white and some streaking on breast. Bill red.
mostly located by calls.
Voice: Flute-like *weela-weeoo*.
Habitat: Deciduous woods.
Similar Species: None.

Red-backed Shrike *Lanius collurio*

stubby hooked bill

grey crown

rusty back

grey rump

dark ear coverts

rusty back

♂

♀

J F M A M J J A S O N D

Status: Summer visitor; virtually extirpated Britain where
a few pairs remain East Anglia.
Identification: 16–18cm (6½–7in). Sits on top or side of
bush waiting for prey. Male has grey crown and broad,
black mask; back rust-red; tail black with white outer
feathers; underparts white. Female sandy brown above
with dark mark through eye and barred underparts;
outertail feathers white. Juvenile similar to female, but
barred above and below.
Voice: Harsh *chak-chak*.
Habitat: Heaths, hedges, scrub.
Similar Species: Other shrikes.

Lesser Grey Shrike *Lanius minor*

black mask
extends over
forehead

no white
supercilium

dark mask

crescents

JUVENILE

ADULT

Status: Summer visitor south and east Europe.
Identification: 19–21cm (7½–8½in). Grey and white
shrike marked by black wings and tail. Shorter in tail and
sits more upright than Great Grey. Major distinction is
black mask in Lesser Grey is larger and extends from
forehead rather than lores. Also lacks white supercilium.
Males in summer have pinkish wash over breast; juvenile
greyish-buff above, marked with fine crescents.
Voice: A harsh rattling.
Habitat: Scrub, fields with hedges.
Similar Species: Great Grey Shrike as above; juvenile
with similar plumage Masked Shrike.

J F M A M J J A S O N D

Great Grey Shrike *Lanius excubitor*

grey forehead

black mask

fine supercilium

grey back

short black wings

long tail

Status: Resident temperate Europe; northern birds
migrate.
Identification: 23–25cm (9–10in). Medium-sized, grey
and white bird with long black tail. Crown, back and rump
grey; wings and tail black, marked with white patches.
Bold black mask through eye. Underparts white. Often sits
openly on top of bush or telegraph post, where glistening
white breast visible at considerable distances. Invariably
solitary.
Voice: Harsh *chek-chek*.
Habitat: Heaths, open scrub, hedges.
Similar Species: See Lesser Grey Shrike.

J F M A M J J A S O N D

Woodchat Shrike *Lanius senator*

chestnut crown

pale scapular
patch

white scapulars

white
rump

ADULT

JUVENILE

Status: Common summer visitor south and west Europe.
Identification: 16–18cm (6–7in). Male and female similar,
with rich chestnut cap, black facial mask and upperparts,
and white underparts. White scapulars form two distinct
ovals on back, and white outertail feathers and white rump
show in flight. Female slightly duller than male. Juvenile
and first winter birds buff-brown and scaled above and
below like juvenile Red-backed Shrike but with two pale
ovals on back.
Voice: Harsh chatter.
Habitat: Scrub, orchards, fields.
Similar Species: Masked Shrike lacks chestnut crown.

Masked Shrike *Lanius nubicus*

white
forehead

black crown

greyish-brown

pale ovals

white ovals

bold primary
patch

peach
flanks

long
tail

ADULT ♂

JUVENILE

Status: Summer visitor to south-east Europe; common
Turkey.
Identification: 16.5–17.5cm (6½–7in). Male has black
upperparts with white forehead, supercilium and chin; two
white oval patches on wings; and boldly white outertail
feathers. Face white, breast and flanks with wash of rich
rufous. Female similar, but has greyish cast on black areas
of plumage.
Voice: Scratchy song; harsh *keer-keer*.
Habitat: Groves, orchards, parks.
Similar Species: See Woodchat Shrike, especially
juvenile, which also shows white ovals on back.

Eurasian Jay *Garrulus glandarius*

streaked crown

brownish pink

black moustache

white rump

whitish patch
in wing

Status: Widespread woodland resident that is absent only
from most of Scandinavia.
Identification: 33–36cm (13–14in). Large with
rounded wings and long tail. Crown streaked black
and white; black moustachial streak. Back buff-brown;
underparts pinkish buff. Wings and tail black; in flight
shows white rump and white patches on innerwing.
Small but distinctive blue and white barred patch
on primary coverts.
Voice: Harsh *kaaa*.
Habitat: Forests, woodlands, heaths.
Similar Species: See Siberian Jay.

J F M A M J J A S O N D

Siberian Jay *Perisoreus infaustus*

dark 'face'

rufous rump

rufous outertail

rufous wing patch

long tail

Status: Resident spruce forests Fennoscandia with only
local movements southwards in winter.
Identification: 30–32cm (12–12½in). Largish bird of
northern forests that is self-effacing in summer, but bolder
in search of food in winter. Dull grey above and below with
untidy dark brown crown extending below eye. Rust-red in
wing, rump and outertail. Rump and tail pattern best
means of identification as bird flies away through thick
forest.
Voice: Harsh *chair*; hard *kook-kook*.
Habitat: Conifer forests, especially spruce.
Similar Species: Eurasian Jay has white rump.

J F M A M J J A S O N D

Azure-winged Magpie   *Cyanopica cyana*

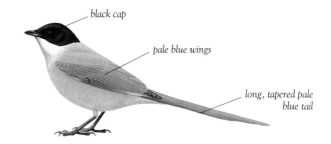

black cap

pale blue wings

long, tapered pale
blue tail

J F M A M J J A S O N D

Status: Locally common resident Iberia that is otherwise found only in China.
Identification: 33–35cm (13–14in). Large, highly gregarious bird. Combination of black cap, vinous-buff body and pale blue wings and tail unique. Wings short and rounded; tail long and graduated. Shy birds that melt into forest when disturbed, giving mainly fleeting views among tree trunks under canopy. Frequently feed on ground; loath to fly in the open.
Voice: Noisy, repeated *zhree-zhree.*
Habitat: Groves, orchards, woods.
Similar Species: None.

Magpie   *Pica pica*

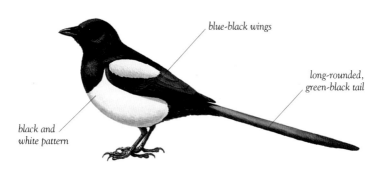

blue-black wings

long-rounded,
green-black tail

black and
white pattern

J F M A M J J A S O N D

Status: Widespread resident, though absent Iceland, northern Scotland, the Alps and Corsica and Sardinia.
Identification: 42–50cm (16½–20in). Large black and white crow, with distinctive long, wedge-shaped, green-glossed tail. Black head, breast and back; wings black with glossy blue wash and bold, white oval patches. Belly white.
Voice: Harsh *chak-chak-chak.*
Habitat: Hedges, woods, gardens, parkland and open grasslands and arable with adjacent thickets.
Similar Species: None.

Alpine Chough   *Pyrrhocorax graculus*

short yellow bill

red legs

Status: Gregarious resident high mountains of south when often associates with Red-billed Chough.
Identification: 37–39cm (14½–15½in). Very similar to Red-billed Chough, though slightly smaller with narrower wings. Whole plumage black. Bill yellow and shorter than Red-billed Chough; legs and feet red. Narrower wings with swept back primaries useful, but should be confirmed by viewing yellow bill.
Voice: Whistled *churrish*; abrupt *chupp*.
Habitat: Mountain crags, cliffs.
Similar Species: Red-billed Chough as above.

J F M A M J J A S O N D

Red-billed Chough   *Pyrrhocorax pyrrhocorax*

square wingtips with fingers

long decurved red bill

square tail

red legs

Status: Localized resident mountains and sea cliffs of south and west.
Identification: 36–41cm (14–16in). Black, crow-like bird with thin, decurved, red bill and red legs. Wings broad and square, with deep fingering at tips. Masterful flight involves diving, soaring and aerobatics. Gregarious sometimes in mixed flocks aith Alpine Chough on Continental parts of range.
Voice: Ringing *keear*, repeated.
Habitat: Mountain cliffs and gorges; coastal cliffs.
Similar Species: Alpine Chough.

J F M A M J J A S O N D

Nutcracker *Nucifraga caryocatactes*

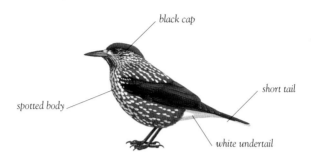

black cap

short tail

spotted body

white undertail

J F M A M J J A S O N D

Status: Gregarious bird, resident conifer forests, but with some regular and irregular wandering in winter.
Identification: 30–33cm (12–13in). Chunky bird of northern and Alpine forests that occasionally erupts in autumn. Like overgrown Starling or undersized Jay with black-brown plumage boldly spotted with white; bold white undertail coverts. Wings large rounded and black; tail showing bold black and white pattern; bill pointed.
Voice: Harsh *kror*.
Habitat: Conifer forests.
Similar Species: None.

Jackdaw *Corvus monedula*

short bill

grey nape

white eye

rounded wings

longer tail than Chough

J F M A M J J A S O N D

Status: Locally common, gregarious resident. Absent northern Scandinavia; winter visitor to many areas.
Identification: 32–34cm (12½–13½in). Smallest crow; black plumage broken by grey nape, not often visible at distance. Short, stubby bill distinguishes from Crow and Rook. Performs aerobatics along cliffs and gorges and in towns around churches and cathedrals.
Voice: High-pitched *kya*; distinctive *chak*.
Habitat: Mountain and sea cliffs, towns and villages with tall buildings.
Similar Species: In mountains watch for gregarious, aerobatic choughs.

Rook   *Corvus frugilegus*

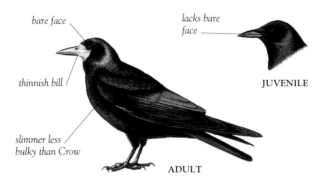

bare face

thinnish bill

slimmer less
bulky than Crow

ADULT

lacks bare
face

JUVENILE

Status: Widespread, locally common resident through
temperate Europe.
Identification: 44–47cm (17–18½in). Highly gregarious
crow, forming large flocks, roosts, and colonial rookeries in
clumps of trees. Crown has distinct peak above eye. Bare
skin around base of bill main distinguishing feature; absent
in juvenile. Similar to Carrion Crow, but slimmer and
more angular, especially in flight. Feeds mostly on arable
land, taking more pests than crops.
Voice: Cawing *kaah*.
Habitat: Arable land with copses.
Similar Species: Carrion Crow as above.

Carrion Crow   *Corvus corone*

heavy bill

Carrion Crow

grey body, black
wings

Hooded Crow

Status: Widespread resident, but only summer visitor to far
north of Scandinavia.
Identification: 45–49cm (18–19in). Large, familiar all-
black bird with heavy bill and aggressive habits. More
strongly built than Rook and usually found in pairs, though
larger numbers may roost together and gather at rubbish
tips. In northern, eastern and southern Europe, replaced by
subspecies *C.c.cornix* (Hooded Crow), which has grey
back, belly and rump.
Voice: Loud *kraa-kraa*.
Habitat: Virtually ubiquitous.
Similar Species: See Rook and Common Raven.

Common Raven *Corvus corax*

thick heavy bill

ragged beard

ragged beard

wedge-shaped tail

J F M A M J J A S O N D

Status: Widespread in wilderness areas, now mainly mountains.
Identification: 60–67cm (23½–26½in). Similar to Carrion Crow but considerably larger with more powerful head and bill, and shaggy beard. Large wedge-shaped tail particularly obvious in flight is surest means of separating from other crows. Frequently soars like bird of prey. Mainly a scavenger but also kills birds and mammals.
Voice: Hollow *pruk-pruk*.
Habitat: Mountains, sea cliffs, lowland wastes.
Similar Species: Carrion Crow and Rook are smaller with less marked bills and tails.

Common Starling *Sturnus vulgaris*

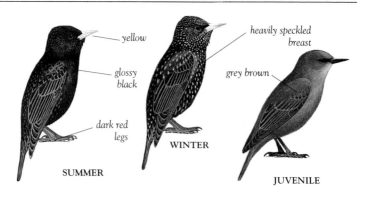

yellow

glossy black

dark red legs

SUMMER

heavily speckled breast

WINTER

grey brown

JUVENILE

J F M A M J J A S O N D

Status: Abundant, widespread resident, summer and winter visitor.
Identification: 20.5–22.5cm (8–9in). Highly successful; gregarious outside breeding season forming huge flocks, particularly at roosts. Upperparts glossy black with brown margins to wing feathers. Head, back and underparts glossy black in summer, spotted white in winter. Bill yellow, legs dark red. Juvenile grey-buff with white chin. Pointed wings and short tail give characteristic flight silhouette.
Voice: Variety of wheezing calls; much mimicry.
Habitat: Virtually ubiquitous.
Similar Species: See Rose-coloured and Spotless Starling.

Spotless Starling *Sturnus unicolor*

yellow bill

pale-based bill

unspotted plumage

faint body spotting

pink-red legs

SUMMER ♂ **WINTER ♀**

Status: Resident replacement of Common Starling in Iberia, Corsica, Sardinia and Sicily.
Identification: 21–22cm (8½in). Similar in shape and size to Common Starling, but shiny black, lacking spots in summer and marked by dull spots in winter. Bill yellow, feet red; usually more obviously so than Common Starling. In all plumages, appears 'blacker' than Starling, even at distance. Behaviour like Starling, and forms mixed flocks with that species in winter.
Voice: Variety of wheezing calls.
Habitat: Wide variety from towns to wild cliffs.
Similar Species: Common Starling as above.

J F M A M J J A S O N D

Rose-coloured Starling *Sturnus roseus*

boldly black and pink

dark wings, pale margins

short bill

ADULT SUMMER **JUVENILE**

Status: Summer visitor Balkans; eruptive westward late summer.
Identification: 20.5–22.5cm (8–9in). Adult pale pink with black head, wings and tail. Legs pinkish, bill shorter and more thrush-like than Common Starling. Juvenile sandy-buff above and paler below, with some fine streaking on breast. Pale supercilium over darker ear coverts; pale wing covert tips form wingbars; and short yellow bill separates from similar plumage of Common Starling.
Voice: Various wheezing calls.
Habitat: Agricultural land, farms.
Similar Species: Common Starling as above.

J F M A M J J A S O N D

House Sparrow   *Passer domesticus*

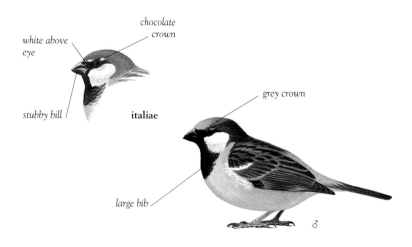

white above eye

chocolate crown

stubby bill

italiae

grey crown

large bib

♂

pale supercilium

♀

Status: Widespread, common and familiar resident throughout Europe except Northern and montane Scandinavia and Sardinia.

Identification: 14–15.5cm (5½–6in). Male streaked brown and black above with chocolate nape extending to eye. Crown is contrasting grey. A black bib widens out to form a clear-cut breast band. Female buffy and brown with black streaked back, prominent pale supercilium and double wingbar, bill chunky and pale horn. Female resembles female Common Rosefinch, but with paler bill and no streaking on breast and flanks. Italian Sparrow *P.d.italiae* of Italy and Corsica has chocolate crown, broken white supercilium and more extensive black bib. Generally regarded as stabilized hybrid of House x Spanish Sparrows in area formerly occupied only by Spanish Sparrow. House Sparrow still not found in more isolated Sardinia. Hybrids found elsewhere where the two species overlap show variable sizes of black bib and variable degrees of breast streaking.

J F M A M J J A S O N D

Voice: Distinctive chirrup, also a brief *tu-tu* and various twitterings.

Habitat: Cities, towns, farms wherever people have permanent residence.

Similar Species: Tree and Spanish Sparrows. See also above for hybrids and Italian Sparrow. The allocation of the latter to a subspecies of either House or Spanish Sparrows remains a matter of debate by systematists and may even be allotted full specific status.

Spanish Sparrow *Passer hispaniolensis*

bold supercilium

bold braces on back

chunky bill

chocolate crown

flank stripes

black bib extends to breast and flanks

♂

♀

J F M A M J J A S O N D

Status: Gregarious, but localized, Mediterranean sparrow.
Identification: 14–15.5cm (5½–6in). Slightly larger version of House Sparrow, but obviously blacker, even at distance. Male like House Sparrow, but with full chocolate cap. Back heavily streaked black; bib extending to breast with heavy black streaking along flanks. Female similar to House Sparrow, but with light streaking on breast and flanks and distinctive braces.
Voice: Variety of chirrups.
Habitat: Scrub, fields, copses.
Similar Species: House Sparrow as above and its Italian subspecies.

Tree Sparrow *Passer montanus*

brown crown

black cheek 'comma'

white half collar

small neat bib

Status: Widespread, but localized resident.
Identification: 13.5–14.5cm (5½–6in). Both sexes resemble male House Sparrow, but slightly smaller with upperparts more clearly streaked black and brown. Crown chocolate-brown; tiny black bib; black comma on white cheeks. White half-collar visible at considerable distance – best field mark when picking out from mixed sparrow flocks. Underparts white. Often associates with flocks of House Sparrows. Colonial.
Voice: Distinct *chup-chup*.
Habitat: Old copses, orchards, hedges.
Similar Species: Male House Sparrow as above.

J F M A M J J A S O N D

Dead Sea Sparrow   *Passer moabiticus*

distinctive
face pattern

chestnut
in wing

small
bill

supercilium broadens
behind eye

contrasting
back stripes

♂

♀

J F M A M J J A S O N D

Status: A well-marked, true sparrow, resident in southern
Turkey, but spreading westwards and has reached Cyprus.
Identification: 12cm (5in). Male is supremely well-marked
with yellow, grey, white and black face pattern that
precludes confusion. Female resembles female House
Sparrow, but is smaller, supercilium broader behind eye,
larger head and smaller bill, and clear broad back stripes.
Sometimes has yellow at side of neck and in supercilium.
Voice: Sparrow-like chirrups, higher pitched.
Habitat: Trees and thickets near water in dry landscapes.
Similar Species: Female resembles female House and
other sparrows.

Rock Sparrow   *Petronia petronia*

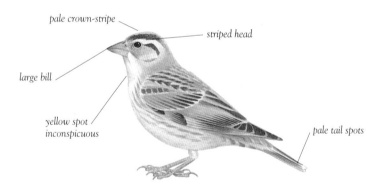

pale crown-stripe

striped head

large bill

yellow spot
inconspicuous

pale tail spots

Status: Localized resident Mediterranean Europe.
Identification: 14cm (5½in). Similar to female House
Sparrow, but with boldly marked crown. Adult streaked
buff and brown above, with distinctive pale spots near tip
of tail. Characteristic pattern of brown and buff stripes on
crown, dark ear coverts and chunky pale bill. Underparts
streaked buff with pale yellow spot on chin.
Voice: Sharp *tut, chwee.*
Habitat: Rocky slopes and fields; hill villages and towns.
Similar Species: Crown-stripes separate from female
House Sparrow; see also Pale Rock and Yellow-throated
Sparrows.

J F M A M J J A S O N D

Pale Rock Sparrow   *Petronia brachydactyla*

pale bill

pale supercilium

double wing bar

pale panel

dark flight feathers

white moustache with fine dark line

white outer-tail tips

pinkish legs

Status: Summer visitor to mountains of south-eastern Turkey.
Identification: 14cm (5½in). Seemingly featureless washed out buffy sparrow. Note pale supercilium; pale moustache with fine dark double white wingbar; dark flight feathers; pale panel on secondaries; white tips to outertail; pale bill; pale pinkish legs.
Voice: Repetitive buzzing song; trilled flight note.
Habitat: Scrub-covered rocky hillsides; descends in winter.
Similar Species: Rock Sparrow and female/juvenile Yellow-throated Sparrow.

J F M A M J J A S O N D

Yellow-throated Sparrow   *Petronia xanthocollis*

pointed black bill

chestnut shoulder patch

double wingbar

yellow throat patch

ADULT ♂ SUMMER

J F M A M J J A S O N D

Status: Summer visitor to south-eastern Turkey.
Identification: 13cm (5in). Adult male is grey-brown above marked by chestnut patch at bend of wing and double white wingbar. Yellow patch on lower white throat. Bill narrow, longish and black. Non-breeding male, female and juvenile have pale brown bill, but pointed shape remains important feature.
Voice: A sparrow-like *chip* and more pleasing song.
Habitat: Gardens, dry rivers with trees, open woods, groves.
Similar Species: See Pale Rock Sparrow.

Common Waxbill *Estrilda astrild*

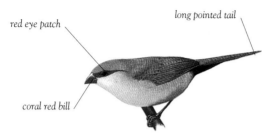

red eye patch

long pointed tail

coral red bill

J F M A M J J A S O N D

Status: Tiny African finch introduced to Portugal, now established and spreading to Spain.
Identification: 10cm (4in). Gregarious finch-like bird marked by conical coral-red bill and bold red eye patch. Upperparts heavily barred black and brown extending to long, pointed tail. Underparts finely barred brown on white with variable red belly patch.
Voice: Characteristic nasal *cher-cher-cher* with buzzing quality.
Habitat: Waterside margins with reeds and adjacent arable fields.
Similar Species: See Avadavat.

Avadavat *Amandava amandava*

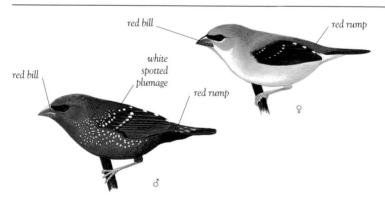

red bill

red rump

white spotted plumage

red bill

red rump

♀

♂

J F M A M J J A S O N D

Status: Small African finch introduced Portugal; established and spreading to Spain.
Identification: 10cm (4in). Male unmistakable tiny red bird marked by white spots on breast, belly and on black wings. Tail black, but rump and uppertail bright red. Female very similar to Common Waxbill with red bill, but brownish plumage unbarred, rows of white spots across wing and bright red rump and uppertail coverts.
Voice: Twittering song. Call *chirp* repeated.
Habitat: Usually near water, among reeds and other vegetation, in much same areas as Common Waxbill.
Similar Species: Common Waxbill.

Chaffinch *Fringilla coelebs*

blue-grey crown

white double wingbar

white outertail

buffy crown

creamy breast

pinkish breast

broad wingbar

♂

♂

♀

J F M A M J J A S O N D

Status: Numerous and widespread resident and summer visitor to north and east.
Identification: 14.5–16cm (5¾–6¼in). Male has blue-grey crown and pinkish breast. Female duller, in shades of buff. Both with bold white double wingbar. In flight shows bold wingbars and white outertail. Forms large winter flocks, often in associaton with Brambling on forest floor.
Voice: Delicate song ends in flourish; loud *pink-pink*.
Habitat: Woods, gardens, groves, fields, hedges.
Similar Species: Female similar to female House Sparrow, but bold wingbar of Chaffinch quite distinct.

Brambling *Fringilla montifringilla*

black head and back with scaling

black crown and back

scaled black on buff

white rump

orange double wingbar

♂ SUMMER

♂ WINTER

bright orange breast

♂ WINTER

♀

Similar Species: Summer visitor Fennoscandia; widespread over most of Europe in winter.
Identification: 14–15cm (5½–6in). Similar to related Chaffinch, often associating in winter flocks. Winter male has blackish upperparts, liberally edged buff on crown and back. Tail black; shows square white rump in flight. Breast bright orange; belly white. Buff margins lost in summer; head and back become pure black with broad orange band below. Female more heavily edged buff at all seasons.
Voice: Hard *tswick* and *chik*.
Habitat: Birch scrub, fields and hedges.
Similar Species: Chaffinch.

J F M A M J J A S O N D

Red-fronted Serin *Serinus pusillus*

streaked black over buff

red crown patch

black head

JUVENILE

ADULT

J F M A M J J A S O N D

Status: Dainty, high-altitude, black-faced finch resident in Turkey.
Identification: 12cm (4¹⁄₂in). Unmistakable with black head, neck and upper breast broken only by bold red crown patch. Upperparts streaked brown and black, underparts white and black. Juvenile streaked brown on pale buff, plain buffy face becomes streaked during first winter, when resembles Twite.
Voice: Serin-like jingling.
Habitat: Above tree line among junipers and bare ground.
Similar Species: None.

European Serin *Serinus serinus*

large head, tiny bill

bright yellow breast

streaked, often little yellow

yellow rump

♂

♀

J F M A M J J A S O N D

Status: Resident Mediterranean and summer visitor northwards.
Identification: 11–12cm (4¹⁄₂–5in). Tiny yellow finch with bright tinkling song; pure yellow rump a bold field mark. Male has yellow head, back and breast, marked with variable amount of brown streaking. Wings dark with yellowish edges. Less yellow on female, but heavier streaking, particularly on breast. Short stubby bill creates large, round-headed appearance.
Voice: Tinkling jangle of notes.
Habitat: Orchards, groves, hedges.
Similar Species: Siskin and Citril Finch

Greenfinch *Carduelis chloris*

thick bill

dark around eye

green

yellow at wing edge

green underparts

♂

yellow tail sides

♀

Status: Common resident through most of Europe.
Identification: 14–15cm (5 ½–6in). Chunky, thick-set finch with substantial white bill. Male green above, with bold yellow margin to folded grey wing; yellowish below. Female paler and browner. In flight, shows yellow at base of primaries and incomplete yellow edges to tail. Largest and most common of green-yellow finches.
Voice: Nasal *skeer*; *chup-chup* in flight.
Habitat: Woods, gardens, orchards; often among the commonest birds at garden feeders.
Similar Species: Check smaller yellow-green finches.

J F M A M J J A S O N D

Goldfinch *Carduelis carduelis*

yellow wingbar

crimson face

white rump

bright yellow in black wing

lacks face pattern

JUVENILE

ADULT

Status: Widespread resident; summer visitor north and east.
Identification: 11.5–12.5cm (4 ¾in). Attractive, easily identified finch with distinctive face pattern of crimson, white and black. Back warm brown; wings black with broad yellow band apparent both at rest and in flight. Juvenile lacks bold 'face' pattern, but shows uniform brown back and gold in wings. Shows bold white rump in flight.
Voice: Sweet tinkling song and call.
Habitat: Wasteland, heaths, scrub.
Similar Species: None.

J F M A M J J A S O N D

Citril Finch *Serinus citrinella*

grey crown
and nape

yellow rump

yellow
wingbars

♂

♀

J F M A M J J A S O N D

Status: Resident or summer visitor mountains of western Europe and at lower levels Corsica and Sardinia.
Identification: 12cm (4¾in). Tiny 'green' bird marked in all plumages with wash of pale grey on crown, nape, back and sides of head; and in female on breast and flanks. Yellow margins to inner flight fethers and bold double wingbar. Variable yellowish rump. Underparts greenish yellow, with variable grey wash. Rather featureless 'face'.
Voice: Fast twittering.
Habitat: High, bare mountain slopes above tree line; except Corsica and Sardinia where also lower.
Similar Species: Serin and Siskin.

Siskin *Carduelis spinus*

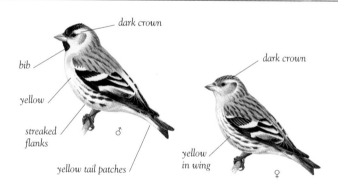

dark crown

bib

yellow

streaked
flanks

♂

yellow tail patches

dark crown

yellow
in wing

♀

J F M A M J J A S O N D

Status: Small, arboreal finch that breeds much of temperate Europe; winter visitor to south and west.
Identification: 11.5–12.5cm (4¾in). Particular liking for damp areas with alder and spruce. Male greenish above, yellowish below with streaked flanks. Crown black, forming distinct cap; small black bib. Wings show yellow wingbars; yellow rump. Female duller with yellow only in wings and tail; upperparts grey-green, underparts buffy with streaking above and below. Agile feeder.
Voice: Twittering *tsu, tsu-weet*.
Habitat: Waterside trees and flooded woodland.
Similar Species: European Serin.

Linnet *Carduelis cannabina*

red forehead

white wing flashes

white in tail

brown back

red breast

♂ SUMMER

♀

Status: Widespread resident; summer visitor to north and east.

Identification: 13–14cm (5–5½in). Small finch often abundant in open areas. Summer male distinguished by red forehead and breast; grey head, brown back. Female lacks red; streaked above and below. Male loses red in winter. Both sexes show white in tail and wings in flight. Gregarious, often forming huge flocks in association with Twite in coastal areas.

Voice: High-pitched twittering.

Habitat: Open wasteland, coastal marshes, heaths.

Similar Species: See Twite.

J F M A M J J A S O N D

Twite *Carduelis flavirostris*

buffy throat

distinctly streaked

yellow bill

pink rump

double wingbar

♂ SUMMER

streaked

♂ WINTER

Status: Resident or summer visitor to northern hills; winter visitor nearby coasts.

Identification: 13–14cm (5–5½in). Northern, upland equivalent of Linnet; and shows similar markings in flight. In all seasons and plumages, Twite warm, buffy brown bird, especially on face, heavily streaked above and below. Linnet never as heavily streaked, even in juvenile plumage. Twite has pink rump and double wingbar. Juvenile and winter birds have yellow, not grey, bill.

Voice: Harsh nasal *twoo-eek*.

Habitat: Open moors; coastal marshes in winter.

Similar Species: Linnet as above.

J F M A M J J A S O N D

Common Redpoll *Carduelis flammea*

red forehead

streaked back

tiny black bib

pink breast

SUMMER ♂

♀

J F M A M J J A S O N D

Status: Arboreal finch; northern resident and summer visitor; widespread in winter.
Identification: 11.5–13cm (4½–5in). Small, streaked finch; hangs tit-like among trees when feeding. Forehead red; small black bib. Heavily streaked buff and brown above; lighter flank streaking below. Summer male has pink wash on throat and upper breast. Generally gregarious at all times.
Voice: Buzzing nasal trill.
Habitat: Conifer and mixed woods, birches, heaths.
Similar Species: Siskin also arboreal; see Arctic Redpoll.

Arctic Redpoll *Carduelis hornemanni*

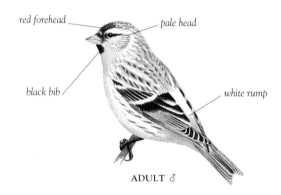

red forehead

pale head

black bib

white rump

ADULT ♂

J F M A M J J A S O N D

Status: Replaces Common Redpoll in high Arctic, moving southwards through northern Fennoscandia in winter.
Identification: 12–13cm (4 ½–5 ½in). Like Common Redpoll, Mealy race of which shows characters intermediate between the two. Arctic Redpoll much paler than Common Redpoll, but with similar red forehead and black bib. Head and nape almost greyish-white, underparts virtually devoid of streaking, two white bars on wing, rump white.
Voice: Rasping like Common Redpoll.
Habitat: Scrubby dwarf trees.
Similar Species: Common Redpoll as above.

Crimson-winged Finch *Rhodopechys sanguinea*

ivory bill

black crown

pink wings

mottled back

♂

barred flanks

dark legs

much white in tail

♀

Status: Chunky, pink and black-winged finch, resident in mountains of eastern half of Turkey.
Identification: 15cm (6in). Sexes similar. Upperparts mottled buffy-brown with black crown; plain face with prominent dark eye and variable pink wash; stout ivory bill. Bold pink panel in folded black wing. Tail black with white edges. In flight pink wings and largely white tail obvious.
Voice: Sweet trilling song. Call a liquid *tireep*.
Habitat: Mountain fields and dry plateaux.
Similar Species: Desert Finch uniformly grey with black bill.

Desert Finch *Rhodopechys obsoleta*

black bill

plane face

uniform upperparts

♀

black lores

♂

pink and black wings

Status: Resident pink-winged finch found in our area only on Turkish–Syrian border.
Identification: 14.5cm (6in). Superficially similar to Crimson-winged Finch, but uniformly buffy-grey with no mottling or barring. Bill black, legs pale. Pink wings with white-edge black tertials. Tail white with black centre. Male has black loral streak, lacking in female.
Voice: Nasal flight-note.
Habitat: Orchards, shelter belts and bushes.
Similar Species: Crimson-winged Finch lacks black bill.

Two-barred Crossbill *Loxia leucoptera*

streaked

pinkish red

double white
wingbar

white-tipped
tertials

streaked
flanks

♂

♀

Status: Resident Finland; in winter Scandinavia.
Identification: 14–15cm (5½–6in). By far most distinctive of all crossbills; others differing almost entirely in size and shape of bill and head. Two-barred Crossbill marked by bold, double white wingbar, but also by white tips to tertials. Male paler, pinker bird than Common Crossbill, with thinner, less bulky bill. Female more yellowish-green than Common Crossbill, paticularly on rump; streaking of upperparts produces more contrasting effect.
Voice: Common Crossbill-like *jip-jip*.
Habitat: Conifer forests, especially larch.
Similar Species: Other crossbills lack wingbars.

Common Crossbill *Loxia curvirostra*

chunky crossed
bill

chunky crossed
bill

♂

♀

Status: Widespread resident of conifers that erupts spasmodically.
Identification: 16–17cm (6–6½in). Chunky, thick-set finch with large head and substantial bill. Crossed mandibles, visible at close range. Male dirty reddish on crown and underparts; wings dark brown. Female grey-green with light streaking above and below. Large head and shortish tail useful in flight. Mostly gregarious.
Voice: Distinctive *jip-jip*.
Habitat: Conifer woods.
Similar Species: Scottish, Parrot and Two-barred Crossbills.

Scottish Crossbill   *Loxia scotica*

larger
crossed bill
than Common
Crossbill

♂

♀

Status: Endemic resident of pine forests of north Scotland.
Identification: 16–17cm (6–6½in). Almost identical to
Common Crossbill; recognized as separate species (and
Britain's sole endemic bird) only in 1970s. Differs in larger
bill, though this is a fine point that requires close
examination. Identified in the field only with greatest
care; habitat the most certain confirmatory criterion. Birds
in old Caledonian forests are most likely this species.
Voice: As Common Crossbill, *jip-jip*.
Habitat: Forests of Scot's Pine.
Similar Species: Common Crossbill also occurs in
Scotland.

J F M A M J J A S O N D

Parrot Crossbill   *Loxia pytyopsittacus*

flat crown

ivory cutting
edges to bill

top and
bottom of
bill virtually
parallel flat crown

♂

♀

Status: Resident conifer forests Fennoscandia, but
sometimes erupts south and west.
Identification: 16.5–17cm (6½–6 ¾in). Slightly larger
than both Common and Scottish Crossbills; differs mainly
in size of bill and head. Bill huge, with upper and lower
mandibles virtually parallel, a shape accentuated by
flattish crown that almost continues into top of bill. Both
mandibles have pale ivory cutting edges. In other respects,
plumage very similar to that of other crossbills.
Voice: Deep *chook-chook*.
Habitat: Pine forests.
Similar Species: See other crossbills and above.

J F M A M J J A S O N D

Trumpeter Finch *Bucanetes githagineus*

variably red face

black in wings and tail

deep stubby bill

sandy with pink wash

deep stubby bill

♂

♀

J F M A M J J A S O N D

Status: Colonizing North African finch that has spread to Spain and occurs as vagrant farther north.
Identification: 13–14cm (5¼in). Small, but stoutly built finch with large head and pronounced stubby pink bill. Male washed pink above and variably on face. Wing feathers, especially primaries show much black. Female and first winter birds have pink bill, pale eye-ring and sandy plumage.
Voice: Distinctive, rasping, nasal wheezing.
Habitat: Desert or semi-desert.
Similar Species: Other desert finches.

Common Rosefinch *Carpodacus erythrinus*

silver bill

pink

featureless face

silver bill

pinkish wingbars

SPRING ♂

double wingbar

♀

J F M A M J J A S O N D

Status: Brightly marked summer visitor north and east Europe that is fast spreading westwards.
Identification: 14–15cm (5½–6in). Male pinkish on head, breast and rump. Belly white, wings and tail brown; has pinkish wingbar. Female and first-year birds dull grey-brown above and whitish below, streaked with brown on breast. Pale conical bill, double wingbar and black eye best field marks on what is otherwise rather sparrow-like bird.
Voice: Quiet *tu-ick*.
Habitat: Meadows and floods with trees.
Similar Species: Female like female sparrows.

Snow Finch   *Montifringilla nivalis*

black bill

grey head

black bib

yellow bill

WINTER

white in wing and tail

white in wing

SUMMER

Status: Resident highest mountains, southern Europe.
Identification: 17–19cm (6½–7½in). In summer, head grey with black chin and pale moustachial streak. Back mottled in shades of brown; wing largely white with black primaries. Tail white, with black centre and tip. Underparts silvery white. In winter, bill yellow, not black as in summer. Only confusable with Alpine Accentor, which inhabits same high altitudes; and Snow Bunting, which has much white in wing.
Voice: Repeated *sitti-char*.
Habitat: Rocky mountain slopes.
Similar Species: See above.

Pine Grosbeak   *Pinicola enucleator*

chunky bill

chunky bill

orange wash

double white wingbar

♂

white-tipped tertials

♀

Status: Resident northern forests with some winter movements.
Identification: 20–22cm (8–9in). Large, reddish finch, similar to crossbills, but without crossed mandibles and with longer tail. Male reddish on head, back and underparts; black wings marked by white-edged tertials and white double wingbar. Tail black and considerably more substantial than in crossbills. Black bill short and chunky. Female similar, but greenish-buff instead of red.
Voice: Whistled song; high *tee-tee-tu*.
Habitat: Conifer forests mixed with deciduous species.
Similar Species: See crossbills.

Bullfinch *Pyrrhula pyrrhula*

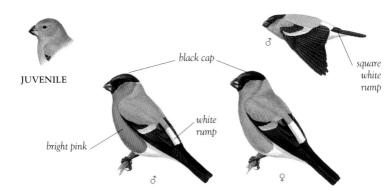

JUVENILE

black cap

white rump

bright pink

♂

♀

square white rump

♂

J F M A M J J A S O N D

Status: Portly, bull-necked finch; widespread resident though absent northern Scandinavia and most of Iberia.
Identification: 14–15cm (5½–6in). Most often seen singly or in pairs. Male has black crown with thick, black conical bill and bright pink breast; upperparts blue-grey. Female similar but with pale buffy breast. Both sexes are chunky, thickset birds with black wings, broad white wingbar, black tail and square white rump.
Voice: Soft *heu*.
Habitat: Orchards, groves, gardens, woods.
Similar Species: None.

Hawfinch *Coccothraustes coccothraustes*

massive thick bill

short tail

thick neck, large head

broad wingbar

J F M A M J J A S O N D

Status: Widespread, but elusive, resident; summer visitor in east; absent most of Fennoscandia.
Identification: 16–17cm (6–6½in). Stout finch with huge, thick, silver-grey bill. Large head and bill, thick-set body and short tail obvious in flight; broad wingbars above and below diagnostic. Crown rufous, back brown, wings black, rump and underparts buff. Often perches immobile near top of tree for long periods.
Voice: Robin-like *tic*.
Habitat: Deciduous woods, parks, groves.
Similar Species: None.

Lapland Bunting *Calcarius lapponicus*

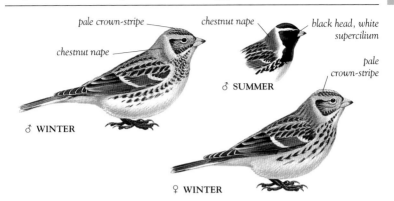

pale crown-stripe

chestnut nape

chestnut nape

black head, white supercilium

pale crown-stripe

♂ SUMMER

♂ WINTER

♀ WINTER

Status: Summer visitor northern mountains and tundra.
Identification: 14–16cm (5½–6 ½in). Ground-dwelling bunting that often perches on large stone or similar object. Summer male has black head with rich chestnut nape and prominent creamy supercilium extending behind eye. Back streaked black and white; wings rufous; underparts white. Female, juvenile and winter male similar to female Reed Bunting but with pale central stripe on crown, rusty wings and (in male) rusty nape.
Voice: Rolling *rrrp*.
Habitat: Open mountainsides, tundra; winters coasts.
Similar Species: See Female Buntings pages 310-311.

J F M A M J J A S O N D

Snow Bunting *Plectrophenax nivalis*

white in wing

buffy marks on head

white head

white in tail

buffy marks on head

♂ WINTER

♀ WINTER

♂ SUMMER

Status: Summer visitor Fennoscandia mountains; winter visitor Baltic and North Sea coasts.
Identification: 16–17cm (6¼–6¾in). Winter flocks fly like pieces of white paper blowing in wind. At all times shows much white in wing and tail. Summer male mainly white with black back; wings black and white. Female, juvenile and winter male have mottled upperparts and variable amounts of streaking or buff on head. Feeds low on ground.
Voice: Loud *sweep*.
Habitat: Mountain plateaux; winters beaches.
Similar Species: Only Snow Finch shows as much white in plumage.

J F M A M J J A S O N D

Yellowhammer *Emberiza citrinella*

rusty back

very yellow head

more yellow on head than Cirl ♀

rusty rump

♂

♀

J F M A M J J A S O N D

Status: Widespread resident, but summer visitor only to northern Scandinavia, and winter visitor to Mediterranean.

Identification: 16–17cm (6¼–6¾in). Yellow bunting mostly seen perched openly on top of bush. Male bright yellow head marked with black, and yellow underparts streaked chestnut; brown wings and prominent rusty rump. Female similar but with less yellow; more extensive head markings. Forms winter flocks.

Voice: Familiar *little-bit-of-bread-and-no-cheese* song.

Habitat: Heaths and hedges.

Similar Species: See Female Buntings pages 310-311.

Cirl Bunting *Emberiza cirlus*

black and yellow head

black chin

rusty back

buffy rather than yellow

♂

♀

J F M A M J J A S O N D

Status: Resident south and west.

Identification: 15.5–16.5cm (6–6½in). Male distinguished by bold head pattern of black and yellow; greenish breast band, pale yellow underparts and rusty, streaked back. Female rufous buff above, creamy buff below – heavily streaked. Face pattern resembles that of female Yellowhammer, but is bolder and lacks yellow background.

Voice: Song a rattle, lacking terminal flourish.

Habitat: Bushy slopes, hedges, parks, gardens.

Similar Species: Female with female Yellowhammer. Cirl lacks rusty rump.

Rock Bunting *Emberiza cia*

black and white striped crown

prominent eye-stripe joins moustache

grey throat

♂

FIRST WINTER ♀

chestnut flank streaking

J F M A M J J A S O N D

Status: Resident hills southern Europe.
Identification: 15–16.5cm (6–6¹/₂in). Male has silver-white head boldly striped black on crown, through eye and moustache. Upperparts streaked buff and brown, with rust-coloured rump and longish black tail edged white. Underparts warm reddish-orange. Female subdued version of male, though with similar striped head pattern and lightly streaked underparts.
Voice: Song a descending *zi-zi-zi-zir*.
Habitat: Rocky slopes with trees and bushes.
Similar Species: None with such a clear-cut and pronounced head pattern.

Cinereous Bunting *Emberiza cineracea*

green face

blue-grey bill

unstreaked breast and flanks

yellow chin and moustache

♂

grey rump

♀

Status: Summer visitor to south-western and eastern Turkey showing similar pattern to Ortolan Bunting.
Identification: 16.5cm (6¹/₂in). Male has greenish head with yellowish chin and moustachial streak. Back, breast and rump grey. Thus similar to Ortolan, Cretzschmar's and Grey-necked Buntings. Female more subdued; lacks breast and flank streaking of females of other species. Juvenile has breast streaks, but in all plumages bill blue-grey not pink.
Voice: Repetitive *dip-dip-dip-dree-dreee*. Call a sharp *jip*.
Habitat: Dry, rocky hillsides with scant vegetation.
Similar Species: As above; blue-grey bill diagnostic.

J F M A M J J A S O N D

Ortolan Bunting *Emberiza hortulana*

grey-green head

pale yellow bib
and moustache

pinkish
bill

pale eye-ring

SUMMER ♂

JUVENILE

pink legs

J F M A M J J A S O N D

Status: Widespread, but scarce, visitor.
Identification: 15.5–16.5cm (6–6½in). Summer male grey-green on head and breast with yellow throat and moustachial streak. Remaining upperparts brown, streaked with black; dull yellowish rump. Underparts orange-buff. Female and winter male similar, but duller coloured, with spotting on breast. First-winter birds paler, less rufous above, with streaking on sides of head and breast. Pink bill and legs and pale eye-ring useful field marks.
Voice: Six or seven notes ending on an odd note.
Habitat: Scrubby and bare hillsides; fields.
Similar Species: Cretzschmar's Bunting.

Cretzschmar's Bunting *Emberiza caesia*

grey head

orange bib and
moustache

greyish
head

hint of facial
pattern of ♂

♂

♀

streaked
flanks

J F M A M J J A S O N D

Status: Summer visitor to hills of south-east.
Identification: 15–16.5cm (6–6¾in). Similar to Ortolan Bunting. Male has grey-blue head and breast marked by pale orange bib and moustache. Underparts rich orange-rufous. Female similar, but less boldly marked with blotched or streaked underparts. Juvenile streaked with clear moustachial stripe and pink bill, very similar to juvenile Ortolan Bunting. Warmer coloration may be helpful, as is less pronounced eye-ring.
Voice: Clear notes with differently pitched final note.
Habitat: Rocky hillsides, upland fields.
Similar Species: Ortolan as above.

Rustic Bunting *Emberiza rustica*

broad supercilium

crest

♂ SUMMER

rust
breast band

flank
blotches

crest

WINTER

rusty
streaks

J F M A M J J A S O N D

Status: Summer visitor Fennoscandia.
Identification: 14–15cm (5¹/₂–6in). Marked in all
plumages by raised crown feathers that form crest. Male in
summer has black head with bold white supercilium
behind eye, and white chin. Broad chestnut breast band
extends along flanks to form series of blotches. Female,
first-winter and winter male resemble other female
buntings more closely, but have pale supercilium behind
eye, dark brown cheeks and dark moustachial streak.
Voice: Repeated high *tsip*.
Habitat: Arctic thickets, woodland margins.
Similar Species: See Female Buntings pages 310-311.

Little Bunting *Emberiza pusilla*

striped crown

chestnut cheeks
with black outline

thin
bill

♂ SUMMER

white,
streaked
black

♀ WINTER

Status: Summer visitor northern Scandinavia.
Identification: 13–14cm (5–5¹/₂in). Small version of
female Reed Bunting, with shorter tail than most buntings.
Upperparts brown rather than rufous, with bold clear-cut
black streaking. Underparts white, with fine black streaks
on breast and flanks. Head pattern with black lateral
crown-stripe and chestnut cheeks outlined with black. Bill
thinner and more pointed than in most buntings; legs
pink.
Voice: Thin *tic*.
Habitat: Thickets around marshes.
Similar Species: See Female Buntings pages 310-311.

J F M A M J J A S O N D

Reed Bunting   *Emberiza schoeniclus*

black head, white moustache

white collar

♂ SUMMER

♂ WINTER

streaked crown

black moustache

♀

J F M A M J J A S O N D

Status: Common and widespread resident and summer visitor.
Identification: 14–16cm (5½-6 ½in). Male black head marked by white moustache and collar; upperparts streaked black and brown. Female heavily streaked buff and brown above, buffy below. Bold supercilium and smudgy black moustache helpful distinguishing features. Both sexes have white outertail feathers.
Voice: Several deliberate notes ending in hurry.
Habitat: Marshes, wetland margins, gardens.
Similar Species: Lapland Bunting; see Female Buntings below.

Identification of Female Buntings

Though many buntings are well-marked birds even some males, in full summer plumage, can cause problems. Females, being less well-marked, are even more problematical and should be separated with great care. Bill colour is a primary feature in separating groups of species – some clear pink, some definitely silver. A prominent supercilium is another major field mark. And the ear-covert box (ECB) is better defined on some than it is on others. A combination of these three major factors will whittle down the identification task to one or two species. The text should clinch an identification of all regular female buntings of our region.

LAPLAND: Yellowish, black-tipped bill. Dark triangle (ECB) created by eye-stripe and moustachial streak being joined across ear coverts, heighten by pale surrounds. Chestnut nape and pale coronal stripe. Malar-stripe consists of spotted streaks that widens to form breast band.

REED: Dark bill. Brown head with well-marked supercilium and pattern of white moustache and bib separated by boldest malar-stripe to form ear-covert box. This is the darkest faced female bunting and should be confused only with yellow-billed Lapland.

RUSTIC: Dark silver, pale-based bill. Dark ear coverts surrounded by white supercilium and upturned moustache form rounded ECB. Clear malar-stripe and white bib. A pale spot at the rear of the ear coverts, combined with a truncated supercilium, creates a patchy effect.

LITTLE: Tiny dark silver bill. Chestnut crown-stripe and ear coverts, latter highlighted by black horseshoe around rear end. similar to, but less clear-cut, than male. Plain, pale lores create an 'open-faced' appearance quite unlike any other bunting.

ROCK: Silver bill. Similar, but less contrasting, head pattern (ECB) to male, but in grey and black rather than white and black. Black line passes through eye; and 'in-fill' of ear-covert box and bib a distinctive dusky-grey contrasting with warm pink of breast.

YELLOW-BREASTED: Horn-coloured bill. Bold dark eye-stripe joins edges of ear coverts to form distinct triangular outline (ECB). Hint of warm yellow in moustachial-stripe that extends to sides of breast and flanks and along lower edge of ear coverts.

YELLOWHAMMER: Silver bill. Pattern of stripes; eye-stripe, moustachial-stripe, faint malar-stripe on yellow head. Similar to Cirl, but much more yellow in background creating a less contrasting effect. Add rusty rump to clinch identification.

CIRL: Silver bill. Pattern of stripes; eye-stripe, moustachial-stripe, malar-stripe on dirty, yellowish head. Similar to Yellowhammer, but much more clearly cut and of equal prominence on a buffy-yellow rather than pure yellow background.

ORTOLAN: Pink bill. Dull brown head with yellowish moustache and bib. Insignificant eye-ring. Face pattern much more streaked than any other female bunting, though bill and moustache stand out as a result. Malar stripe streaking widens to extend over breast and flanks.

CRETZSCHMAR'S: Pink bill. Pinkish-orange moustache and bib on greyish head with hint of warmth on ear coverts. Eye-ring stands out more than that of most other female buntings by contrast with overall greyish pattern of head. Grey nape.

GREY-NECKED: Pink bill. Pale grey head with pale yellow moustache and bib, the latter becoming warm pinkish as it fades to breast. This is basically the same pattern as the male and care should be taken in separating from male and female Cinereous and Cretzschmar's.

CINEREOUS: Dark bill. Grey-brown, featureless 'face' with hint of yellow in moustachial-stripe and bib separated by fine malar-stripe. Spotting on crown, around neck and onto breast creates a scruffy appearance, but is not diagnostic.

Grey-necked Bunting *Emberiza buchanani*

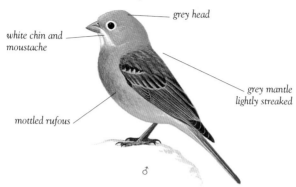

grey head

white chin and
moustache

grey mantle
lightly streaked

mottled rufous

♂

J F M A M J J A S O N D

Status: High-altitude summer visitor to far eastern Turkey.
Identification: 15–16cm (6–6½in). Like Cretzschmar's
Bunting with grey head and mantle; but mottled rufous
underparts extend to chin and lack grey breast band of
Cretzschmar's. Chin and moustachial streak white. Grey of
mantle extends to chestnut scapulars broken only by
narrow band of fine streaking. Rump grey, bill pink.
Female similar, but duller.
Voice: Song *ze-ze-ze zee-zoo* with a pause between third
and fourth notes. Call a *tetchup* or *chip*.
Habitat: High-altitude bare hillsides and steppes.
Similar Species: Cretzschmar's, Ortolan, Cinereous Buntings.

Yellow-breasted Bunting *Emberiza aureola*

black 'face'

bold double wingbar

breast
band

bold supercilium

black line
encloses ear
coverts

flank
streaks

♂

heavy
flank
streaks

♀

J F M A M J J A S O N D

Status: Scarce summer visitor Finland.
Identification: 13.5–14.5cm (5½in). Marked by yellow or
yellowish breast in all plumages. Male in summer
distinctive with chestnut crown above black face; yellow
underparts cut by narrow, but distinct, breast band.
Upperparts mottled chestnut with bold white double
wingbar. Female streaked buff and black above; head
pattern similar to other female buntings, but with
prominent supercilium and striped crown washed yellow.
Voice: Liquid song; hard *tic-tic*.
Habitat: Marshy scrub.
Similar Species: See Female Buntings pages 310-311.

Black-headed Bunting *Emberiza melanocephala*

chestnut back

black cap extends to cheeks

plain 'face'

yellow undertail

♂

♀

J F M A M J J A S O N D

Status: Common late summer visitor south-east Europe.
Identification: 16–17cm (6½–7in). Male colourful and obvious with black cap that extends below eye and over ear coverts. Upperparts chestnut with much white in wing. Underparts bright yellow with chestnut wash at bend of wing. Female buff and brown above with rather plain 'face' and hint of cap. Underparts unstreaked, undertail coverts yellow.
Voice: Pleasant warble; hard *zit*.
Habitat: Hillsides with woods and groves.
Similar Species: Female with female Cinereous Bunting.

Corn Bunting *Miliaria calandra*

short, thick neck

stubby bill

both sexes streaked

pink legs

J F M A M J J A S O N D

Status: Locally abundant, widespread resident.
Identification: 17–18.5cm (6½–7½in). Chunky, thick-set bunting that appears almost neckless. Streaked buff and brown above and below; both sexes similar to other female buntings. No white in tail. Perches openly, usually near ground in fields and open bushy areas. Sings with head thrown back; legs trail in fluttering flight.
Voice: Jingling rattle.
Habitat: Fields, hedges, heaths.
Similar Species: Larger and plumper than other female buntings.